G000024019

Praise for **IT'S NOT ALL ROSEY**

"This extraordinary account of an award-winning businesswoman's journey from council house to luxury mansion, surviving trauma after trauma, is notable for its honesty and for the total, almost unnerving clarity of its self-regard… A compelling read."

Jonathan Lamb
Author of 'The Ugly Baby'

"Rosey's story must be one of the most gripping real-life accounts it has ever been my privilege to hear. We sat one evening over supper and a bottle of wine and she had me captivated for hours. Her eventual triumph over adversity was a warming inspiration to me, as it will be to many others. I am delighted that she has now made it accessible to a wider audience, and warmly commend her personal narrative to the reader."

Anne Atkins
Broadcaster, journalist and novelist

"Let Rosey take you by the hand and lead you on an enchanting journey through her life. Sometimes this is a delightful meandering then, very suddenly, a corner is turned and it becomes a head-first flying-blind charge into the blackest of nights. Each of us can relate to a life that isn't all a bed of roses and is sometimes an undeserved crown of thorns. As the pages turn, you will feel as if you are making a wonderful new friend."

Ron Lexander
Author of 'Seduction by the Stars'

Praise for IT'S NOT ALL ROSEY

IT'S NOT ALL
ROSEY

ROSEMARY BENSLEY

The Book Guild Ltd

First published in Great Britain in 2017 by
The Book Guild Ltd
9 Priory Business Park
Wistow Road, Kibworth
Leicestershire, LE8 0RX
Freephone: 0800 999 2982
www.bookguild.co.uk
Email: info@bookguild.co.uk
Twitter: @bookguild

Copyright © 2017 Rosemary Bensley

The right of Rosemary Bensley to be identified as the author of this
work has been asserted by her in accordance with the
Copyright, Design and Patents Act 1988.

All rights reserved. No part of this publication may be
reproduced, transmitted, or stored in a retrieval system, in any form or by any means,
without permission in writing from the publisher, nor be otherwise circulated in
any form of binding or cover other than that in which it is published and without
a similar condition being imposed on the subsequent purchaser.

Typeset in Minion Pro

Printed and bound in the UK by TJ International, Padstow, Cornwall

ISBN 978 1911320 524

British Library Cataloguing in Publication Data.
A catalogue record for this book is available from the British Library.

FSC
www.fsc.org

MIX
Paper from
responsible sources
FSC® C013056

To those I have loved, lost and still long for.
And my big sister, Joan, who encouraged me,
fed me, cried with me and never doubted me.

CONTENTS

PROLOGUE

The car stopped turning. What on earth had happened?

Silence. Darkness. Momentary silence. Then my senses return.

I hear the deafening sound of quiet moaning. Who is hurt? What did we hit? We were driving fast, but not too fast, and the road had been clear. There were no lights coming towards us in the black of night. No noise but our singing.

I sit quietly for a moment. Am I hurt? What can I feel? Who is moaning?

I have to get out of the car. My chest hurts. I must climb out. But so must everyone else. Someone is lying in the footwell on my feet. No one is saying anything, only moaning. But I'm not moaning. I'm okay. Just fine. I am the strong one. I must help everyone.

I was always the strong one.

1

THE HELPER OF STRAY DOGS

I entered this world on a cold day in December, with the cord wrapped round my neck and turning blue. I was born on the landing of our council house in Sevenoaks, and if I'd known how I was to spend my first eleven years of life, I probably would've asked to be put back. Being one of seven children – four brothers in bunk beds, three girls sharing a second room, while our parents took the smallest – there were plenty of people, but not enough love to go around.

Roger, Joan, John

Marjorie, Rosemary, Peter, Paul

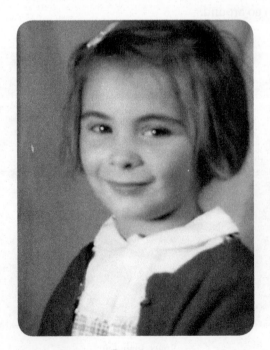

Rosemary

Mum and dad worked constantly. We saw them little. The cosy affection that enveloped my friends' homes never warmed my own. My friends' mums would give them kisses and cuddles, listen to their stories, and were genuinely interested in their lives. This was unfamiliar territory in our noisy, untidy, ramshackle abode. If you strode into my childhood home at any given moment, you were more likely to find Mum shouting, Dad ignoring, and the seven of us avoiding the lot of it.

School was my escape; I loved learning and was a good pupil, devouring my education as though it were sustenance. I strove to be top of the class and was so proud when I earned certificates, racing home to show them off, not that anyone else was interested. The only one to exhibit an ounce of enthusiasm was my sister, Marjorie, and only because she was always happy to help me spend a shiny new sixpence on sweets: sherbet dab, rhubarb and custard, gob stopper, and milk bottles.

Having no pocket money, apart from the occasional penny here and there, is difficult for a youngster to understand. Everything is comparative in youth. Most of my friends had pocket money, so where was mine? I wanted to be like the other girls at school who had shiny new shoes, the latest colouring pencils, books, sweets, and toys. The only way I came into the latest fads was to take them from someone else. I knew it was wrong to steal things that didn't belong to me. I knew I would be found out. I knew I would get in trouble. But I also knew trouble meant attention; it never mattered to me that it was the wrong kind.

When I went to my senior school, I had to wear a school uniform. This was an improvement upon wearing my old clothes. You're not singled out and called 'rag bag' when you're dressed like everyone else. But with anonymity in numbers, I began to blend into the wallpaper in other ways, as well. It soon became evident that at senior school, there was more competition, and I was no longer the cleverest – just one of a number of bright girls. With even less to write home about than before, I started to cry out for attention through theft. I got away with it a few times and even felt a buzz when the culprit would be sought out, but at some point, every thief's prints are found.

Mine were found the day the school got wise to the thieving and decided to position staff in the cloakroom. I had looked for a purse, found one, and tucked it in my knickers. Behaving as though I had nothing to hide, I removed my coat and hung it on the hook. My heart was pounding, as it always did, and I smiled to myself, *I got away with it, yet again*. But, as I turned around, a shiver ran up my spine.

No one was leaving the cloakroom; in fact, everyone was being searched. Panic rose with hot blood. My heart thumped like thunder. I looked round and realised there was no escape. *Someone must hear my telltale heart,* I thought. *They must hear my fear.* But all I could hear was the occasional whisper.

"They are looking for the thief!"

"Who do you think it is?"

"Whose purse is it this time?"

Clever as can be, I joined the excited chatter, "It can't be mine – there's nothing in it!"

How I had the gall to join in when I was guilty as hell, I'll never know. My head knew I was guilty as much as my hammering heart, and when I'd finally heard the words, "They've taken Jane to one side. It must be her," my heart steadied and my mind sighed with laughter.

The relief was fleeting. It was too soon followed by a protestation from Jane's best friend, Jill, "No, it can't be Jane. Don't be silly!" And, though people continued to murmur, Jill was spot on. None of the few people in that cloakroom who mattered – those searching, that is – had thought it was Jane, and the line in front of me had not stopped dwindling. As it dwindled further, I grew more and more afraid. What on earth had I done? I never even kept any of my stolen goods; I always threw the purses away. The act of theft was no longer for need or even want; it had become purely for the thrill. Nothing a clever girl like me should ever have succumbed to, and, yet, here I was, my heart fit to burst.

The sound of it was making my guilt known again. I knew my heart would betray me in the end. But, then again, maybe not. My friends hadn't noticed anything different about me, had they?

My heart was racing when I was taken aside into a cubicle. I thought I would die of embarrassment and shame. I was stripped searched and there was the stolen purse. I cried non-stop, was taken to the headmistress's room. Through my tears I explained that I only did it for attention and waited for the police to come. With the police being involved it meant that I left the school that day and didn't go back. Thank goodness, I couldn't have faced any of the girls. I showed the police where I threw the other purses into a garden on my route from school and was scared stiff of what would happen when I got home. Surprisingly, apart from being sent to bed and told that I wouldn't get any treats for a week, little was said. Later that week I did have to attend a meeting though and was left in a room with lots of other people. This was daunting and at the age of eleven years I was scared. I was asked my name and very clearly said, "Rosemary Anne, with an 'e'." My mum always told me that it was important people were told that bit. They wrote something down and I went back to my seat. I thought it strange they hadn't asked me my last name. As each name was called out I sat tensely waiting for mine. I waited and couldn't understand why I was being left to last. Then I heard Rosemary Anne Witheney being summoned, I looked round and there was no response from anyone else. I stood up slowly and said "My name is Rosemary Anne Gilbertson and my middle name is spelt with an 'e'. Is it me you want?" I saw a smile appear and was beckoned down and ushered into a side room by the lady that would become my probation officer for the next two years.

***

I may have entered the world in 1953, but it was when I left for boarding school in '66 that my life really began. I was given a second chance, a fresh start, courtesy of the UK Education Authorities.

Royal Wanstead School for Girls was in Sawbridgeworth, Hertfordshire. To me, it would be an escape from home life, where attention and affection was scarce. The school would also steer me in the right direction. Unknowingly, my kleptomania may very well have thrown me off-course towards juvenile delinquency. Royal Wanstead would eventually redirect my head, right my choices, and recalibrate my moral compass. But, first, I would have to get in.

A week before my boarding school interview, Mum took me out to buy a new coat. This was a rare occasion; my family could hardly afford stamps, let alone a garment that wasn't second-hand. Somehow, my mother had scraped the funds together, but of course I was limited to the sales rack, and of my limited selection, my fashion sense steered me toward one that was lime green. This was at a time when no one I knew wore neon, but somehow I was attracted to the vibrancy of it. If nothing else, I would definitely stand out. Perhaps another cry for attention? Whatever the case, I was pleased to own something new, as all my life, my clothes had been hand-me-downs from my two older sisters. In my lime green coat, I was truly going to knock those interviewers dead… or, at the very least, blind them.

The following week, Mum and I took a journey across to East London on trains and the Underground to a place called Snaresbrook. Mum explained that I would be interviewed and, if I did well and answered all of the questions correctly, I might be offered a place at the girls' boarding school. I was an avid Enid Blyton fan and also loved the St. Trinian's books about boarding school, so I was excited and, at the same time, nervous to win this chance at boarding. I promised my mum I would be well behaved and do my best to win everyone over.

When I first saw the school, it loomed before me, immense and overwhelming, but even in its enormity, it felt welcoming. A glittering lake spread before the front lawn, and the imposing stone building rose like a castle, with me being but a poor girl, dreaming. Was I really going here to school? Or was I only dreaming? I hoped not.

Mum and I were led into a meeting room on the first floor, where three interviewers sat round an oval table – one gentleman and two ladies. I was petrified, but a glass of milk and a biscuit revived me enough to answer the panel's questions.

"What lessons do you enjoy in school?" asked the man.

"Why would you like to go to boarding school?" asked the stately woman.

The third sat in judgmental silence, looking over her specs at me with an arched brow.

This carried on for a week and a half – or so it seemed to my anxious twelve-year-old brain – until the stately woman commented, with a hint of a grin, "What a coat you have on."

Without missing a beat, I replied feeling bold, "It's the best coat I've ever had."

They smiled at each other and probably felt sorry for me. Once the doors closed upon my interview, I'm sure they had a good laugh about my enthusiasm for such a blindingly hideous coat. When we weren't given a tour of the school, I assumed I'd failed. My shoulders sank, and my excitement drained into the glittering lake, as we left the pristine courtyard behind us. I kept thinking I had failed my mother; I had failed myself. I knew I wouldn't be attending school there. I was right about that last point.

Days later, my mum told me I'd been accepted and would soon be on my way to the Royal Wanstead School for Girls. The interview had been conducted at the boys' school, which is why we'd not been given a tour. The girls' school was in the country many miles away, and I couldn't wait for what this mysterious institution held in store for me. I began the countdown to the next decade of my Enid Blyton-esque boarding school years. Little did I know how much this adventure would shape my life.

***

It was 26th April 1966, and at twelve years old I said goodbye to everything that had gone before. I was starting anew: a new home, a new school, a new life, and a new me. When the big day arrived, I kissed my little brothers, Peter and Paul, and my sister, Marjorie, and was happy that Dad had given me a big bear hug before he went to work. I don't know that I felt I would be missing out on much at home; I was too excited about what was to come.

I was also thrilled that Mum was driving me to school in her old Ford Prefect, because I'd never gone on a long road trip with her. This trip to boarding school would be the furthest I'd ever travelled in her car. My dad couldn't drive because of an injury to his arm, so Mum took us anywhere necessary, but it was a rare occurrence. I didn't know much about my mum, to be honest. I knew she was clever, because she'd been nominated to be the Labour candidate for Sevenoaks in the 1964 elections. She didn't win, I was told, because Sevenoaks was far too snobby to vote in a council house tenant. Not long after this, Mum had a nervous breakdown from overwork. She didn't have enough time to look after us, so I don't know why she took so much time out to help other people. She was a conundrum, my mum, and I watched her drive me to the school in silence, curious about this conundrum, delivering her daughter to the possibility of a better life.

When I saw the sign for Sawbridgeworth, Mum signaled to turn off the road. Butterflies began to flutter in my stomach, and I squirmed in my seat, as my nerves took hold. We entered through the school gates, where I saw the words 'Hyde Hall' emblazoned in gold. Up a long windy road, bordered by trees on both sides, the imposing building soon rose into view on the right, appearing like a stately home. I crawled out of the car, the smell of newly mowed lawns made me smile and I couldn't wait to start my new life. Scanning the grounds, I spotted tennis courts to my left and a large modern detached house. I assumed the teachers lived there. About them, I wasn't too wary. I did think they might be horrible, but I would cope. It was the girls who gave me cause for concern. What if they didn't like me? What if I wasn't accepted? What if I had no friends? The thought of being ostracized and isolated made me want to crawl under a rug.

"Your name?" a kindly woman asked when we'd approached the office.

"Rosemary Anne Gilbertson," my mum answered.

After scrolling the attendance sheet and landing upon my name, the woman announced, "You've been assigned to Roden House. Your form mistress is Mrs Lamb." I later discovered that Mrs Lamb was the wife of Mr Lamb, the headmaster.

After a tearless farewell and hardly any fanfare, Mum left and I was shuffled to my dormitory where my bed was labeled 'Rosemary'. I tipped my bag onto it and emptied the contents, placing the few items neatly into the bedside drawers. My soap, toothpaste, and underwear looked quite pathetic in its drawer, but I didn't need much else; I knew that I was going to be kitted out for my school uniform soon. I sat down on the edge of the bed and waited nervously. I'd joined midway through the school year, so I was the newest member of a dormitory where all the girls had been together for two terms already and so had formed friendships, bonds, and inside jokes. New girls, like me, had to arrive earlier than the rest, go through an induction process, and be schooled in the routine. I would also be introduced to other new girls who, for whatever reason, had also started at the school late. Soon, I was rushed off, along with the rest of the newbies, to be measured for my new green uniform. Moreover, I was given a daily timetable, which informed me that supper would begin shortly.

The dining hall was a newer building, but no matter how new, the girls found something to complain about; mainly the food. I couldn't understand what there was to scoff at. To me, the meal was tasty, and there was a lot of it, including a pudding. Though I kept my opinions to myself, I couldn't help but think, *What more could you ask for?*

All around the dining hall, a counterfeit conversation unfolded repeatedly:

"What did you get for Christmas?" one pretty blonde girl asked her neighbor and mine.

"I got a Sindy doll, a watch, and grandma knitted me the usual cardigan," said the brunette. "Not what I asked for."

"Oh my goodness, I got the same. Don't our families have any imagination?"

"Well, my mum is really into music, so I get a share in the new record player and was allowed to go and buy records. I chose the Beatles' 'Help' and Tom Jones' 'It's not Unusual.' I love the way he moves, don't you?"

For once, I was pleased not to have anyone's attention. I'd rather avoid taking part in this banter. Belonging to such a large family, presents were thin on the ground in the Gilbertson household, which was made worse for me, in particular, by the fact that my birthday was in December. I was always told I only had something small for my birthday, as I would have a bigger present for Christmas. This was never the case, of course, but I learned to live with it. Still, it was painful to hear of Santa's generosity to others, when I rarely got much more than reindeer pellets. Apart from the obvious wealth gap, everyone seemed friendly enough, and I was looking forward to becoming part of the "inner circle."

When I entered the dormitory, I was surprised to find everyone crying. *What happened?* I thought. *Was there a death?* No, far from it. What I deciphered through the sobbing was that everyone felt homesick and wanted to return to their happy families. I was mortified; I felt the exact opposite and had been ready for pillow fights and late night snacks with my dorm mates, like I'd read about in all those boarding school books. Instead, I would have to make myself well up in order to fit in. Homesickness seemed pretty silly to me, but I decided I must play the cards I was dealt.

I slipped out of the dorm and fled to the bathroom. Seating myself in a toilet, I made myself cry. I thought about being smacked for the umpteenth time because I had wet my bed. I thought about how sad I'd been when our dog ran away. I thought about the saddest memories I could conjure up, until a single tear slipped down my cheek. And then another and another, until I was sobbing.

Eventually, I heard a knock and a soft singsong voice echoed through the bathroom.

"Whatever is the matter, my dear?" the voice rang like a bell. It was Mrs Lamb.

Being the right little actress I was, I blubbered, "I w-w-want to g-go ho-o-o-o-ome."

After a pause, Mrs Lamb said gently, "That may be how you feel now, but I can assure you that you'll be very happy here, once you've settled in. When you've made some friends, the school will seem an improvement on home."

I gave another fake sob. "What if nobody likes me, and I don't have anyone to help me?"

"Well, that won't happen," she answered, readily. "I will always be close by to help you. The first night is strange for new girls, especially when you've arrived halfway through the school year. Open the door, and I'll give you a welcome cuddle."

I couldn't resist affection and slowly opened the door. She took me in her arms and said, "I understand why you're unhappy. We all miss home, but you're at home now."

For the first time in my life, I felt wanted. In the space of fifteen minutes, I bonded with Margaret Lamb like I never had my own mother. She became my surrogate mum and would play a pivotal role in my life during my formative years.

Margaret Lamb, my surrogate mum

***

I soon settled into the school's routine, and because I'd always loved learning, I embraced whatever was put in front of me. I became best friends with Louise, who made me laugh and was a brain box. Louise and I were competitive. We were equally intelligent and wanted to be top of the class, so our exam results were always eagerly awaited and compared. If Louise didn't come out on top, then I did; any other ranking was unusual. I was thrilled to bits when I won the writing prize during my first year, and I wondered if Mrs Lamb had a hand in it. She certainly enjoyed taking me to Bishops Stortford to spend the money I'd won. She was so kind and gentle, like a lamb – everything I would have liked my mum to be. Mrs Lamb hadn't any children of her own, so maybe I was filling a hole in her life too.

Every Saturday, we were allowed into the local village to go shopping. Soon enough, Mrs Lamb asked if I'd like the responsibility of helping the teacher distribute the tuck shop pocket money. I was surprised to be asked, as I was a first-year pupil, but I jumped at the chance. It turned out there was a reason no one wanted the responsibility; it took up a good portion of my Saturday morning and who really wanted to shell out money on their day off? Never mind, I took my responsibilities seriously and, looking back, this was certainly one of the ladder rungs leading to my love of accounting. Something inside me enjoyed counting out the money and obtaining a signature from the older girls and my classmates to confirm that they'd received the right amount. I didn't mind being the last to receive mine, as my pocket money was a pittance; I then had less time to look at things in the shops that I couldn't afford. Everyone was eager to go to the village and do so, but there was a downside to these trips, and I got caught up in it early on.

"Over here, girls," one of the seniors whispered, nastily, outside of Woolworths one day. She drew me and my two form mates to the store window. "That Nivea cream – two jars for me and Ruth."

This happened all the time; children of the lower forms were left in little doubt that if they didn't steal for these upper classmen, they would be crushed like bugs. Woolworths was the easiest target, but it was still frightening. With my past, shoplifting was not something I wanted to be caught up in ever again. But just as you'd expect, the need to be accepted outweighed the repercussions of thievery.

The senior girls were never seen with us when we did the pilfering. They were far too clever for that. We had to walk up the long drive, stolen goods in our bags, and put the swag in a predetermined place, usually in the gym. On the day in question, we didn't make it to the gym; someone had seen us in the village and reported us to the headmaster.

Our punishment was to sit in the library. Not too shabby for a bibliophile, but the shame of being exposed to the other girls was worse than a lashing. The library was beside the main staircase, which led to the dormitories – the main thoroughfare for getting anywhere in the school. We, the thieves, were reprimanded, but the older girls in question faced even graver punishment. They were given detention and made to do menial tasks, like cleaning and washing dishes, while their parents were also informed. Some of the girls were forced to leave before the end of term, and those who remained laid off of forcing us young'uns into shoplifting. Thusly, peace was restored, and my hands were clean again.

***

This peace was short-lived. The world came crashing down during my second year at boarding school. The governors had decided that a girls' boarding school should not have a male headmaster. Most of the students were devastated to hear this. We did not want to see Mr and Mrs Lamb go. But go, they did, along with several of the senior staff. In their stead, Miss Clarkson stole into our lives.

Miss Clarkson's first address to the pupils included a religious story featuring a small mouse. If the audience had been half our age, this fable may have gone down well, but we were teenagers. My classmates and I did everything we could to stop ourselves laughing. Her seeming obliviousness to the general maturity level of her audience sealed her fate for me, and I disliked her from that day onward. I sensed she was a weak individual, because she never once praised the outgoing staff. Her weakness did work in my favour from time to time, but as she replaced the strong, strict staff with young, less experienced teachers, my education suffered.

It was because of this that, at fourteen years old, I staged a protest march against Miss Clarkson the Headmistress. I gathered interest from pupils, both old and young, and we decided we would walk from Sawbridgeworth to the boys' school in Wanstead. The plan was to leave while the first sitting of lunch began, as that would give us more time away before they sent out a search party. My theory was, the longer we talked about it, the more likely we were to be found out, so the planning process was short-lived. Moreover, the longer we left it, the quicker people's feet would grow cold. If this happened, the plan would be dead on the ground.

And, sure enough, the day of the march, my two best friends suffered from cold feet and locked themselves in the bathroom. No matter, the rest of the pack marched on. We set off that day – twelve rebels and their protest... twelve rebels who were totally unprepared. Apart from some posters that we brandished while passing people in the street, I'm not sure it was clear to anyone that we were rebelling; we probably just looked like we were on a school outing.

Eventually, the police became interested enough to pick us up, and we were taken to Epping Police Station. I was identified as the ringleader, and the friendly police station staff took no time at all to nickname me 'Sandie Shore,' being that I had long, dark, straight hair and was barefoot. Although I couldn't sing, this seemed an apt comparison.

We were collected by transport sent by the school and left without a hint of a police record, but back at school, we were treated with the respect of hardened criminals... or, at least, that's how we saw it at the time. The other pupils welcomed us as heroes, but Miss Clarkson saw our heroic march in a different light.

"Detention in the library for three weeks," she commanded. "You're lucky that I'm not expelling you all!" When it came to parental discipline, however, she didn't let me off the hook completely. In her end-of-the-year report, she'd jotted in an angry red pen, 'Rosemary should refrain from antisocial disputes'.

When my mum read this out to me and asked what it meant, my acting skills came to the fore. "There must have been a mistake, Mum. There's another Rosemary in my class, and she's always mixing us up."

Mum had too much to worry about to interrogate me on the matter, so my punishment went undealt. And, yet, the leader in me had made herself known.

***

Towards the end of the term, in December 1968, Miss Clarkson spoke the always-dreaded words, "Will Rosemary Gilbertson come to my office straight after supper?"

"Now what have I done?" I turned and whispered to my friends. "I'm sure the old bat will have made something up."

When I arrived at her office, she asked me to sit down and began, "God moves in mysterious ways, and sometimes he challenges us, doesn't he?" I nodded. *Oh no,* I thought, *a religious telling-off this time.* "Take John, for instance," she continued. John was the school's elderly gardener. "We all thought he was going to die after having that long bout of illness, but he miraculously pulled through and is now on the way to recovery." I had no clue why she was telling me all of this. I shifted in my chair and then, through my discomfort, heard her say, "I'm sorry to inform you that your mother has just lost her husband."

I stopped fidgeting for a moment. *'Just lost her husband'? What does that mean?* I fleetingly imagined that they'd been shopping, and he'd disappeared.

"With it being so close to the Christmas holidays, your mother has agreed you should stay here and travel back with your escort as planned."

Suddenly I realized what she'd meant. My mum's husband wasn't 'lost'; my dad was dead.

I jumped from the chair, opened the door, and ran as fast as my legs would carry me. I dodged past anyone who was in my path, no idea where I was headed, finally landing in the horsebox in the gym. I hid there, silencing my tears, as I heard staff and girls searching for me. But they couldn't find me; I was as quiet as a mouse. Through my pain and shock, one vivid feeling pierced through me: I hated that old witch. *Let her worry,* I thought. *What a horrible way to tell me that my father is dead.*

***

Miss Clarkson left not long after that at the end of the Spring term (I assumed she was sacked for the way she'd dealt with my father's death) and was replaced by Mr Hall. The governors had gone full-circle and returned to male leadership. Nearly everyone breathed easier, as Mr Hall was a breath of fresh air. His positive attitude won the pupils and staff over straight away. With someone competent in charge, I was willing to flourish again.

My Dad. Gone too soon

I'd always taken pride in working hard, and my leadership skills were developing, as I came to care, more and more, for others. One member of staff labelled me a 'helper of stray dogs', as she'd noticed I'd always try my best to help the school's underdogs and was well respected by my peers for it. One of my proudest moments was helping a girl in my house who wasn't very bright and was often the victim of bullying. I made her part of my close group, and she was so much happier. Still, it surprised and delighted me, when Mr Hall appointed me head girl. I was determined to succeed in my new role. At the same time, it turned out I was equally determined to take advantage of the position. Drunk with power, I think they call it.

I'd often find a way to excuse myself from completing certain school tasks on time. "Oh, I'm really sorry, Miss Cook, but there was an incident I had to deal with last night, and I didn't get to reading the chapter."

I cherry-picked my work, favouring the subjects I enjoyed and not worrying about those yawn-worthy subjects; geography, for starters. But, don't get me wrong – I didn't shirk my duties as head girl. In fact, my private bedroom received regular visitors, usually younger pupils who were struggling. And struggle greatly, some did.

One of those struggling was a talented pretty young girl from Sevenoaks – an amazing pianist, with above average intelligence, who seemingly had everything she could ever want. However, something was stopping her from fulfilling her dreams. At first, I thought she maybe felt pressured by her parents, but coming from the same hometown, I had talked with them and could see they were proud of her, not pushy. But, still, she struggled.

One day, she walked into my room, and at first glance, it looked like she was drenched in ketchup. If only it had been a condiment. She was covered in blood, having attempted to slit her wrists.

"My god! What have you done?" I sprang from my bed and raced to her, my heart thumping and my stomach turning. I had never seen such gore.

Through her tears, she blubbered, "I am so sorry. I shouldn't have come to you, but I was scared what the matron would do. I don't want my mum and dad to know I did this. I'm sorry, I'm really sorry."

I started to stem the bleeding and asked her to apply pressure, which made me realise she'd avoided cutting the main arteries.

"Honey, calm down and don't apologise. Once the bleeding stops, you can stay in my room. If you want to talk about it, we will. If you don't, we won't."

The bleeding soon stopped and, after she fell asleep, I went to tell the matron what had happened. The girl was taken under the wing of an adult, but seemingly her troubles didn't end. It was not long after this that I discovered a letter in my underwear drawer.

"I am running away to London," it said. "I'm sorry for all the trouble I've caused."

She never returned to Sawbridgeworth.

**

Being head girl allowed me instant access to the headmaster, and I loved being in a position to see how far I could push the boundaries.

"Please, Mr Hall," I begged one day during the last spring of my schooling. "May the senior girls attend the end-of-term dance at the boys' college?" Boys were rarely seen at the girls' school, so the prospect of meeting several all at once excited many.

"I'm not opposed to the idea," Mr Hall replied, "but each girl must write to her parents and ask permission and ensure that the replies are postmarked to me. You'll have to do the legwork and arrange it."

I think he assumed this would dissuade us, but he'd underestimated our interest in boys. After two weeks, I was summoned into his office. Letters were piled in front of him on his desk and, as he leaned back in his chair, worry settled in the pit of my stomach. He looked grave and serious as I walked in – too grave for my liking – and, without a word, he beckoned to a chair. I sat down unsteadily. Surely, with the dozens and dozens of permission forms stacked before him, he couldn't now rescind his promise?

"I've had a response from your mother." I held my breath. "She says she thinks you're old enough to keep your head." He continued to appear on the verge of pulling the rug out from under me, heightening my anticipation. Then he said, "The only problem is, it's not your head I'm worried about!" I must have looked puzzled, for he gave in and said, "I've written to the boys' college, and they're happy to have you ladies attend, if accompanied by a female teacher. "

Brimming over, I couldn't wait to escape Mr Hall's office to inform my classmates. And, more importantly, I couldn't wait to meet some boys!

**

On the first outing to attend the dance I had my first proper kiss from a blond haired, blue-eyed boy whose nickname was Fritz. His parents lived near Lake Lucerne in Switzerland. I didn't get to know him very well, as my best friend decided she didn't like the boy she'd met, so we both ended the friendships before they'd started.

After mixing with the boys at the dance, my interest redoubled. I began to seek out reasons to be around them and frequently attended functions at the Royal Wanstead School for Boys. The head boy, Chris, was a handsome mixed-race lad, and he and I became a 'couple'. He used to come over to visit me in Sawbridgeworth whenever he got the opportunity and vice versa. A few weeks before I was due to leave school I got gated for the first time ever. This was for the heinous crime of being seen walking with Chris up to the hockey pitch. Although I'd never done anything to make the matron believe otherwise, she suspected it wasn't an innocent walk.

Chris was very clever, and my classmates were a tad jealous. He really fitted the bill of tall, dark, and handsome. I was well pleased with myself and when, on one of his visits, he had a present for me, I was even more thrilled. "What have I done to deserve this? It's not my birthday." I was so excited; I could burst! No one ever bought me presents.

"You shouldn't question why. Just open it, and let me know if you like it." He hesitated, "You might not, and then I'll have to think of something else."

"Don't be silly," I said, peering into the bag. "Of course I'll like it!" I pulled out a reggae LP, one that I was fairly sure none of my friends would have, which made me like it even more. "Wow, this is fantastic! This will be the start of my record collection. I've never been given one before." I gave him a quick kiss and a big squeeze. "Thank you so much, my handsome hero."

The nearest Chris and I ever got to consummate the relationship was after we'd left school, and he came to stay at my house in Durham which was where the family had moved to from Sevenoaks the year before. He was a perfect gentleman and didn't take advantage of the fact that we had the opportunity to make love when my mum was out. I am ashamed to say that I didn't treat him as well as I should have. I was encountering racial prejudice for the first time and found myself distancing myself from him in public. I was influenced by my colleagues, who should have known better, and it's one of my biggest regrets.

***

All good things must come to an end, as the saying goes, and it was too soon that my one good thing did. My tenure at boarding school came to a close, and the glaring prospect of leaving the safety of Royal Wanstead and moving to Durham, where I knew no one but my family, made me feel dead inside. I dreaded the idea of reverting back to my old life – how could I live like I'd done before, having had all of these experiences? Having grown into myself? How could I return to a home that was never a loving one and a family that no longer knew me… if they ever had in the first place?

One glimmer of light shone to save me. "Would you like to stay boarding at the school and attend Harlow College of Further Education?" Mr Hall called me into his office and asked me at the end of term.

I jumped at the chance, only to be disappointed when my mum crushed my dreams in two seconds, flat. "No, I don't think so, Rosemary. I need your income to help run the household." I hated her for that, especially since I was her child and felt she should have been financially stable enough to support herself.

After my dad died suddenly when I was fourteen, it had only taken her four months to marry a man thirteen years her junior. I didn't understand it then, but later realised she'd thought it would make things easier. As often happens, he was a waste of space and a womaniser. My mum finally saw the error of her ways and ended up divorcing him, but not until he had spent all her money and a lot of damage had been done. It came to light in 2013 that he was a paedophile and worse still caused great distress to my younger brothers. I had been oblivious to this.

I was even more proud of being head girl of the Royal Wanstead School for Girls, when years later I found out that the governors had sold both this and the boys' school to form a charity in 1971. The charity funded children from disadvantaged families to attend mainstream boarding schools. Such institutions give children, like me, a chance to become more than what the world had in store. And I would soon prove in my career, that I had benefitted for sure.

2

THE BOY WHO LOVED BOB DYLAN

"Pack your bags, Rosemary! We're shooting off to Skegness for a week!"

I read Lucy's thin script over again, just to be sure. On holiday for a week with my dear friend? No obligations? That sounded like an extravagant and lavish gift to myself. I never would have thought to give myself such a generous break, but neither had there ever really been an opportunity. Nor an invitation.

It was the summer after I'd left school, and I was working for a clothing transport company called Tibbett and Britten. In my first job, I'd quickly progressed from office junior to office manager, after the previous office manager was caught stealing from the petty cash tin. I had only been with the company for five months, but my eagerness to tackle any job prompted the Managing Director to throw me into the role and see if I could sink or swim. And I was swimming.

By the ripe old age of seventeen, I was already hiring staff and managing them. I'd even been able to set a bit of money aside, which is shocking, as Mum kept 80% of my take-home pay. Either accounting was in my blood or financial management skills were forced upon me by my family's need, but whatever the case, I've always been able to live on whatever means I could scrounge together and learned to manage my money well. In fact, I'd made it my life's mission not to be poor, so I didn't spend where unnecessary. Never did I treat or pamper myself. I rarely went out of an evening and, if I did, it was to the local Amateur Dramatics Club in the city centre. To go out for an occasional drink afterwards meant I'd splurged.

So it came as a surprise, even to myself, not only that a good friend had suggested a week's vacation to someone as frugal as me, but that I was seriously considering it. And it didn't even take me long to make up my mind. Soon, not only was I planning my budget, but I was daydreaming about our splashing out at Butlins Holiday Camp.

***

Butlins Skegness was the flagship resort and one of the first of its kind. When the resort launched in 1936, it was unique in that it catered to all ages, particularly to families; but by the time we showed up for our holiday in 1971, other companies were competing for the family holiday business, and it was no longer novel. Still, Butlins was competitive, with a daily programme and a leaflet that catalogued dozens of activities, ranging from bingo to water sports to knobbly knee competitions. Though the wealth of choices may have been overwhelming, there was certainly no excuse to be bored. You could join in whichever activity you pleased or opt out. And if you had no clue what to do, red-coated teenagers employed by the resort were at your beck-and-call. The Red Coats were on hand to entertain and/or encourage anyone who looked like they were at a loose end. They were also the stars of the evening shows, the primary form of nightlife at the resort.

Lucy was already there when I arrived, and it didn't take us long to unpack our bags in our chalet and start exploring. We chatted non-stop and caught up with each other's news whilst discussing the timetable of events for the day.

"Oh my goodness, Lucy – look at those old folk over there making fools of themselves! Are you sure this was a good idea?"

Lucy looked up from the brochure and burst out laughing. "Oh, come on. What are they doing? Maybe the conga? But very badly. Let's follow them. Anything for a laugh, hey?"

We tried to be discreet but the Red Coats were having none of it. "Hey, girls, come and join in. We need some judges." We looked at each other and ran the other way. We hadn't come on holiday to spend it with wrinklies. Instead, we dropped in at one of the bars to watch the talent show auditions.

"Are you really only going to have grapefruit juice?" Lucy teased.

I sipped my juice. I didn't mind her teasing. I knew who I was, and if I didn't want to drink, I wouldn't. "To be honest, I have tried a few drinks, but I don't like the taste of alcohol. I don't see what all the fuss is about. It's the same with smoking. You know how it is, sneaking into the woods and lighting up a Consulate. Of course I've had a puff or two, but I didn't like that either, so now I don't waste my hard earned money on cigarettes or booze."

"I know what you mean, but don't you feel left out when your friends are all doing it?"

"Not really. As it happens, I don't go out much so don't have that problem. Do you like boys who smoke and drink?"

Just as Lucy was about to respond, she nudged me, and I looked up. Two boys – or should I say young men – were walking in our direction. One was smoking, and both had drinks in hand. I glanced behind me, assuming they were meeting their girlfriends and couldn't believe my luck when they instead turned toward us, just as I'd imagined some mystery men would in my pre-travel daydreaming.

"Can we join you?" the fair-haired man asked.

Instead of vocalizing our approval, Lucy and I looked at each other and nodded.

"I'm Phil," said the man, tossing his long fair hair. He was scruffily dressed, probably intending to be trendy. Seating himself next to Lucy, the pair started chatting and soon they were acting as though they'd known each other for ages.

"Mark," said the dark-haired man, who sat down alongside me, presenting his hand for me to shake. The man's darkness didn't end at his hair; he was the moody type, but much more handsome than his counterpart. His skin was kissed by the sun and his black mane waved by the wind. He was slim, sexy, and as he turned to me, he smiled. I could have died, right there.

I was okay-looking, I suppose, with my long, straight, dark hair. But never had I considered myself at all beautiful. My plainness didn't seem to bother Mark. He was quite happy to watch the talent show and chat about his musical preferences.

"Bob Dylan," he said. "Have you heard of him? Genius. Mind-blowing. And Leonard Cohen. 'Suzanne,' 'Bird on the Wire'. Just unparalleled talent. Have you heard of them?"

His enthusiasm was attractive, and now I wished that I'd paid closer attention to pop culture. Instead, I had to shake my head and mutter sheepishly, "I know 'Mr Tambourine Man'." After a beat, I asked, "Do you play?"

"What?"

"Guitar?"

"Oh, yes," he answered. "Owning a Les Paul is my dream."

"Is that a brand of guitar then?"

Mark laughed. I thought my ignorance about music had made us incompatible, but my lack of knowledge about his passion didn't scare him off. Although I soon realised he was shy, he stayed with me until it was time for us girls to head back to our chalet, and as we reached the night's end, he pulled me toward him and pecked me on the lips. "Goodnight and see you again, I hope."

The moment the boys left, I turned to Lucy. "Well? What did you think of Phil?" I asked, and before she could reply, I plastered a big knowing grin on my face, "He looked very interested in you."

Lucy laughed. "He didn't really give much away, but I learned a lot about him and Mark. They're good friends, and music is their common denominator. I like music, but I don't know much about the artists Phil mentioned. I'm a 'Pan's People', dance music kind of girl," she grinned. "You remember our dancing days on Sunday nights in our school uniforms? We all thought we were brilliant dancers." We both laughed. "What about you? You looked star-struck when Mark sat down."

"I was, but don't tell him that. I'm going to play it cool. Well, that's assuming he wants to see me again, of course. They said they'd see us tomorrow evening, but a lot can happen in twenty-four hours."

"Yes, a lot can happen," Lucy nodded, knowingly. "They could both fall deeply in love with us."

***

Unfortunately, the very next day I went down with a lurgy of some sort. Lucy met Phil and Mark when she went out for a walk, and when she told the boys that I was sick, Mark asked for our chalet number so he could check I was okay and see if I needed anything. I was so thankful that he wanted to bother with visiting me when we had only just met that he went up even further in my estimation. The scene was set for our holiday. Neither Mark nor Phil seemed to have any desire to chat up any other girls, and we were having fun getting to know them. With two chalets available, we could pair off and enjoy one-on-one time together without being disturbed. Mark and I spent time canoodling, as one did in those days – nothing more than a kiss and a cuddle – and at the end of each day, Lucy and I would catch up and compare notes on the budding romances. Neither of us felt so overpowered with love or lust to let it takeover our holiday. Instead, we continued to participate in activities, including swimming events and quizzes, and before we knew it, the week had reached its end. Parting from our boys, saying our goodbyes, and promising to keep in touch, I didn't imagine we'd ever see each other again.

But, surprisingly, Mark kept his promise. Not long after, he phoned me to see if I wanted to meet up. He lived in Woodford Green in Essex, which was an eight-hour coach journey from Durham. Although the commute was long, and our schedules were difficult to manage, we met up a few times. Neither of us had money to waste, so we were happy having a drink and a cheap meal at the local pub. My brother, Roger, gave me keys to his flat in Ilford, and it was there that our feelings for each other grew and the relationship went to the next stage. I didn't take much persuading to move down south the following summer.

My boss was disappointed but encouraged me to continue working for the firm at its head office in Tottenham, London. I had no idea where that was in relation to where Mark lived or to where I would be staying with Roger's ex-girlfriend in Rainham, Essex; but I would make it work.

Leaving meant upheaval in the household. My mother was angry, because she would be losing my salary. But I was sick of suffering and being unhappy. She had been the one to drain her savings by wasting it on that man. I had sacrificed enough for her choices, and nothing would deter me from striking out on a new adventure. Though I was somewhat apprehensive, I was naïve and left home feeling assured that life would be simple, and I would be happier without my difficult home life to contend with. I relished a new challenge and looked forward to being with someone who loved me.

***

Mark was an only child. His parents, Maureen and David, welcomed me into the family and became my new mum and dad. Maureen was the most elegant lady I had ever met, She had long blonde hair, which she always wore up and a figure to die for. Not an ounce overweight in my opinion. She owned the Gift Shop, which was situated below their smart flat, and I knew I had been accepted as part of the family when I was asked to help her with the takings.

David was several years older than her and I wondered what it was that had drawn Maureen to him. He worked hard as a money collector, which meant his hours were varied. Like a lot of husbands he took a back seat when it came to cooking and cleaning and it made me question why us females put up with that. *Something to change if I ever get married*, I thought. Mark and I got on well enough, and whilst we didn't have much in common, I enjoyed being with him. Even better, his parents treated me like a princess, and I'd never felt so loved. Soon, I was part of the family and proud to be a member.

What's more, I had a good-looking boyfriend who wanted to be with me. But I always wondered what he saw in me. "You're a beautiful person," he'd insist whenever I'd ask. "I'm the lucky one."

"Don't you think you'd like someone who enjoys music more? I feel I let you down by not joining in when you and your friends are in the zone."

"Don't be silly. They're my pals, but you're my special lady. You're much more important to me."

Not long after this, I was invited to live in his parents' home so that we could save money for a house of our own. I often stayed the night and slept on a mattress on the floor of Mark's room, but it didn't take long before we were sharing his bed.

It was easy to think I was in love with Mark. He was so sweet and vulnerable. I liked that. On my nineteenth birthday, he put my jacket over my shoulders and said, "I'm taking you to London." Whisking me through the city streets, he wined and dined me, and when we arrived at Oxford Circus, we decided to have our photo taken by a professional photographer inside a silver-lined booth. We were asked to smile into a large silver disc while the camera flashed. Then we strolled around the bustling shops until it was time to collect the black and white photos. The night was a whirlwind of flashing lights, laughter, and joy and when, on the Central Line back home, Mark pulled out the box – a diamond engagement ring glinting inside. I can't pretend it wasn't expected. The night seemed as though it had been leading up to this point.

"Will you marry me?" he asked. In grand Mark fashion, no one was getting down on one knee, not much romance, but certainly, excitement. After I'd said yes, he leaned over and whispered in my ear, "I sold one of my guitars to buy you that ring."

He'd sold his first love for me? All right, so there was *some* romance.

Our Engagement 1972

3

A REVELATION

We burst through the door of his parents' home, thrilled to share the good news.

"We're getting married!" I informed them, shrilly.

"Are you now?" asked David, a mild look of concern drifting into his features.

"Well, isn't that lovely..." Maureen trailed off.

My excitement seemed to trip down the stairs. I expected enthusiasm. I expected them to congratulate us with genuine delight. They'd always treated me like a princess... didn't they want a princess for their prince? Though I was more than a bit disappointed by their reaction, I put it down to the lateness of the day and exhaustion.

But as I lay awake in bed like a deflated balloon, I wondered if the magic and weightlessness I'd been floating on all night was nothing but helium.

**

The next morning, I passed Maureen and David's bedroom and greeted them hesitantly, "Good morning."

"Can you come in here for a minute, Rose?" Maureen called out to me. Wondering what this could be about, I entered the room. "Have a seat, dear. I want to talk with you." I sat at the foot of the bed and waited. A moment passed before Maureen said, "I want to explain why we reacted the way we did to your big news last night. I have to tell you that Mark... Mark was a difficult baby. Very difficult. We could tell since birth that there was something different about him. But it wasn't until he was a teenager that his illness materialised."

I furrowed my brow. *'Illness'? Does Mark have some fatal disease? Is he dying?* A million illnesses marched through my mind until Maureen saved my sanity by answering my unasked question.

"Mark went on a trip to Utrecht, Holland in 1968. While he was there, he joined a group of hippies – they played music, sang, and smoked pot all day long. When he returned, something was… off."

"Off? How do you mean?" Though I'd posed the question, the posing was somewhat mechanical. On some level, I already knew what she meant. Mark did act a bit strangely at times. One moment, he was there, the next he was off in his own little world, talking to himself. But this had never given me great cause for concern.

"If you're going to get married, I need to take you to Claybury Hospital so that you can hear what Mark's psychiatrist has to say about his condition. You should be aware that he has a mental illness, and he must take medication for the rest of his life. If he stays on top of it, the illness will remain under control."

I nodded slowly and said, "I doubt a visit with his doctor will stop me wanting to be part of Mark's life."

Maureen smiled, "I'm delighted that you and Mark have found each other. There is nothing I would like more than for you two to be happy."

***

Claybury Hospital was an imposing Victorian building only a few miles from where Mark's family lived. Being a psychiatric hospital, it didn't have the usual sounds and smells of a medical hospital but was surprisingly quiet. I expected to hear screaming and doors slamming, but everything seemed normal… or at least more normal than might be expected from a general ward in a National Health Hospital. We climbed the stairs to an office, not unlike my old headmaster's, and sat down opposite Mark's psychiatric doctor.

"This is Rosemary, Mark's fiancée," Maureen introduced me. After the usual formalities, Maureen pressed him, "Please, doctor, if you could help explain to Rose about Mark's condition."

The doctor turned to me and said, "First, can you tell me a little about yourself? What's your background? Tell me about your life."

I hadn't expected to be interrogated; rather, I'd expected to do the interrogating. Squirming a little in my chair, I kept it short and sweet. "I'm the office manager at a clothing transport company called Tibbett and Britten. I'm one of seven children and attended Royal Wanstead School for Girls. Mark and I met while on vacation. We've been dating for a year and a half. He proposed yesterday. That's why I'm here…" I really had no idea what else to add. All the while, the doctor sat back in his chair, listening, smiling, and writing the occasional note.

"In your mind, will you and Mark have a successful marriage?" the doctor asked. "And why?"

"Of course we will. I wouldn't have said yes to him otherwise. Both Mark and his parents have made me feel very special. I can honestly say I've never been happier."

When I'd finished, the doctor's face fell serious, as he launched straight into the specifics of Mark's illness. "As I'm sure you are aware, Mark took drugs in Holland. He had an adverse reaction to the drugs, which sometimes makes him act strangely. In my opinion, Mark's illness is a drug-induced psychosis. Provided that he takes his prescribed medication, he will lead a relatively normal life. This is the important point – he must take his medication. But, if he stays on top of it," he stressed again, "he can lead *a normal life.*"

Though the weight of this information hung heavy in the air, we chatted for a while longer, and at the end of the session, the doctor wished me and Mark the best of luck and a long, happy life together. The visit had been strange, but in no way did I reconsider my acceptance of Mark's proposal. I was in it for the long haul. Or so I thought.

***

Mark and I chugged along quite well, but life together wasn't anything thrilling; it mainly revolved around my work, his family, and a limited number of friends. Phil, who Lucy and I had met in Skegness, was really into American folk music, as was Mark, of course. I was happy to do my own thing while they spent time together. We had our holidays in Norfolk with his family, and the occasional day out to places like Woburn Safari Park; otherwise, we were happy just going out to the local pub and visiting friends. Neither of us were high maintenance, so the ol' routine seemed to work for our relationship.

In the meantime, I had left Tibbett & Britten and moved to Rio Tinto

Zinc, a much larger corporation quoted on the stock exchange. During my interview, I learned that the company described itself as 'finding, mining, and processing the earth's mineral resources,' something I knew nothing about, but I wasn't there for a job as an executive. I was over the moon when I landed a position in the small accounts department. The bookkeeper, Dorothy, became my mentor. She was a shy, lovely-natured, middle-aged spinster who knew her job inside out. She taught me double-entry bookkeeping, and I began to know the thrill of hand-written books adding up to zero at the end of the month. It was even thrilling when I'd sometimes have to spend an hour or two finding a mistake and putting it right. Whatever mistakes I made, I was never late in producing the figures and handing over the ledgers to the accountant. For people who do not like figures, this no doubt sounds boring. But to me, it opened up a whole new world.

***

On the 7th of September 1974, Mark and I were married in a church in Woodford Green. The day was dry but the wind was whipping, so much so that my veil blew above my head and couldn't be tamed for a number of the wedding photographs. My sister, Marjorie, had made my wedding dress, and like every bride, I felt like a million bucks. Marjorie's two-year-old daughter Julie, sang 'Winnie the Pooh' repeatedly to herself during the wedding ceremony which made everyone smile. Mark's two cousins were bridesmaids, and there were over seventy guests. I'm not sure if anyone noticed my tears walking down the aisle, but in hindsight, I think I realised at that point that I was in love with the family more so than just Mark.

Mr and Mrs Lamb and friends from my Royal Wanstead days attended, as well as all of my brothers and sisters. This was unusual, as I couldn't remember when we'd last been together, probably at my dad's funeral. If only he could have walked me down the aisle instead of Sid, my stepfather, whom I disliked. As Mum was paying for the wedding, I didn't really have a say in the matter. Regardless, everyone seemed to have a good time, and with no calamities, I deemed it a successful wedding.

As was tradition then, Mark and I left for our honeymoon after the reception that evening. It was my first time traveling abroad, and when we landed in Majorca, the smell, sounds, and warmth made me feel that this really was the first day of a new life.

Our Wedding 1974

4

THE MAD HATTER'S TEA PARTY

The next two years were nothing to write home about, so here's the skim version. We'd bought our first house in Harlow, Essex a month before the wedding, and there was decorating to do and furniture to buy on a budget. I quickly discovered that I didn't like housework, and my cooking skills were abysmal. I realised I was never going to enjoy being a housewife. Instead, I focused on my work outside the home and excelled at it, which preoccupied me more than anything else. Mark didn't mind, as he had his music, and we still spent a lot of time with his family and friends.

Another thing I realised was that marriage was not all it seemed. I had found myself withdrawing from Mark in the bedroom and put it down to being tired with traveling to London every day. I knew I needed to make more of an effort to make the marriage work. I changed jobs so that I could work near home, joining a local Jewish clothing manufacturer as their bookkeeper. I found the work easy and my colleagues friendly enough.

Mark, meanwhile, had changed jobs a few times. Due to his personality disorder, holding a job was not easy for him. Although he was a willing employee, the disorder reared its ugly head now and again. He worked as an HGV driver delivering soil but soon wanted to train to become a bus driver. He enjoyed this work and, for a while, everything was on an even keel.

One thing that was throwing a kink in our mechanical relationship was our love life. Or, at least, it seemed to me. Mark never complained, and we never talked about the infrequency or lack of excitement in the bedroom. As Mark was my first love, how was I to know our sex life was unusual? I figured the novels I'd read had always exaggerated, making sex sound more exciting than it actually was. I assumed that a roll in the sack once a week was completely normal. And, yet, I wasn't satisfied.

***

Nearly three years into the marriage, I woke up one morning at 2 a.m. to find Mark staring out of our bedroom window, muttering to himself. I blinked my sleep away, and to my astonishment, found he held a French sabre bayonet in one hand and a ghurka knife in the other. These were part of a collection he had previously had hanging in his bedroom wall behind the headboard at his home. I was disorientated and thought I was dreaming. It took me a few minutes to understand that Mark was anxious and getting more and more upset.

"Mark, what's the matter?" I asked tentatively. "Come to bed."

He must have sensed my concern, for he replied, "Come and look outside, Rose. There are people in a car down there, and they're coming to get us!"

A chill ran down my spine. Slowly, I arose and crept to the window, choosing to go along with what he was saying so as not to anger him. Sure enough, cars were parked down in the street; but only in the spaces cars had always been parked. None of the cars had people in them. I returned Mark's wild look with an exasperated one, which only exacerbated his agitation.

"We're in danger, Rose! If you don't believe me, come and look at this." He crouched down on the floor and lifted the draping blanket, gesturing beneath the bed. Reluctantly, I knelt down beside him and peered under. "Look at our poor little rabbit all covered in blood," he pointed with his knife. I spotted a rolled-up, red sock in a shadowy corner.

This frightened me more than the imaginary people. I assumed Mark was having a paranoiac schizophrenic attack. In the past, he'd had the occasional blip when he'd forgotten to take his medication. At those times, he acted a bit strangely but never like this. This bloody rabbit was a different story. And not one of which I wanted to know the end. I had to get out of the room and fast.

But I didn't want to move too quickly and alarm him. After all, he was gripping two sharp blades so hard his knuckles were white, and I was unarmed. So, instead, I stood slowly and began inching towards the door.

But he beat me to the punch. He raced in front of it, barring my way and looking increasingly menacing as he brandished the sword and knife.

"You can't go down there!" he screamed out in panic. "They're coming to kill us, and they're going to rape you! I can't let them do that to you." He was pacing and stopped abruptly. "I must kill you first."

I don't know what made me do it – a guardian angel perhaps – but what I did in the next few moments may have saved my life. I calmly approached the door, turned the lock, and looked Mark in the eye. "Look, I've locked us in," I said to him, firmly. "They can't get us now."

He looked at me quizzically, reminding me of a dog trying to work something out in his mind.

"Put the knives down very quietly. We must both get into bed. It's important we don't make a sound when they come to the door." He did as he was told and followed me to bed.

Don't ask me how I fell asleep, but I did. And it must have been almost immediately. I don't remember lying awake or being afraid once Mark had slipped in beside me, but I awoke two hours later to find myself alone again. I looked toward the window and beside the bed, where he'd shown me the "bloody rabbit." Not there. My eyes then scrambled to find the weapons. They were still on the floor where Mark had left them.

The relief that flooded through me was immeasurable. Although I knew he wasn't a bad person, he would have done anything to make sure no one harmed me, even if that meant he had to take my life himself. He must have decided no threat existed and killing me was unnecessary. But where had he gone?

I needed to go to the bathroom, so I crept out of bed as quietly as I could. When I was finished, I opened the bathroom door, and Mark stood before me.

I was startled for a moment, "Mark, are you okay? Did you get some sleep? You look very tired."

"All the relatives are downstairs," he told me, "but don't worry, I've made them all a cup of tea."

I breathed a sigh of relief. *Thank god,* I thought, *he must have called his parents.*

"Who's here?" I asked, feeling reassured already.

"Mum, Dad, Nanna…"

Immediately, my heart began, again, to race. His darling Nanna had died two weeks prior. I knew he was still hallucinating. I went downstairs and, sure enough, a tray full of teacups was set on the table, but with no people surrounding it.

I sat Mark down and called his parents, explaining what had happened. His dad drove the thirty-minute journey to our house, and after spending some time talking to Mark, he took me to one side and asked me to pack a suitcase for him. He was going to take his son to their house to be nearer the hospital.

"Go to work as usual, dear, and don't worry," he said. "Later today we'll let you know what is happening."

***

I knew when Mark and his dad drove away that I wouldn't be able to go to work. I tidied up the house and then waited until it was time for my office to open so I could call in my absence. I then called Mark's parents' house and spoke to his dad.

"How's he doing?" I asked.

David breathed a deep, pained breath. "He was agitated the entire ride over," he answered. "At one point, he grabbed the steering wheel, because there were people waiting for a bus, and he wanted me to stop and pick them up. I had to convince him it was his day off and that there would be a bus coming along very soon. He went quiet, but I knew he was the worst I'd ever seen him."

Although I was worried that Mark's behaviour had extended beyond the four walls of our home, I was somewhat relieved David had seen his son's disorder in action. What had happened that night was so crazy, I was concerned no one would believe me when I told them.

"We'll be calling his psychiatrist first thing," David continued on the other end of the line, "and we'll call you when a decision has been made about how to treat Mark. By the way, Rose, do you know if Mark has been taking his medication?"

I shook my head, even though he couldn't see me and answered, "I'm so sorry, David – no, he hasn't." By then, I had checked and realised Mark had gone off it. I felt terrible that I'd never checked before.

"Don't blame yourself," David reassured me. "Mark is an adult. He felt he was better and didn't need the medication, so he made the decision himself. No one could have seen this coming."

No, no one could have seen it, just as I certainly couldn't have seen the demise of my marriage approaching. But, before I even heard the whistle, it was barrelling down the tracks.

***

Mark spent three weeks in a psychiatric ward at our local hospital and, during this time, he met a lady patient named Caroline. He often talked to me about her, and I remember feeling relieved that he was interacting with people. I liked to listen to him describe the day-to-day goings-on of patients. He explained the hospital's routine, but because different people had different mental challenges, no two days were the same. "One old boy thinks he is still fighting the war, and there are spies everywhere," Mark told me. "He points them out, but of course the 'spies' are just other patients."

When Mark was ready to come home, Maureen and David decided they wanted us to live nearer them and encouraged us to sell the house in Harlow. They even helped us buy a pretty end-of-terrace house in one of the most prestigious streets in Loughton. I loved it and tried my best to make Mark happy and be a good little wife but, unfortunately, I knew by then that I couldn't stay in the marriage. The undeniable fact was I'd outgrown Mark intellectually, and my career was on the rise. I didn't want to be in a marriage with someone who had no interest in my life, someone I didn't love the way a wife should.

Mark's friendship with Caroline enabled me to pluck up the courage to ask for a divorce. Mark didn't protest much; in fact, we remained friends. But his relatives were another story. I dreaded bumping into his mum or auntie who had decided not only to hate me, but to completely shun me. I felt totally humiliated one day when I walked into the local bakery and said hello to Maureen's sister. She glared at me, turned her back on me, and walked away. I felt like a pariah.

Although I'd never realised I was suffocating in our marriage, suddenly, without Mark, I was allowed to breathe again. I moved out of my pretty home and into a dreadful bedsit near my work. I may not have had many material things, but I did have something new: a new lease on life.

5

A HAPPY BIRTHDAY: DECEMBER 1978

Birthdays never meant a great deal to me. This is because, every year, someone else's birthday overshadowed mine.

On December 19th, six days before Christmas, I'd inevitably be let down. Year after year, the same ol' thing. Unremarkable. Mundane. Outshone by the birth of a baby, a couple thousand years my senior. Acknowledged alongside Christmas parties, drinks and family gatherings, but nothing special and certainly nothing worthy of fanfare. In fact, on my fifteenth birthday, my family forgot me altogether and, with that, I gave up. I accepted I'd drawn the short straw. But, for whatever reason, on my twenty-fifth birthday, my luck changed.

The girls at work told me they were organising an office birthday party for me. I was, at that time, employed at Norwoods, a meat wholesaler and family-run business. When I first joined the company, I worked in the accounts department with Mr Stiff and Mr Sheath, both of whom had the same first name. You couldn't make it up really, could you? Mr Stiff left and was replaced by a handsome new accountant. This caused some speculation amongst the girls about his marital status (separated), while the grapevine also reported on the new manager appointed to the meat wholesale division, a master butcher by trade, brought in to try and stem the tide of pilfering. His name was Brian, and he made his mark straight away as a no-nonsense manager. The report that came down the line was that Brian was thirty-five and divorced.

Having just left Mark, I wasn't as enthusiastic about these eligible bachelors as the other girls were. I wasn't in a good place. Mark's parents had been my idols. They'd always treated me like their daughter, but now they weren't talking to me. Louise, my best friend from school, had moved into my rundown flat with me. She had her own relationship issues, and we consoled each other. This transitional period was not pretty, and I was grateful to my friends at work for making my big day special.

The office party would take place in the basement of the building, which had been decorated with Christmas paraphernalia and birthday banners. One of the lads had even brought in his music system so we could dance. On the day of the party, I descended the stairs to find sheets draped over the desks, the girls prettying up the banquet tables, tables that were laden with buffet food made by them, including a small birthday cake. In a separate corner were the drinks – beer, lager, and wine, together with an assortment of non-alcoholic beverages, which were probably meant for me. I always said I could get giggly enough on grapefruit juice, so why waste money on booze?

Once the party had started, one of my colleagues handed me a glass, despite my sobriety. "It's a white wine spritzer," she said. "Enjoy yourself." I gave in but made sure that any future spritzers were more soda water than wine. I was happy to see everyone having fun, but I wouldn't be the one with a hangover in the morning.

The party was in full swing, when the girls started passing out cards and presents to open. I slit one of the cards open and read, 'Sex is like rain. You never know how long it will last or how many inches you're going to get!' Smirking, I passed it to one of the girls. As her smile broadened, one of the lads snatched it up and read it out to everyone, a spectacle that was met with a roar of laughter. My blush deepened with each guffaw. Sex wasn't a subject I was happy discussing in private, let alone in public, with me at the centre of the discussion.

"Who sent it?" the lad who'd read the card out asked, searching front and back for a name.

"Guess," said the warehouse supervisor with a wink.

"It doesn't matter who sent it," I said, blushing furiously. "Whoever did, don't embarrass him." Really, I meant *don't embarrass me*.

"Oh, it's too late now," one of the girls laughed. "I bet it's Brian, the new manager. He fancies you. I could tell that when he was dancing with you."

My face was on fire as I searched for Brian amongst the lot, but he was nowhere to be seen. I hadn't noticed him dancing with me any differently to anyone else. Actually, that's not true. He stood out in my mind, because he was a good dancer, twirling me about the dance floor, as though I was feather-light. But as to whether or not he fancied me, what could anyone have seen in our conservative dancing to suggest it? *Honestly*, I thought, *how easily actions are misinterpreted.*

"Happy birthday to you, happy birthday to you…" Lynn came to the rescue, approaching with the cake fully lit with candles, as everyone was still chuckling about Brian and the card. Instead of persisting in their teasing, they all chimed in, and the boys followed it up by hoisting me into the air, so they could give me the bumps. Thank goodness I'd chosen to wear trousers!

I was in my element and enjoying every moment, but all the while, I wondered why Brian had sent me that card. *Does he really like me?* I thought. *He treats me just the same as the others girls.* I'd felt special when he was dancing with me, but then he disappeared as if he'd done his bit and could leave. *He's too old for me anyway*, I decided, putting him out of my mind.

As the party came to a close, I thanked everyone and insisted, "I'll finish the clearing up," and in response to their protests, added, "I live the nearest. Besides, it'll take me no time at all. You've made me feel very special today; it's the least I could do. Now, go on home."

To be honest, I wanted to be alone. You know how it happens sometimes, when you're being celebrated, and you're meant to be happy, but in the deep down depths of you, you know that you're not? My heart felt leaden with this discordant sorrow, and as it grew heavier, I imagined everyone heading home to their loved ones, their families, their relationships, their happily-ever-afters. And, me? I was heading home to a cold, dark, empty flat. Louise was likely out for the night, leaving me to sit alone, wondering what had become of my life. I reminded myself that I was at fault for it all. I was the one who had put myself in this position. I could have been going home to Mark. But, then again, had that ever really made me happy?

As the tears fell, knowing I'd never really loved Mark the way I should have, I wondered why I'd married him in the first place. I had cried walking down the aisle, not tears of joy, but of angst, in realising too late that his parents' attention is what I craved. This loneliness and sheer isolation was the price I had to pay for the choices I'd made. I'd never really understood the term 'having a heavy heart,' but that was what I had. More appropriately, my heart was empty with no one to care for and no one to care for me.

After clearing up, I climbed the stairs, trudged to my desk, and collected my things. I wrapped up warm, and as I was just about to leave, a door creaked open, making me jump out of my skin. I looked up, and there was Brian. It took me a moment to comprehend why he was still there, and I finally realised it was out of necessity; I didn't have keys to lock the office.

"Are you all right?" he asked, a note of concern lifting his brow. "You look like you've been crying."

"I'm okay, thanks," I turned away. "I was just getting ready to leave."

"Are you sure you're okay? Has someone upset you?" he came nearer me, forcing me to return his look. "This isn't the bright-eyed girl I was swinging round the dance floor earlier."

"I'm fine, honestly," I shrugged. "I'm just feeling sorry for myself – nothing that a brisk walk home in the cold won't put right."

"Is your boyfriend collecting you?"

Oh, so he doesn't know my tale of woe then? I thought. *There's no reason he should, I suppose. I don't know anything much about him either.*

"No, no boyfriend," I answered. "I live close by and share my flat with a friend."

"Well, it's just as well I've finished what I was doing. I'll walk you back to your flat then." At my look of apprehension, he added, "I can't allow you to walk home at this time of night on your own."

"It isn't even ten o'clock yet," I replied. But he wouldn't take no for an answer. This old-fashioned gentleman felt it was his duty to escort little ol' me – the weeping damsel in distress – home. And in my distress, I didn't have the strength to argue.

As we walked, Brian did most of the talking. The conversation came round to his past. "I'm divorced," he revealed, "and I have two boys, ages nine and eleven, who live with their mother in a pub near Little Venice. I accepted the job at Norwoods so that I'd be a bit closer to them. I also have a house in Reading that I return to on the weekends. Every other weekend, I look after the boys and usually take them to visit their grandparents in Surrey." With this thorough history as our icebreaker, we arrived at the flat in no time.

"Would you like to come in for a coffee?" I asked, feeling obliged and hoping he needed to get home. I was tired and could easily have fallen asleep standing up.

But he took me up on my offer, and so I invited him in, praying that the flat was tidy and, if Louise was home, that she was suitably dressed. I needn't have worried; there she was in her dressing gown with fluffy slippers on and a mug of hot chocolate in her hands. I introduced her to Brian and sped to the kitchen to make our coffee. When I returned, the two of them were chatting away merrily.

"Louise tells me you were the head girl at school, so are you a bit of a brain box?" Brian asked with a smile and a wink. "I always thought you were the brains in the accounts department."

"Being head girl doesn't make me brainy. In fact, Louise showed me up in the brain department a time or two."

"Here you go again, Miss Modesty," Louise grinned. "Don't believe her, Brian. She just talks herself down, when she's feeling sorry for herself."

"Well, she should be feeling good today, because it's the first day of the rest of her life, and I, for one, will make sure of it. But for now, I must be getting home. I have an early start tomorrow."

Coffee consumed, Brian said goodnight to Louise, and I walked him to the front door.

"Thank you so much for walking me home," I smiled at him. "I'm sorry I've made you late."

"It was my pleasure. I was sorry that I wasn't able to spend much time at your birthday party. Perhaps you'll allow me to buy you a drink before we close for Christmas?"

"That would be nice," I heard myself saying. Again, my thoughts contradicted my response. *Would it be nice? Would it, really? Why did I say yes? He is way too old for me.*

After saying our goodbyes and goodnights, I raced back up to the apartment and told Louise that Brian had asked me out for a drink. Her response was positive, "He's a really nice man. I hope you said 'yes.'"

"I sort of did," I replied. "He is nice but a bit old for me, don't you think? He's thirty-five."

"That's hardly one foot in the grave, is it? He's only asked you for a drink. Promise me you'll go if he asks you again."

Suddenly, I remembered the card he'd sent me. I showed it to Louise, and she laughed hysterically. "Ask him if he's got a friend as handsome, funny, and charming as he is."

I laughed in response and went off to bed, smiling. My mood had changed, and I no longer felt sorry for myself. It had been a happy birthday.

I replayed the evening's events in my mind and wasn't surprised when Brian appeared and reappeared in my memory on repeat. I was happy to be happy again and fell asleep before my head touched the pillow.

***

When I woke up the next morning, I remembered Louise was leaving to spend the Christmas holidays with her mother in Chesterfield. She wasn't looking forward to it, as they had a fractious relationship. I'd seen this first-hand, having been to their family home several times on our school holidays. So as she was leaving, I gave Louise an extra hug and handed her a Christmas present. "Enjoy the break and don't worry about leaving me here to fend for myself."

She laughed, "I bet you can't wait to get into work this morning and see if Brian asks you out for that drink."

"I don't—"

"Don't you dare tell me that you won't go," she interrupted. "It's not every day that someone is going to show an interest in you, you know."

It was a cold, frosty morning, and as I walked briskly through the underpass onto George Lane, I thought about what she'd said. *I suppose she was right; I shouldn't dismiss Brian entirely without getting to know him better. Anyway, knowing my luck, he probably wouldn't talk to me today. It will be business as usual.*

Being that everyone was winding down, ready for the Christmas break, a lot of chattering was going on in the office when I walked in. But the work didn't stop. Every time another batch of sales invoices came in from the warehouse, a unanimous groan rumbled through the room. This was a busy time of year, of course; turkey, duck, beef, chicken, sausage, bacon, lamb and pork were all in demand. We only had three days to go until Friday, the 22nd of December, the last working day before Christmas. I rallied the troops and made sure everyone was pulling their weight. To my dismay, every time Brian came into the office, the lot of them made a point of chanting in unison, "Hello, Mr Turner, is it Rosemary you want to see?" Although I blushed crimson, Brian took it all in his stride, and apart from giving me a wink when no one else was looking he went about his business, joining in with the girls' banter now and again.

Just before the end of the workday, he brought in the last batch of paperwork and placed it on my desk. On top was a note that read, 'Would you like to have a drink with me after work? Check 'Yes, No, Tomorrow, Friday, Sometime or Never.''

A smile twitched at my lips, as I said, "I'll stay a bit later tonight and try and get these entered before I leave. Will you be around if I have any queries?"

"I'll be here until six o'clock as usual," Brian answered. He sauntered back into the warehouse.

Considering everyone's daft antics that morning, I was certain some snide comment would be made, but they were all far more interested in clearing their desks ready for going home. Most of my colleagues were married and had families, so the fact that they were first out the door was understandable. I, on the other hand, had no one. I decided a drink with Brian would be better than being miserable at home.

When everyone had left and I'd finished the paperwork, I struck out to find Brian. He was deep in conversation with one of his staff, and I sensed some friction so decided to leave them to it. But, as I turned to go, Brian called out, "Would you mind waiting five minutes for me? I'll have the answer to your query."

I simply nodded and returned to my desk. When he joined me, he looked harassed and worn out.

"Difficult day?"

He nodded, "Let's go for that drink and forget about work." As we left the office, Brian turned to me with a swift change of heart. "Let's have dinner instead. Nothing fancy. I don't know about you, but I'm starving."

As I headed home to ready myself for a seven o'clock pickup, I realized I was very much looking forward to learning more about this mystery man who was certainly kicking up a storm in the warehouse. Now, what to wear? I'd never been into fashion and didn't have the money to be, anyhow. I changed several times, finally landing upon a smart dress, one I'd never worn to the office. As I looked into the mirror, I realised I was actually nervous. *Why?* I asked myself. *We're only going for dinner, after all.* I attempted to calm my nerves before he arrived.

We ended up at The George a bar with good pup grub that I knew would be quite lively. I suggested the place, because the Norwood team lunched there often, particularly if there was something to celebrate or sometimes just because it was a Friday. After making the suggestion, I began immediately to question it. What if someone from the office was there? I didn't want to fuel the fire that had already been kindled yesterday with Brian's card and the purported close dancing.

But, it turned out The George was an excellent choice; no one we knew was there, the food was cooked well, the pub wasn't too noisy, and Brian was a good conversationalist.

After ordering, Brian looked around the room. "No Norwoods folk," he grinned. "Now, we can trade some stories and get to know each other in peace. What do you think?"

I nodded, "I'll let you start the story-telling, since you're older and wiser."

"I'm young at heart," his smile was infectious and made me grin. "Hm, let's see. Where to begin? Oh, I know," he sat back in his chair. "I used to be a master butcher in Pangbourne, which is a lovely village in Berkshire. A well-dressed man would come in once a week and ask for a bag full of bones and a small amount of braised steak. Nothing else, the same each week. I was curious so asked him why. He looked embarrassed, but in his very posh English accent, he told me he'd fallen on hard times and that the bones and meat made delicious soup which lasted most of the week." Brian paused, "I felt bad for asking but made sure I put extra meat in the bag each week after that."

My heart warmed. I was planning on telling him one of my funny stories but now felt obliged to tell him of a good deed. I knew I had some but none came to mind, so I went with the story I'd planned. "I can't top that, so I'll regale you with a story about my twenty-first birthday dinner, organised by work friends. They took me to an Italian restaurant called Topo Gigio. There were about fifteen of us, and the banter was quite loud and raucous. When it came time for dessert, I was told mine had been specially prepared, so there was no need to look at the menu. When the handsome waiter arrived with a rude version of a banana split, everyone erupted in laughter, while I sank into my chair. Then I was forced to eat the strawberry from the end of the upright banana with my hands behind my back."

Brian roared with laughter, so infectious that even the tables near us joined in. To this day, I'm not sure why I chose that story, but it soon livened things up. By the end of the evening, my face hurt from smiling so much. Brian had kept the subject matter light and had loads of funny stories to tell.

"What are you doing at Christmas?" he asked, as the evening was wrapping up.

"I'll be driving to Durham with my brother, Roger, to stay with my mum."

"What about New Year's Eve weekend?"

"Oh, I haven't thought about it yet. There's usually something happening I can join in with." That was a white lie, really. When I was with Mark, his family always had something going, but I wasn't part of that something anymore. For the first time that evening, my spirit sank. "What are you doing?" I asked Brian, attempting to recover myself.

"I have tickets for a dance on the Saturday, and then it's tradition that all the neighbours get together for a New Year's Eve party."

"Will you have your boys with you?"

"Yes, they love the party. It allows them to meet up with the friends they've grown up with and don't otherwise get to see very often." He hesitated a moment, then said, "If you don't receive a better offer, I would love to twirl you around the dance floor again. I can promise you a fun few days."

"Well, maybe—"

"Don't give me an answer now," he cut me off. "Think about it. We can talk when you come home from Christmas break."

"Thanks," I agreed. "I'll think about it." I decided right then and there that Brian was a real gentleman.

And he proved this further when we arrived at my flat by kissing me on the cheek. "Thank you for your company. I've had a lovely evening and look forward to your answer."

***

I'd promised my brother Roger that I would drive him up to Durham for Christmas. I had forgotten to tell him that the heating wasn't working in my mini. It was a tortuous journey for me although Roger was fine as he could sleep anywhere. After an uneventful Christmas holiday, I realised why I had left the northeast for London. I didn't belong there, and I didn't want to be there. The entire time I was home, I counted down to Boxing Day, when I could head back to South Woodford to my cold, uninviting flat. Before I knew it, my countdown had ended, and I was packing my things in the car. As I shoved my suitcase in the trunk, my mum hollered, "Rosemary, someone's on the phone for you!" *Strange*, I thought, *I'm not expecting a call.*

"Hello?" I questioned the phone.

"Hello, Rose, sorry to disturb you…" It was Brian. I smiled when I heard his voice; it was like a breath of fresh air sent to lift me out of the doldrums.

After the usual banter back and forth about Christmas, he asked, "So, have you given any thought about the New Year?"

I hadn't really, but spending the holiday with people was going to be tons better than spending it on my own. I hesitated just long enough before replying, "Do you have room for me at your house with the boys there?"

"Sorry, I should have pre-empted that question. The small bedroom will be yours. Does that mean you'll join us?"

"Yes, thanks for asking. I would like that very much."

When I set the phone down, I was grinning from ear to ear; I now had something to look forward to. I hoped 1978 would end on a happy note and that 1979 would be the start of me learning to live life to the full.

6

THE DANCE

On the Saturday before the New Year, I woke up in a cold sweat, wondering whether the decision to spend the next three days with Brian had been a good one after all. I don't know why I had doubts; I knew he liked me, and I had a good feeling about him. But my mind nagged me relentlessly. I hadn't asked many questions about the weekend at all. I wasn't even sure when he was collecting the boys from their mother. I didn't think he would try anything on, but what if he did? How would I react?

A couple of days before he was to pick me up, Brian called again, and his upbeat demeanor made me feel better about everything. "I'm really looking forward to spending time with you, Rose," he said. "Remember that we're going dancing." I had remembered and had even bought a new dress for the occasion as a Christmas present to myself. "I'll pick you up mid-morning. Don't eat a big breakfast."

The morning of our getaway, Brian arrived as promised, and as we drove through London, I grew nervous about meeting his boys while the two of us were just beginning to know each other. I had heard from friends who had stepchildren that any enmity between the children and the new addition could be a rocky road to disaster. Having no children of my own and having never had a partner with a family, I didn't know what to expect. When we arrived at our destination, I waited in the car, wondering what the boys would be like and what they would think when they saw me. I didn't have long to wonder; within five minutes, the two came sailing out of the pub they lived in, their bags launched into the car boot, the doors flung open, and like trained trapeze artists, they catapulted into the back seat.

"Say hello to Rose," Brian commanded. "She's going to stay with us for the weekend."

"Cor blimey, Dad, not another one?" said Russell the younger of the two. Out of the mouths of babes, as the saying goes. Clearly, I wasn't the first girlfriend Brian had introduced to his sons.

"You cheeky monkey," Brian laughed. "She's the nicest one though, you wait and see."

I swiveled in my seat and greeted them, my nerves evaporating. "Hello, you two. Nice to meet you." eleven-year-old Darren had a broad grin on his face and looked friendly enough. He was a good-looking boy with tousled brown hair, and Brian had already told me he loved spending time away from the pub they now lived in with his mum and stepfather. Russell looked nothing like Darren. He had blonde hair, blue eyes, and a cheeky demeanour. He was also a mummy's boy and thus was less likely to be friendly with me. But I didn't let that stop me from trying to win him over. "Did you get the Christmas presents you were hoping for this year?" I asked. This was obviously a good icebreaker, as it broke through any and all shyness. The rest of the car journey entailed a rundown of the toys and games and presents they'd received from Santa.

While the boys' lists unfurled, the scenery changed as we left London, heading south. We weren't on the M4 towards Reading, as was our plan. This left me to ponder silently where our detour would lead. When we arrived at our destination and pulled up outside a three-bedroom, semi-detached house, I was even more confused. I knew it couldn't be Brian's home. Were we stopping off at a friends'?

The mystery was soon solved, however, when a grey-haired lady opened the door with a big smile.

"Hi, Mum," Brian said as he escaped out his car door to greet her. He collected a bag of shopping from the boot, before walking me to the front door, while the boys rushed on ahead of us. "I bought meat from Norwoods for my parents," Brian explained, under his breath. "My mum insisted on cooking lunch for us."

This was not quite what I was expecting. I hadn't anticipated meeting anyone's parents, least of all Brian's. *Am I going to be interrogated?* I wondered. *What will his parents think about their son's new friend? Girlfriend? How is Brian going to introduce me?*

"This is Rose, the friend I told you about from the office," he answered that question straight off. I smiled and extended my hand to his mother, thinking, *So I'm a 'friend'; at least we've got that much figured out.* "Rose, this is Joan, and Jim will no doubt be putting the kettle on." His mum nodded. With a grin on his face and a wink at me, Brian joked, "Rose is a wiz with numbers but doesn't know much about butchery yet. I bet she can't cook pork chops quite like you can." *A mama's boy, through and through,* I thought, as he handed over the shopping bag to his mum, who was delighted with the compliment.

She ushered us into the lounge, where I met Brian's dad. I could tell straight away he had a quiet personality and was happy to blend into the background, while his wife bandied about, fussing over Brian with a smile always on her face. Joan was taller than her husband, while Jim had maybe a tad too much weight around his middle. He shook my hand and poured my tea, after which Brian and the boys took centre stage, ensuring no lull ever crept in the conversation. I was on my best behaviour and genuinely enjoyed playing games with the boys, particularly Connect Four, which was their favourite. I made sure to lose in order to hold their favour.

"Jim, have you made the apple sauce for the pork chops?" Joan asked her husband, as I helped lay the table, determined to make a good impression. Jim hovered in the kitchen, expecting orders to be forthcoming. "Oh, yes, and don't forget Brian likes cranberry sauce so find that as well."

It was evident who wore the trousers in this relationship, and I felt sorry for Jim who kept the peace in order to get on with it. Brian looked over and winked at me, "Dad does as he's told but he's the boss, really. Isn't that right, Mum?" Joan grinned but didn't say anything. As Brian watched Joan busying herself over the pork chops, he reminded her, "Remember, we're going to a dance and can't stay long, Mum."

"I wish you'd invited me. You know how much I love you to spin me round the dance floor."

"This is Rose's first real chance to see me in action," Brian replied, smiling at me, "so you wouldn't have got a look in. Especially considering she's already confessed she has two left feet, so she'll take a while before she catches you up. Isn't that right, Rose?"

I appreciated that Brian was trying to engage the two of us in a conversation. I decided to play my part even though, inside, I was growing concerned that Joan didn't like me. I could feel it. "Absolutely," I said, smiling. "I'll no doubt embarrass Brian tonight, and he'll soon be regretting making this our first proper date." I left it at that, but I could tell Joan wasn't charmed by me.

After a lunch of delicious pork chops, we said our goodbyes and headed for Reading. The sky had grown grey, threatening snow. Brian turned to the boys in the back seat, "I'm taking Rose out for the evening. You'll be staying with Pete and Brenda. Behave yourselves." This information barely registered on their radar. It seemed that staying with the neighbours wasn't something new to the boys. I began to think Brian must be a player. *How many girls has this guy brought round?*

We pulled into a cul-de-sac, and my first impressions of the house and neighbourhood were positive. Though barren now, I envisaged the small, manicured lawns and flowerbeds filled with colour at springtime. Some of the houses were lit up with Christmas lights, and Brian's front door was decorated with a holly wreath spotted with red berries and a robin perched on top. I felt at home already, and I hadn't yet been inside.

As I entered, I could feel the warmth of a coal fire. *Warm already?* I thought, the mystery of Brian growing. *Does this man have worker elves, slaving away in his absence, readying our arrival?* I was just about to ask who had prepared the fire, when Brian said, "The great thing about living here is that all I have to do is ring Pete, and he'll pop on over and light the fire for me. There'll be plenty of hot water for you to have a bath before we go out if you'd like."

"That would be perfect," I replied, looking forward to some alone time before the party. "Is there anything I can do before I disappear for a soak?"

"Nothing at all," Brian's words were music to my ears, "you're our guest and so you can expect to be spoiled."

I was led upstairs to my room at the front of the house, which was exactly as Brian had described: small, but with a cosy feel. Perfect for me. After a short-guided tour, Brian ran my bath, checking with me before adding bubbles. *Spoiled is right,* I thought. *I could get used to this.*

***

To my dismay, the house was empty when I came downstairs after bathing and dressing. But before I could panic, I found a note on the table in Brian's scribbled hand, "Gone next door to settle the boys in. Won't be long just make yourself at home. There's wine in the fridge." I skipped the wine and made myself a coffee. I didn't want to establish myself as a wine-o, which was far from the truth.

Before long, Brian bustled through the door, whipping his coat off and wiping his shoes. He was all smiles. "Your dress is lovely," he said. "I'll pop up for a quick shower so that you don't have to dance with a tramp."

The dance was being held a forty-minute drive away, out in the country. We started out as evening was falling, and when we approached the venue, snow started to drift to the ground, an appropriately romantic beginning to our night of dance. The event was taking place in a country pub with a large dance floor, and the festivities were in full swing when we arrived later than expected. We navigated round the bystanders to the bar, where the publican and friends immediately greeted Brian. He took great care to introduce me as his new dancing partner and friend. *Yikes,* I thought, *he really wants to impress upon me and everyone else that we're nothing more than good pals.*

From start to finish, it was a never-ending round of introductions, since Brian seemed to know most of the people there. Apart from a plump lady who stepped in to dance with Brian, I can't pretend that I remember anyone I met that night. I watched them dancing and when Brian returned, he explained who she was. "This is the friend that helped me get over Mandy, and we became close," he said. He then whispered, "She really wanted me to fall in love with her, but the chemistry wasn't there. I think she's finally accepted that we're just friends."

Though we hadn't spoken much about Mandy, his previous love, I sensed it was a painful break up for him. I decided we'd come far enough to probe the issue some. "What happened with you and Mandy?" I asked. "I mean, if you don't mind my asking."

"She..." he hesitated before admitting, "she ended the relationship. I didn't want it to end. She was young – younger than you, even. I was her first long-term boyfriend. After three years together, she wanted to travel and have the freedom to go out with other people. She didn't want to settle for being the step-mum to two small boys. She said she needed to spread her wings."

I weighed my response, trying not to be too involved or judgmental. "Oh, Brian, I'm sorry. Such a sad story. But her feelings are understandable, I guess."

"Understandable, yes, but it came as a complete shock to me. I was devastated. I thought I'd found the love of my life. I was so happy waking up every morning to her beside me. It was because of that love I had to let her go."

"I can't even imagine what that must be like. I don't think I was ever in love with Mark, although I cared for him and loved him in a way. Has she found happiness, do you know?"

"I think so. We're still friends, and I see her once in a while. It took some time for me to face the fact that she would never be mine again. It hurt so much; I thought I would die. Life goes on though, and I knew I would eventually get over her. I'm much happier now than I was six months ago."

With that, Brian reached for my hand, held it tightly, and steered me toward the dance floor. After a few lively dances, where Brian impressed me with his jiving (and I trod on his toes more times than I care to admit), 'Don't Go Changing' began to play. As Brian pulled me close, my heart skipped a beat. I'd never felt this way before, nor had I ever danced with anyone like this before. Though it was thrilling to feel as though I was floating on air, I didn't know whether or not it was real or if I even wanted it to be. I had no idea what I wanted at this stage of my life, but it wasn't to fall for the first person that made my heart flutter, and it certainly wasn't to be going out with someone older than my big brothers. To put it mildly, I was confused. Though I liked Brian and adored the way he treated me, I felt myself withdrawing from the idea of being a couple, which I could feel happening the more we danced.

All at once, the music stopped, and the DJ made an announcement, "I don't want to worry any of you, but I must warn everyone that the snow is falling thick and fast now. The roads around here are bad enough without snow, so I recommend that those with long journeys leave earlier than planned. Be safe out there and drive carefully."

I looked at Brian, and he shrugged his shoulders. "I've driven snowy roads plenty," he said. "I was a professional bus driver at one point. I'm comfortable driving, whatever the conditions." He must have sensed my continued trepidation, because he added, "Let's have one last dance and then we'll make a move."

The journey home was scary. Brian demonstrated that he did know exactly how to drive in a snowstorm, but I wasn't convinced about anyone else on the road. We made slow progress; a forty-minute journey had taken us double that by the time we'd arrived a stone's throw from where he lived. At that point, cars had stopped at the top of a small hill, clearly not confident to continue over it for fear of skidding. A minor car collision had occurred halfway down the incline. Drivers were standing outside, craning their necks. Brian popped out as well, surveyed the situation, and got back in.

"Hold on to your seat," he said, his eyes glowing. "I'm going to get you home!" He steered the car into the middle of the road, cautiously passed the mishap, made a couple of right turns, and we'd arrived in his cul-de-sac. "Home, safe and sound," he smiled at me, as we pulled up alongside the curb, and we rushed inside, shaking the snow from our winter coats. "Didn't I tell you I knew how to drive? I wouldn't have risked it if I didn't know it would be easy for me. Most UK drivers can't navigate snow, since we get so little of it. Understandably, traffic slows down and drivers panic and stall, too scared to continue. But I just remember what my training taught me."

I smiled and attempted to congratulate him, but my response turned into a yawn. The dancing, the socialising, the excitement of the evening, and the tense drive home had taken its toll on me. "Do you mind if I go straight up to bed? I've had a really lovely evening, but I am dead on my feet."

"Of course you can. Would you like a drink to take up with you?" I shook my head. "I'll just leave you to lie in tomorrow morning. Being a butcher, I'm an early bird so will probably be up and about by five o'clock. I won't make any noise, but you might hear the boys later in the morning." He approached me at the foot of the stairs and kissed me gently on the lips. "Thank you for a lovely day," he said, ever the gentleman. "I've enjoyed it very much. Sleep well, and I'll see you in the morning."

As I made my way upstairs I felt like my life was beginning all over again, and I didn't know why I'd been confused earlier on in the evening. Brian was the nicest person I'd ever met. A true prince in shining armour, perhaps sent to Norwoods strictly to rescue this damsel in distress. If he was sent by fate, I was grateful. As I climbed into bed, I hoped the memories of the evening would continue on in my dreams.

***

I woke the next morning feeling refreshed and excited about whatever the day had in store. Reaching up, I pulled the curtain to one side. The snow had continued through the night, and a winter wonderland now spread its sparkling scape across the cul-de-sac. Below, Brian's footsteps led from the front door of the house to the neighbours and back again, but judging by the fact that no boys' footsteps accompanied his I assumed we were alone. I rose from the bed and put on my fleecy dressing gown. If Brian intended to take advantage of the absence of his children and expected me to float downstairs in a negligee, he would be sorely mistaken.

Hearing me wake, Brian called up the stairs, "Would you like coffee or tea? I'll bring it up to you."

"Tea, please," I answered, "but no sugar."

When he entered my room with the tea tray, he asked, "Would you like to come into my room? It's warmer in there, and we can both sit on my bed." For some reason, I was not at all suspicious of Brian's intentions, and as I was feeling a bit chilly, the invitation was welcome. The house hadn't yet warmed up, but I could smell that Brian had lit the fire, so it would soon be pleasant enough. But for now, I followed him to his room and snuggled under the covers of his bed. "No sugar in your tea?" he asked, handing me my cup. "Are you sweet enough then?"

"You took the words right out of my mouth," I grinned. "But, really, would you like to know why?" He nodded. "I was eleven years old, and my oldest brother, Roger, was nineteen. With such a large age gap, he was an enigma to me. He was into pop music and girls, of course, but I never really got to know him until I was fourteen. One summer, he invited a new girlfriend to stay. She was from Sweden, and her name was Astrid. I remember thinking she was so exotic and beautiful. I liked to talk to her, because she had a pleasant singsongy voice, and she told me once that she never took sugar in her tea and coffee, because she was always watching her weight. She was quite short and didn't want to look dumpy. Ever since, I've never taken sugar in my drinks. It has yet to make me look like Astrid though."

Brian laughed, "You look pretty good to me. Did their romance last?"

"No, but I could tell you another funny story, if you're interested."

"Of course I'm interested. I'm happy you're happy to share stories with me. We should make the most of this time together, as it'll be bedlam when the boys return."

"All right, this one's funny," I began with confidence. "I usually slept like a log at that age, but while Astrid was visiting, I woke up in the middle of the night and needed to go the bathroom. So off I went and no doubt made enough noise to wake the dead, because when I came out of the bathroom, my mum was on the landing. I heard her say to my dad, 'Bill, wake up, Astrid isn't in her bed!' As quick as a flash, I said 'Don't worry, mum, she's in bed with Roger!'" Brian laughed. "Well, I didn't know that was not the right thing to be happening, did I? Chaos ensued with Mum growing more and more insistent that my dad go into the boys' room to boot Astrid out of there. Dad insisted that it would cause more problems doing that than leaving it. He said, 'Cora, think about it – three boys are in there with them. They can only be sleeping!'"

"So what happened the next morning?" Brian asked.

"Oh, everything was back to normal, and no harm done. To this day, I don't know if either Mum or Dad bothered Roger about it."

As we both laughed, suddenly I realised I was discussing my childhood with someone I hardly knew. Mark had never even heard these stories. A natural comfort existed between Brian and me, one that never had existed with anyone else. Brian shared his life with me, as well. He was the eldest of two boys and his brother, Michael, lived close to his mum and dad. Michael had three sons. "There's obviously a shortage of female genes in our family," he said.

We'd become so comfortable opening up that he even went so far as to share with me the details of his divorce. "I have to confess I'd become a workaholic, which meant I was at home less and less. When I wasn't working in the butchers, I was driving a bus. We needed the money to maintain a reasonable standard of living, and I thought I was doing the right thing. But this left her to her own devices. She decided she'd get herself a part-time job and, eventually, she succumbed to the advances of one of the salesman and started having an affair. I began to suspect something was wrong when my next-door neighbour suggested it might be a good idea to slow up and pay her some attention. By then it was too late. She was cool towards me, and nothing I said was right."

"So what did you do?" I asked, eager to hear more.

"Well, one evening I decided to come home from work early and found Pete's wife, Brenda, babysitting. When I asked her why, Brenda said, 'She said she had an evening meeting to go to. Didn't she tell you?' I answered, 'No, and I suspect it's not an official company meeting.' Brenda put her arm round me and said, 'I don't know for sure, but she has been avoiding me lately, as if she's guilty of something. I hope you can get everything back on track.' I waited up for a while but soon fell asleep. The sound of a key being turned jolted me awake. There she stood, pretty much covered in mud, and shocked to see me up."

Brian stopped short, having noticed the time. "The boys will be back any minute, and we haven't yet had breakfast," he said, "so I'm going to let you fill in the blanks. Besides, you really don't want to start the day with the gory details of my divorce. That's well and truly history, and I have no regrets. The good thing is we're civil to each other because of the boys, and that's all that matters."

I found myself not only wanting to hear the gory details, but all the details of his life. I especially wanted to hear more about Mandy. What's more, I was pleased that Brian had genuinely wanted to get to know me and didn't have ulterior motives so soon, which could have spoilt things. Anyone walking into the bedroom that morning would have thought we'd known each other for a lot longer than a few weeks. We were completely relaxed in each other's company, and my confusion had vanished; I knew I'd made the right decision to come to Reading with this man, and I couldn't wait to see where our relationship would lead.

7

A NEW YEAR

Ready to start my day, I descended the stairs to find the three boys were sitting round the table with a list before them. The New Year's Eve party would take place that evening at the neighbours', three doors up. Everyone who attended had to participate in some small way, meaning that everyone had a job, including me. This tried and tested formula ensured everything was ready ahead of time so we could all ring in the New Year without stress or disappointment. As it turned out, I wouldn't be disappointed in the slightest.

Brian introduced me to the hosts early on in the evening, who then directed me in what to do. My job was to wrap the plastic knives and forks in a festive paper napkin and help with laying out the buffet food – hardly rocket science. The tasks also gave me a chance to get to know some of the neighbours outside the confines of a loud and boisterous crowd. I was grateful Brian had allowed me to dip my toes in, as I would be the stranger in the midst. If I'd been thrown in the deep-end when the party was in full swing, I suspect I would have kept myself to myself, but my enthusiasm about being part of the welcoming committee demonstrated my eagerness to mingle.

The furniture had been pushed to one side and chairs placed round the wall wherever there was room. And soon there was barely any, it was so crowded and noisy. Music played, while the children charged about, hyper on sugar, waiting for the games to start. We ate food off paper plates, and there was plenty of alcohol to keep the adults happy. *Have I ever had a New Year's Eve like this?* I asked myself, as the party whirled around me. My family had always been so fragmented that we never saw the New Year in all together. Mark's family was small, and we tended to meet up and have a sit-down dinner with champagne at midnight. No new year in my life had ever matched this level of raucousness and fun.

I was leaning against the wall, smiling pensively at this thought, when, "Oy, Rose!" broke me from my reverie. I looked across at Pete, Brian's next-door neighbour, and he beckoned me over. He was shorter than Brian, plumper, had thinner hair, and wore black-rimmed glasses; but what he lacked in beauty, he made up for in personality. He was the joker of the bunch, and I could see straight away that you couldn't be miserable when Pete was around. He wouldn't let you. As I approached him, he took my hand and pulled me towards him, saying, "Come and sit on my lap, and we'll talk about the first thing that pops up!"

I sat on his knee, laughing, and responded, "There's no point in trying to shock me, Pete. Your reputation precedes you. I know you're a pussy cat underneath all that bravado."

"Oh, so Brian's been telling you all my secrets then? Shall I tell you some of his?"

"We're just good friends, you know. Brian only felt sorry for me and thought I would have fun at the party, and he was right."

"Just good friends? I'm sure he told me you were in his bed this morning."

"Did he now? I bet he didn't tell you that he was fully dressed, and I may as well have been."

Pete laughed, "I was only winding you up. Brian thinks more of you than to take advantage. Are you sure you don't want to hear some of his secrets?"

"He's probably got far too many to tell, and there is far too much excitement going on to spend time on that. Anyway, I'm sure I'd be required to tell you a few of mine in return, and I wouldn't want to put you to sleep before midnight."

Pete laughed again. I seemed to be on a roll. "You're absolutely right," he said. "Come and have a dance with me instead. But be gentle; I haven't been out of hospital long." Pete had suffered a heart attack recently. He was forty and needed a quadruple-bypass.

"Well, it's a good job that it's a slow record on then. I'll make sure I don't give you any cause for a spike in blood pressure."

Brian saw Pete and I enjoying our banter and decided to muscle in on the action. "Brenda's looking for you, Pete, and she's looking particularly sexy tonight, so I wouldn't leave her alone if I were you."

"Thanks, mate. I was waiting for someone to rescue me from young Rose, here. She was intimating she liked me better than you."

I gave him a friendly clip on the ear, "You promised not to tell Brian that. Off you go. I'll have to make it up to him now."

Pete made heavy weather of getting out of the chair before kissing me on the cheek and whispering to Brian in a loud voice, "Keep hold of this one. She's a little diamond."

Brian saluted, "Will do, captain." He reached for my hand and pulled me to the dance floor.

"Thanks again for including me in this special occasion," I whispered in his ear. Brian pulled me even closer, and I felt happier than I'd ever imagined.

***

Midnight was approaching, when I heard the champagne corks popping.

"I'll help pass out the glasses," I left Brian on the dance floor. I was grateful to get away, as we'd been dancing almost non-stop. Although I was exhausted, I was looking forward to singing 'Auld Lang Syne' and bringing in the New Year with these newfound friends and acquaintances.

"Ten, nine, eight..." Brian found me when the countdown began and stood by my side, holding my hand tightly, as though he was worried I might run away. On the stroke of midnight, everyone roared, "Happy New Year," clinking their glasses, and singing boisterously. We joined hands with the people on either side of us, forming a circle, and as the tune drew to a close, everyone rushed to the middle, still holding hands. The circle was re-established, and each of us turned to our partners and friends, kissed and hugged them, and repeated "Happy New Year" a thousand times over.

As I kissed Brian and wished those around me happiness, I was on cloud nine. This had been the best start to a new year by a mile in my twenty-five years on this earth, and it was thanks to a relative stranger... the relative stranger with whom I was now locking lips. I'd been made to feel as though I belonged to his pack of friends. Brian, too, had unveiled so many sides of himself to me that evening. He adapted to different situations with ease and never seemed phased by anything. Everything I observed in him impressed me so that he seemed too good to be true: a devoted father, a caring son, a helpful neighbour, a hard worker, and from what everyone had told me, a faithful partner. *What must he think of me?* I found myself wondering. *My list is certainly shorter.*

For a fleeting moment, sadness filled me when I realised the next day would return me to my boring life. I chose not to dwell on it; instead, I took Brian by the hand for one last slow dance, my first golden dance of a brand new year.

***

"Pete has become a big fan of yours," Brian told me, as we walked the short distance home. "He said you're the nicest girl I've ever brought around."

Praise indeed, I thought, wondering again just how many notches Brian had in his bedpost. In fact, an attachment had already begun creeping in, and if Brian had been anything but the perfect gentleman, I'm sure he could have persuaded me that I'd be warmer in his bed. But he didn't do that.

"Why don't you go ahead and use the bathroom first, while it's still free. I'll get the boys into their pyjamas."

"Honestly, Brian, I can't keep my eyes open," I replied. "I hope you don't mind if I head straight to bed."

He gave me a big hug and a gentle kiss, sending me on my way. He must have realised that if I hadn't fancied him before I arrived in Reading, I probably did now. But I needed more time to get my head and heart together. I'd only just come out of a marriage that ended in regret. I didn't want Brian to think I was easy prey. Though I wouldn't have admitted it to anyone, what I secretly hoped was that our budding relationship would lead to a blossoming future together.

8

A BUDDING ROMANCE

"A snowball fight!"

"No, a fort!"

I heard the boys arguing downstairs the next morning, in a heated dispute over what to do in the last few hours before they'd be returned to their mum.

"Hush up, you two," Brian's authoritarian tenor entered the fray. "Your room is in shambles. You have to tidy it before you can go out and play. You can finish rowing when you do, but for now, Rose is sleeping."

A short time later, Darren brought me a cup of tea in bed. I'd been lying awake, eavesdropping, smiling at the familiarity of it all. Having two younger brothers, I was used to this sort of exchange and wondered whether Darren, being the elder of the pair, usually came out on top, as my brother did.

When I came downstairs, Brian and the boys were discussing their summer holiday plans. The boys pelted Brian with questions, and he took them all on board patiently before answering. I listened but pretended to be oblivious.

"Are we stopping at the same campsite in France overnight?"

"Will we go back to the same pitch in Spain? It was great last year."

"Are you bringing all the meat for the barbecues?"

Brian hushed the boys, "Hang on a moment! We're talking about a holiday that isn't going to happen until August. I'm sure Rose is not interested in hearing all the details." He turned to me, "I hope you're all packed and ready to go home?"

The boys groaned and traipsed toward the stairs, when suddenly Russell turned to me and pelted me with one more question: "Are you coming with us?"

I looked up at Brian quizzically. *Has he asked him to ask that?* I wondered. Brian answered for me, "Rose probably has other holiday plans, and even if she doesn't, why would she want to spend her holiday with two little horrors like you?" With that, he tickled them both and soon they were wrestling on the carpet.

But the conversation didn't end there. Later that morning, just before we left, Brian brought up the trip again. "You are more than welcome to join us in Spain. You do know that, don't you?"

"Thanks," I answered, grateful for the invitation but unwilling to jump on board just yet. "I have to admit I'm not really the camping type, and I would be a complete waste of space. There's not a practical bone in my body."

"Well, in case you change your mind, the dates are the 17th to the 31st of August, which includes the August Bank Holiday, so you'd only have to take ten days holiday off work."

I thought about it on our drive home, and by the time the boys had been dropped off, I'd come to no conclusion. It was dark by the time we arrived at my flat.

"Let me come up and check everything's okay," Brian insisted. I was pleased that he suggested it; I'd mentioned earlier that I was worried the pipes might have frozen. And so, we went upstairs to find no disasters and, coffee in hand, sat over our cups, chatting.

"What, if anything, should we tell our colleagues about our holiday when we get back to work?" I asked him.

"I don't know. What do you think?"

"I've no clue. That's why I asked."

"How about nothing whatsoever?" Brian suggested. "After all, it's no one's business, and it'll only give rise to office gossip if they know we've shared the same house for two nights. That would be irksome, since we're just good friends. Until we're something more, let's give them nothing to talk about."

So we're friends with the potential to be 'something more,' I thought. I liked the idea of being 'something more' very much, but I needed to take it slowly and not get ahead of myself. If there was a future for us, I had to let it unfold.

***

Over the next two weeks, I realised what Brian had meant when he said he was a workaholic. He started work at 6 a.m. and was usually the last one there at 6 p.m. or later if he wanted to get things done without anyone around to bother him. Understandably, he was tired in the evenings, and whilst we did see each other occasionally for a quick drink after work, romance didn't progress beyond a kiss goodnight.

I was busy at work as well and, to my credit, had been promoted to Senior Accounts Supervisor. This meant I had more responsibility when it came to the day-to-day running of the accounts office and also had more staff reporting to me. It wasn't long before I had to approve holiday dates. It was first come, first served, and many a time I had to refuse someone's request, because it conflicted with others'. This got me thinking about Brian's invitation to Spain. Without telling him, I booked the last two weeks in August. If the relationship didn't develop, I could always change my dates.

I was not the only one with a new man in my life. Louise had recently moved in with her latest boyfriend. He was a handsome intellectual, studying law and politics. When she talked about him, I felt as though she was more in love with having been chosen by such a distinguished man, than by the man himself.

On one of her visits back to the flat and over a mug of coffee, I made an attempt to better understand her situation. "How is everything with James?"

"It's going really well, apart from the amount of time he spends away. He's so busy and rarely has time for me."

'How do you spend your time?"

"Oh, that's easy – I'm educating myself. James said I should be aware of current events, so I've gotten into reading the *Guardian* and the *Observer*, instead of the daily rags. I know a lot more than I want to know about what's going on in the world these days."

"Are you happy?" A long pause ensued, and I detected a tear in Louise's eye. "Come on, you and I can talk about anything, and I certainly won't be judgmental."

Louise sighed. "I just don't seem to be enough for him, and I try really hard. I know he loves me, because he always wants sex... but there's something missing. Why don't I feel like you feel right now with Brian?"

"I haven't even slept with Brian yet."

"No, but you will soon. I'm sure of it. I can tell by the way he looks at you that he cares deeply for you already. You just need to lighten up over the sex bit."

I hoped for her sake that she wasn't going to get hurt again. Louise and I were polar opposites in character. Where I was calm and quietly confident, she was feisty and not afraid to speak her mind. Perhaps this bravado was the reason she'd found relationships difficult to maintain. Her first love had gotten her pregnant. She said she was too young to bring a child into the world, and she was right. She had many boyfriends, most of whom she slept with, but so far no marriage proposals. The mood of our conversation was such that I decided to ask her why.

"Did you always think you were in love with your boyfriends when you agreed to go all the way?"

She hesitated before responding; clearly no one had asked her that before. "Not necessarily, but it always felt right at the time."

This comment moved the discussion to men in general and sex in particular. It became clear that my sexual experience with Mark was sorely lacking in passion and technique. What Louise told me about her sexploits would have made my hair curl if it hadn't been so straight to begin with. *Why have we never talked about this before?* I wondered. Then I realized sex had never been good for me, and I'd assumed it was my fault, so I hadn't wanted to talk about it to anyone. I now found myself not only wanting to hear more about her antics, but wanting to share mine.

"I feel a sexual chemistry with Brian," I confessed, "but I've been nervous about giving out any wrong signals. In fact, I've even gone deliberately out of my way *not* to be alone with him. I want the relationship to go to the next stage, and I don't. I think I'm scared."

"Oh, don't worry about the confusion," Louise consoled me. "Everything will feel right when the time is right."

"But how will I know when the time is right?"

"It'll be the most natural thing in the world when it's right. You won't be able to stop yourselves if you both feel the same way."

Oh, how right she was!

***

On a Wednesday evening in early February, Brian and I had made arrangements to go to see the American comedy *Heaven Can Wait*, starring

Warren Beatty. South Woodford's cinema was right next to The George pub, where we'd had our first meal. Brian joked about us sitting in the back row but, alas, no seats were empty, so we made do with sitting mid-row towards the back… not that it made any difference. We were both in the mood for romance, holding hands and kissing like two teenagers. I didn't want the evening to end.

When he drove me to my flat, I invited him in for coffee, half expecting him to say it was too late, until I noticed it was only 9:30. We chatted away, by now completely relaxed in each other's company. My stereo was playing softly in the background, and the electric fire warmed our frozen toes. Suddenly, Brian pulled me up from the sofa, took me in his arms, and kissed me. 'Don't Go Changing' sang from the radio – the same song we'd danced to the night of the snow. Our song. But tonight, instead of Barry White, it was Brian singing to me. I felt like the luckiest girl on the planet, melting into his arms with every word.

At the end of the song, he lowered me to the floor and made love to me, exploring my body slowly with kisses and gently massaging me until I was tingling all over. "Don't stop," I whispered, when I felt he needed reassurance from me to carry on. I helped him remove his clothes, knowing this moment was right, just as Louise had predicted. In fact, nothing had ever felt more right.

In the afterglow of lovemaking, when we were both spent and lying quietly in each other's arms, Brian turned to me and smiled, running a finger down my arm. "You don't know how much I've wanted to do that. You're amazing, although I must admit I'd envisaged this happening in more salubrious surroundings. You can't be comfortable there. Let me take you into the bedroom."

I didn't want to move ever again. But he was right, as usual; I was getting uncomfortable. We went to my room, and I felt a pang of disappointment when Brian said he'd have to go home soon.

"Do you really?" I asked. I understood why, but I didn't want the evening to end.

"This is just the start of the rest of our lives," he answered. "Don't forget that. Listen to our song again. I wasn't just singing along for the hell of it. I meant every word."

Later when I listened to the words over and over again, they stuck like permanence in my mind.

The sensible me was scared of being hurt though. Would Brian really look after me if I was in trouble? I knew deep down that he cared for me but we had only known each other such a short time. Was this pillow talk or could I really believe it? Would the passion that had been ignited last forever? One thing was for sure I had never felt this way before.

Oh, how my heart raced as I listened, thinking the whole time of Brian. I finally knew what love was.

9

A LEAP OF FAITH

"Mum is likely to interrogate you, but you shouldn't feel obliged to tell all," Brian insisted on the way to his parents' house that weekend. "She means well, but she's a typical mother – she needs reassurance that you're not just after me for my body!"

Brian had promised to bring his parents meat for their freezer, and his mum had encouraged him to invite me to dinner. I'd begun to question the wisdom in my accompanying him; that is, until he made me laugh.

"You horror, you wait until I tell her you've been taking advantage of an innocent young girl."

"Too late for that. She's already aware, it seems. She's offered us her room for the night, and I didn't want her to think I was losing my touch." I punched him playfully on the arm and laughed again.

We arrived just before dark, and Brian busied himself in the kitchen with his mum, while I chatted with Jim. "Brian tells me you're a wizard with wood and can turn a gnarled bit of driftwood into practical art. Is that true?"

Jim looked genuinely surprised. "Well, I am a turner by profession, as well as in name. I love making things from wood, that's for sure. Would you like to see some of my work?"

We were so long out in the chilly garage that Brian had to call us in.

"Your dad is amazing," I said at once. "Have you seen the walnut cracker work? And the pine clock is so pretty!"

"You're lucky Brian came to get you," Joan piped up. "Jim would have had you in there for at least an hour showing you how everything works."

She shook her head at Jim. "There's potatoes to peel for dinner when you can tear yourself away."

I felt awkward. "Can I make you all a cup of tea?" I asked.

"Jim will do it," Joan replied, sternly. "You and Brian sit yourselves down."

I glanced at Brian, and he nodded to the sofa. When they were both in the kitchen, Brian whispered in my ear, "Mum doesn't like Dad getting more attention than her. I should have warned you about that."

"I feel a little sorry for your dad," I whispered back. "He seems a bit browbeaten. Is he happy, do you think?"

"Probably not as much as he should be." We changed the subject for the sake of decorum.

***

The following morning, I was making the bed with Joan in silence, when out of the clear blue sky, she casually mentioned, "Brian will never get over losing Mandy." I felt a stab of pain through my heart, and she drove the knife in further. "You do know she was the love of his life."

I yanked the sheets upward, refusing to look at her and refusing to answer. If she'd set out to upset me, she'd succeeded.

I carried on as if nothing she said concerned me, but my heart felt heavy and tears weren't far away. I bit back the tears and asked, matter-of-factly, "Do you miss Mandy?"

Joan looked up, surprised. Clearly, none of Brian's other conquests had reacted like I had. "Sort of. She was too young for him, really, but I know she broke his heart."

Like you're trying to break mine? I thought, resenting her the rest of the visit and beyond.

***

"Okay, what has Mum said to you?" Brian asked on the way home, when I was uncharacteristically quiet.

"Nothing," I answered, avoiding his look.

"Oh, yes, she has. I've gone through this with every last one of the women I've brought home. I'm not going to let her upset you too. What did she say?"

68

"Just how many women have you brought home?" I asked. Then with tears welling in my eyes, I answered, "She said... she said you'd never get over losing Mandy, the love of your life."

"Oh, for god's sake, Mum," Brian shook his head, his eyes on the road.

"What did I do to deserve that?" I asked him. "I must have upset her, but I don't know how. She really seemed determined to hurt me."

"You did nothing to upset her," Brian assured me. "I wish I'd thought to warn you in advance. Listen, when Mandy left me, I went through a rough patch, to put it mildly. One night, my dad found me standing on Reading station. I don't know what I was doing there or how I got there. I don't think I would've done anything silly, but who knows, I certainly wasn't thinking straight. My mum took her role as mother very seriously and mothered me through the whole thing. Now she feels it's her job to protect me from all the women in the world."

"But was it true?" I asked the question but wasn't sure I wanted to know the answer. "What your mum said – that you'll never get over losing Mandy?"

"I won't pretend it's been easy," he answered and then turned to look at me. "But I can't think of anyone nicer to continue my life journey with than you." I smiled weakly through my tears. "Please don't let my mum get to you. Next time she says anything, just wholeheartedly agree with her. It'll knock her off balance, and she'll stop."

I made myself perk up a bit, but what Joan had said remained steadfast in my mind. Maybe I was falling too quickly for someone whose heart was with another. Regardless of what Brian told me, he'd obviously been in deep with Mandy and maybe still was. Perhaps I was just a rebound and that first night of passion had meant far more to me than it had to him. I resolved to try and be more cool, calm and collected and to distance myself from the intimacy that had occurred. But underneath this resolve, I knew my heart was determined to be the love that would make him get over Mandy.

***

Though it felt somewhat premature, Brian and I became an official couple at work and also began to discuss whether it would make sense to live together. After weeks of reassurance and deep, heart-felt talks, I appreciated that we were both going into this relationship looking forward to the long-term. So why waste money on two lots of rent?

As luck would have it, Mark's dad called me up, asking to meet and discuss the house in Loughton. Mark couldn't afford to run it on his own, and they wanted to sell. I agreed to meet, and without telling Brian what was going on, I set up a lunch date with him to discuss the idea that was formulating in my mind.

"I booked your holiday dates, straight after our New Year weekend," I told him, which made him smile. "I suppose I knew then that we'd be seeing a lot more of each other."

He nodded and admitted, "Well, that's what I was hoping for."

Later at lunch over fish and chips, I wasted no time in revealing my proposal for us buying the house in Loughton. He'd only ever seen it from the outside but knew that it was situated in one of the premier roads in the area. I watched him closely, as he read through the proposal. When he was through reading, I quickly said, "It would mean you selling your house in Reading, but as you only use it every other weekend anyway..." At the look of hesitation on his face, I sighed, "You know what, forget it. Forget I mentioned it. I totally understand if it's not something you want to do. "

"Hold your horses," Brian laughed at my hastiness to drop the proposal altogether. "If I'm being honest, I hadn't thought about selling my place, but that doesn't mean it's not a good idea. Let's go through the numbers." I gave him the rundown, and he sat quietly again, running through the figures without a word. His silence put me on edge; perhaps I was jumping the gun. Had I just scared him off? It was early days, after all.

"Well, Mrs Mathematician, the numbers certainly seem to stack up. I'm all in." I grinned broadly. "First, go talk to your in-laws and see what their thoughts are. They may want to buy it from you." I had to admit I hadn't even considered that, and it was certainly a possibility. But Maureen's gift shop was situated below their rented flat, and I anticipated that they wouldn't want to move, even if they could afford to.

"Would you be happy to have a joint mortgage with me then?" I asked.

"Only if you promise not to default," Brian answered, quick as a flash.

I beamed, "I'll use my persuasive powers to get us a good deal. Leave it in my capable hands."

"I'll leave any bit of me in your capable hands any day," he took my hand, and for a moment, I thought he was going to place it somewhere he shouldn't, but he just kissed it and apologised, saying he had to get back to work. After Brian returned to the warehouse, I went on to make a deal with Mark, agreeing to pay his parents' loan back in full, despite the fact that no legal document existed between us.

***

In May, 1979, Margaret Thatcher was campaigning to become the first female British Prime Minister. On the day of the elections, Brian and I were busy packing up his house, soon to become the joint owners of 1 Upper Park, Loughton. Neither of us were political, but this was a particularly momentous occasion, and as we both considered ourselves conservatives, we were as anxious for the results as the rest of the country. We stayed up all night to watch Maggie's victory. Needless to say, we didn't get anywhere near as much done in the house the next day as we wanted, but it was worth it. This would be a new beginning for Britain and a new beginning for our future.

Our new home in Loughton

Love & laughter with Brian

Our new beginning would start out with a bang – that is, our holiday in Spain. When I told the boys I hadn't been camping since I was at school, they teased me about all the bugs that would creep into the tent and insisted their dad's snoring was so loud, it would blow the tent down.

"Seriously," I turned to Brian when the kids had gone to bed, "I'm really not the camping type. I won't be any use at all."

"The boys are yanking your chain," he laughed. "Once we get off the ferry in France, we stop at a small campsite overnight and then drive down to Pals the following evening, where you can look forward to sunshine, good food, good wine, good company and me for two weeks."

"So are you guaranteeing me no rain then? I don't fancy having to walk across muddy fields to go to the shower rooms. It will conjure up bad memories from when I was on Girl Guide camp from school days."

When we landed in France and it was pouring with rain, I was sure I'd jinxed the holiday. I put on a happy face, whilst quietly dreading what was to come. Brian soldiered on, and when we arrived at the overnight campsite and the rain continued to persist, he asked Darren and Russell, "Do you boys want to sleep in the tent, and me and Rose in the car? Or the other way round?"

"Car, I think," said Darren, to my dismay. I would have preferred the other way round, but I wouldn't despair; instead, I got into the spirit of it all, pegging out the tent, blowing up the mattresses, and making our home cosy by zipping the two sleeping bags together. Though cosy, my sleep was restless, and I, for one, was happy to be woken by the morning.

***

The sun burst through the flaps of the tent at dawn, making the humidity unbearable. But the heat put us on the road early which was good, since the drive through the French countryside to the Spanish border would take most of the day. We arrived at the golden sandy beach of Pals on the Costa Brava, and after setting up camp, the boys led me on a tour of the campsite. Darren and Russell took great delight in unveiling the high diving board and insisted I wouldn't dare to go up there. Basically, they were calling me chicken, and I wasn't about to let them get away with it.

"Oh, yes, I will!" I responded resoundingly, though I cannot imagine why. I was a strong swimmer and had completed basic lifesaving training when I was at school, but I certainly couldn't dive.

When we returned to our campsite, Brian was organising our holiday home. "Here, we have a two-bed residence, with a separate living room and kitchen area, situated in one of the most desirable neighbourhoods in Spain," he said, pretending he was an estate agent. "Sunshine guaranteed."

It was nothing like I'd imagined. My idea of camping conjured up images of all four of us sharing one space at bedtime – not conducive with a couple in their first flush of love. Now I could see we'd have plenty of alone-time together and was happier for it.

As soon as Russell was in sight of the tent, he was off, racing ahead toward his dad. "Dad, Dad, guess what!" he hollered, racing ahead. "Rose said she is going to jump off the high diving board!"

The more excited he became, the more apprehensive I felt, which was compounded when Brian revealed I'd be the first. "You boys are terrible! You haven't even done that yet, so are you going to jump too?"

Darren piped up, "We're probably not tall enough, Dad." *Was that a wink I saw him give Brian?*

"Oh, I see, so all that bravado back there was just to get me on the ledge. Am I to be your entertainment this holiday? Just wait 'til I get my hands on you two." I raced toward them with my arms outstretched. The boys squealed and ran laughing around their friends' tent, shrieking, "We got you! Hahaha!"

When I gave up chasing them and returned to Brian's side, he said, "Well, you seem to have bonded with my two horrors, and they've certainly taken to you. Don't let them walk all over you though, as they'll be happy to take advantage of your good nature."

I laughed. Brian's kids could tease me all they wanted. I was just grateful I wouldn't be forced to jump of the high dive. Since none of them had done it, I had nothing to prove. Right?

***

Waking up in the morning and seeing the cloudless blue sky reminded me of my honeymoon in Majorca… only, one thing was different – I'd smiled more in one day here than I had over that entire two-week holiday.

I stared up at the ceiling, remembering that I'd had a dream about Mark. In the dream, he'd grown enraged about my new relationship and seemed determined to make life difficult for me and Brian. The more I thought back to my relationship with Mark, the more I hated myself. I had to take responsibility for the breakup, even though I ostensibly blamed him for his brief fling. I admonished myself for even thinking about this now, when everything was so perfect. I wondered why I had. Likely, the pending divorce was forefront in my subconscious. I banished my worries and regret and breathed in the fresh new day.

But when we arrived at the pool, I eyed the high dive. It was probably as a punishment to myself that I decided to take the plunge. "We were just joking with you," Darren insisted, when I set off on my march to fear. "You don't have to jump."

"You horrors," Brian again scolded the boys. "Now Rose thinks she has something to prove. You don't, you know!" he called after me. "Let's not be breaking our necks today."

But no amount of persuading from Brian and the boys would change my mind. I began to climb the narrow spiral steps, which wound round the steel pole leading to the top. The board had appeared high from the ground, but the view was nowhere near as scary as it was when I got halfway up and looked down.

"Holy moly," said the guy ahead of me. I wasn't the only one regretting my rash decision. The chatter all the way up the line was trembling. Even the French and German daredevils in front of me must have been scared out of their wits; though I'm not fluent, I could tell by their facial expressions and the tone of their voices that nearly everyone in line was having second thoughts.

Sure enough, at the top of the stairs, two girls were standing on the small square platform, beckoning others to go before them. I tried to ignore what was happening in front of me. If I was going to jump, I would have to do it quickly; no standing at the edge of the diving board, admiring the view, that's for sure. My heart raced as I glanced down to see if I could spot Brian or the boys. Before I could find them, I returned my eyes forward, knowing that if I looked down any longer, my knees would give way beneath me. Too soon, it was my turn, but to my surprise, I didn't hesitate. I went straight to the edge and jumped.

The impact of hitting the water wasn't nearly as memorable as the force of the water ridding me of my bikini top. Embarrassed and proud all at once, I rescued my top and made myself decent before climbing out

I can't believe I jumped!

of the deep end to find my boys. There they were, waving and cheering as if I'd just won an Olympic Gold medal for diving. The respect I earned from all three was certainly worth facing the fear and doing it anyway. From that day forward, I was officially accepted in the eyes of Darren and Russell. And, perhaps more importantly, I was officially a badass.

10

THE GREEN MONSTER

I was the strong one in my family, the glue that held everyone together. Despite being the third youngest of seven siblings, I was always the one to travel from London to Durham to collect Mum if she needed a break or to my brothers' or sisters' houses for a visit. Brian had accepted this, but for whatever reason, I couldn't do the same when it came to his family commitments. Though I never voiced my irritation that I couldn't have him all to myself, I'd discovered I had a tendency towards jealousy, a new emotion for me. But despite my best efforts to keep the green monster at bay, it reared its ugly head on more than one occasion.

The first time was when Brian dropped me off at Louise's flat and then went to visit his ex, Mandy.

"He's going to see *her*," I griped to Louise. "The woman his mum once told me was the love of his life."

"But he's with *you* and obviously loves you," Louise reassured me. "He's over her. The visit will likely be perfectly innocent."

Still, I couldn't shake the thought of them together out of my mind. He'd already told me she was seeing someone else, so I knew I was being irrational; but, because I knew the depth of his feelings for her, I couldn't stop imagining him kissing her… or worse. It didn't help that he showed up after midnight to pick me up, over four hours later. Our journey home was tense.

"I don't understand why you were so long," I whinged. "I thought you were just going to have one drink with her."

"You know how it is when you haven't see someone for a long time. There's a lot to talk about. Neither of us noticed the time."

77

"So it seems. I don't suppose I was even on your mind then?"

"Come on, don't be such a baby. You know I'd already told Mandy about you on the phone. She's really pleased I've met someone new."

"What's her situation then?"

"She is in-between boyfriends right now, and I think she welcomed me being a sounding board."

"I bet she did. Does she want you back?" As soon as I said it, I knew it was the wrong thing to say.

"You know what—" he raised his voice before pausing for a while to calm himself. "You'll just have to sort your feelings out, love. Jealousy shouldn't be one of them. I've given you no reason to be."

The silence during the remaining journey was broken only by the occasional sniffle as I blew my nose, and when we arrived home, he went straight to bed. Once he was fast asleep, I crept in beside him, feeling a bit ashamed of myself.

The second time the green monster roared to life was at a birthday party. Brian had walked in, holding my hand, danced with me most of the time, and was attentive to my needs; but he loved being the life and soul of a party, which meant I had to share him with everyone. I loved and hated him for it, the latter particularly when he was dancing closely with one of the other guests, twirling her around the floor in a way I thought should only be reserved for me. In all honesty, he loved to dance and partnering with someone who knew the steps for a change probably thrilled him. Although I knew his actions didn't justify my glaring, when he came and sat down beside me, he could tell I was annoyed.

"What's wrong now?" I could hear the irritation in his voice.

"Nothing…" I thought about giving him the silent treatment, then, "okay, it's something. I just find it hard to see you with someone else in your arms. It makes me feel insecure."

"For goodness sake, why? I take you home at the end of the night, don't I? I don't know what more I can do to make you feel valued. I can't give you self-esteem. Or trust in me."

"But how could you love me?" I asked, realising that's what I'd been thinking. "I don't understand how someone like you could be attracted to someone like me."

He shook his head in astonishment. "You've got to be joking," he said and gently put his arm around me. "It's entirely the other way round. How could you – an intelligent, all-around-wonderful girl – be in love with a mere butcher ten years your senior? Give us both some credit. You deserve me, and I deserve you."

***

In the months that followed, we had so much going on in our lives and so many people making demands on our time that there was never a dull moment. Ever since the jealous monsters had been put to rest (for the time being, at least), our relationship had grown stronger with each passing day. As I fell further in love, I accepted that I wasn't the only important person in his life, just as he'd come to accept the same about me. But still, I found myself wishing Brian and I could just disappear for a while on our own.

We settled into a routine like most couples do. Brian had taken over cooking the evening meal, which was not the norm in most households. Women were meant to cook, but I had a limited repertoire. On the other hand, Brian could make a banquet out of nothing. What looked like a small sad little lump of meat, well past its sell-by date, would be slow-cooked to melt-in-the-mouth perfection. He knew exactly which herbs worked with different cuts of meat and which vegetables complemented each dish.

Weekdays centered round work, with Brian starting his day two hours ahead of me. He'd changed many of the business practices regarding the purchase and sale of meat products, and the butcher shops were thriving. I, on the other hand, had hit a bit of a rut. I enjoyed what I was doing but didn't feel challenged, and instead of growing in my career, I was spending most of my time sorting out petty squabbles amongst the team.

One weekend in October, Brian announced we were going shopping.

"Where?" I asked. He knew I wasn't keen on wasting a weekend browsing through shops. "You're well aware that I hate shopping. What in the world do we need?"

"Wait and see," he answered, cryptically. "Look on it as an adventure." He drove us round North Circular Road, and I soon guessed our destination.

"Are we going to Brent Cross?" I asked with some irritation. "It's huge, you know. You'll hate it." What I meant was *I* hated it.

Brent Cross Shopping Centre was the first stand-alone shopping mall in the UK and was constructed in a dumbbell shape, with the two largest stores, John Lewis and Fenwicks, at either end and Marks & Spencer –

together with many individual smaller shops – in between. You could find pretty much anything you could imagine there.

"Are we getting our Christmas shopping done early?" I asked, but Brian just smiled and the mystery grew. This was something I loved about him – whatever we did together, he made it special, putting me at the centre of his world.

Once we'd parked the car, we took the lift to the second floor, and I was quickly reminded why I despised shopping. The shopping centre was noisy, blustering, packed with people, and there were so many shops, you didn't know where to start. Brian steered me away from the bluster and the people and the shops and toward the eateries for lunch.

"We can't eat too much," he said. "Dinner's at Mum's tonight, and you know how she likes to spoil us."

By 'us,' you mean, 'you', I thought. But I kept my bite for my food.

When our coffee arrived, Brian finally spilled the beans, "A special friend of mine has a birthday coming up, and I know we'll find something suitable here. Also, as you said earlier, we could do some Christmas shopping early."

Ugh, who's this 'special friend', I thought, *and Christmas shopping? I like to leave that last-minute.* Again, I didn't want to upset the mood, so I kept my feelings to myself. Brian was upbeat and happy, and raining on his parade was the last thing I wanted.

We waded through the crowd, from one shop to another, discussing for whom we needed to buy presents. I was trying to be easy-going as we meandered aimlessly, but I couldn't help myself. "You know, if you'd given me advanced warning, I could've made a list and been more organised." As I said this, we came directly upon a jewellery shop. Looking into the window, I pointed out a pretty brooch to Brian. "Look at that. Both of our mums might like it."

Brian steered me inside, and once we'd captured the attention of the salesclerk, he asked, "Can we take a look at ladies' watches?"

"No, the brooch," I insisted. "I don't have enough for a watch." I'm a bit of a scrooge when it comes to Christmas, I'll admit; the season is overrated and far too much money wasted on items that will neither be liked or used. I left Brian and found the brooches, but he called me back over to him.

"Rose, come take a look." When I returned to his side, he said, "Choose one for yourself. For your birthday."

"What?" I exclaimed, my eyebrows meeting my hairline in surprise. "Now? My birthday's in December."

"I know when your birthday is. We first started getting to know each other on your birthday, remember? But I also know you hate having a birthday near Christmas. So I decided you'll now have two birthdays, like the queen. Everyone else can celebrate your birthday with you in December, but we'll celebrate it on the 19th of October. It'll be our secret tradition."

"You are much too good to me," I squealed with delight, wrapping my arms around him, "and I don't deserve you!"

He winked, "You can reward me later. Now have a look and choose what you want, or we'll be chased out of the shop for taking up space."

***

Our weekends were a never-ending round of visiting friends or relatives. The boys came to stay every other weekend, and with Brian quite often having to work on a Saturday morning, I was left to look after them. Being that I had no children of my own, I found their squabbling hard to handle. To my detriment, I hadn't established myself as an authority figure; instead, I'd tried to be their friend, which meant they felt they could treat me as such. Children are very astute, and they learnt quickly how to manipulate me and wind me up.

"Darren, Russell! We'll have to make a trip into town. I need to do some shopping, before your dad comes home."

"Can we have some sweets?"

"Yes, but only if you tidy up your rooms first."

The trip into Loughton was quick, and apart from me having to stop them putting things they liked into the basket, they weren't awful. But once we returned home, all hell broke loose.

"Darren stole some of my sweets!" whined Russell.

"Darren, did you take your brother's sweets?"

"No, he's lying – *he* took mine!"

A shouting match ensued. The screaming went on for a round or two, before I ended it by raising my voice to them for the first time ever. "Stop it, the both of you!" I hollered at the top of my lungs. "Either be quiet or go to your rooms!"

81

Russell & Darren

Though shocked at my outburst, Darren wasn't threatened. "I'm not going to my room. I haven't done anything wrong. This little pest is lying to get attention." Then he pinched Russell, who cried out, sending the shouting match off for a round or two more. I was livid.

"Wait until your dad comes home!" I cried. "He'll be so cross with you two for upsetting me." As soon as the words left my mouth, I regretted them. How could I have let two young boys get the better of me? I went to my room, leaving them to battle it out.

Ten minutes later, I heard the key in the front door. I pulled myself together before heading downstairs.

"What on earth is going on?" I could hear Brian asking the boys as I descended. "I could hear you from outside."

The boys jumped apart, and before they could put their two cents in, I cut in, "They've been like this for ages, and it didn't matter what I said. They wouldn't take any notice of me."

Brian turned to the boys, and with a face like thunder and a voice to match he ordered them to their rooms. "And stay there until I tell you otherwise." Darren started to back talk, but the look on Brian's face made him run for the hills. With a last kick at Russell, he stomped toward the stairs, scowling at me as he passed.

I expected a cuddle of consolation from Brian, but instead he turned to me, exasperated. "For goodness sake, can't you control two children without getting upset?" He walked past me to the kitchen and put the kettle on.

"I'm sorry you had to walk into that, but they just wouldn't listen to me, and I didn't know what to do. Russell told me Darren stole his sweets, and Darren said— "

"I'm not interested," Brian cut me off. "I'm sorry, but if this is going to work, you need to learn your own lessons. I'm not going to fight your battles for you. You're the adult here, remember? They're the children. I'm not the intermediary. You'll have to learn how to work it out amongst yourselves." He left the kitchen and went up to take a shower.

Brian's reaction threw me for a loop. These were his children, after all; not mine. *Why should he be angry with* me? I thought... but then again, I had to admit I'd been weak. I was sitting in the living room when I heard three sets of feet plodding down the stairs. Brian frog-marched the two boys in and stood them before me. They looked like butter wouldn't melt in their mouths.

"Sorry we upset you," Darren said, begrudgingly, not looking a bit sorry.

"We won't do it again," Russell added.

I nodded solemnly, accepting their apology, all the while knowing full well they would. But if they did, I'd be ready for them.

11

NEW RESOLUTIONS

My mum hadn't been well. She needed some sun, so Brian and I decided to take her on a Canary Island holiday as a Christmas present. Mum was thrilled; she'd never been on an aeroplane before and was as eager for the flight to Lanzarote as she was the vacation. On the day of departure, Brian and I were in the airport lounge, anxiously searching the board for our gate, while Mum was busy doing a crossword.

I nudged Brian and whispered, "I'm going to have a laugh with Mum." Then I turned to her, "Hey Mum, you'd better go and use the toilets here at the airport. The aeroplane only has outside ones."

"Oh, that's okay," she answered distractedly, filling in the boxes of her puzzle. "I've already been. I won't need to go again for a while."

Brian and I just laughed. "Did you understand what I said, Mum?"

She looked up at us, and then the penny dropped, "Oh, you – it's just as well I don't take you seriously, isn't it?" She returned to her puzzle with a smile on her face, as though she didn't have a care in the world.

We were staying in Puerto Del Carmen, the main tourist area with beautiful sandy beaches on the east side of the island. The old town of the picturesque fishing port was close by, and the sun was never far away. I was so glad I could do this for my mum, but we all benefitted from vanquishing the stress of everyday life. Mum enjoyed being in the sun and riding on a camel but was happiest sitting on the beach, reading her book and nodding off under the umbrella, while Brian and I found plenty of alone time. By this point, I was in no doubt that he loved me, but I still had to pinch myself every now and then to check I wasn't dreaming.

Mum enjoying some fun and sun

Monkey business in Lanzarote

We came home from our trip, tanned and happy, and returned to our social ways. We'd gotten to know each other's friends by the end of that first year together – Jim and Pam in West Cornwall, Cliff and Sue in Barnstaple – and were always pleased when we felt we had the same taste in friends. It demonstrated how in tune we were with each other, which made me feel secure somehow. None of Mark's friends had made any attempt to remain in my circle, nor did I want them there. This forced me to admit how very little we'd had in common. Little wonder that no one was surprised when we separated.

***

As 1979 drew to a close, I looked back on how far my relationship with Brian had come in such a short time. He was happy to spend time with my family in the North East and willingly travelled to spend a few days over Christmas with them. Knowing that it was rare for all eight of us to be together in one room he made sure there was a group photo taken. We'd fitted into each other's lives so naturally, it seemed I'd found my soul mate. I couldn't wait to discover what 1980 had in store for us.

Brian no longer lived in the friendly cul-de-sac in Reading, and although Pete had offered to open his home to us for New Year's, we decided to try something different and host a dinner party. We invited four couples to join us, and though I felt nervous, because I'd never really entertained before, the friends we'd invited had met each other previously, so I was confident there would be no awkward silences. I bought everyone a small gift, brooches for the ladies and cufflinks for the men, which I wrapped up and placed beside the plates.

When everyone arrived, cheer erupted as we played charades and silly card games to while down the time to countdown. Everything went smoothly... that is, until it came to revealing our New Year's resolutions, which is when I found out something new about Brian. A new year brings new discoveries, I suppose.

After a unanimous resolution to abstain from the usual suspects – drinking and smoking – while gearing up for healthier diet and exercise, Brian admitted something he'd never once told me in private: "I want to find a new job." I gawked at him. We hadn't spoken a word on the topic. He continued, "I feel I've done what was required of me at Norwoods, and to be honest, I'm bored. Better still, I'd like to own my own business. With Rose's

A Gilbertson reunion: Back Row – John, Roger, Peter, Paul &
Front Row – Marjorie, Mum, me, Joan

finance and admin skills and whatever it is that I bring to the table, I think we could make a success of running a hotel or restaurant." He glanced at me and quickly brought the subject to a close, "Then again, I've had this dream many times before, but it's always vanished in the cold light of day."

While everyone was imagining outrageous things to do if time and money were no object, I was quietly pondering how I'd honestly feel if Brian's dream meant my career went out the window. I assumed I'd give up anything to be with him. Fleetingly, I pictured the two of us, side-by-side, greeting customers who had come to stay at our hotel. It was a beautiful picture – a dream, I suddenly realised, I hoped might one day be realised. It was past 2 a.m. before the evening came to a close.

***

Brian and I never did talk about his New Year's resolution, particularly the part about owning his own business. Maybe he realised the timing wasn't right, or maybe he sensed my lack of enthusiasm to abandon my career. We did talk about him looking for a new job, and as it happened, he encouraged me to do so as well. In fact, he was proactive about my search, bringing the local paper home one day and pointing at an advert he thought I might like.

"'Assistant accountant required for busy accounts office,'" I read, "'Salary AAE and company car provided.' What is this?"

"It's a firm that specializes in repairing doors and windows and the salary would be a step up. They're based in Walthamstow. You should call for an application form. Honestly, Rose, you're wasted doing what you've been doing. You're capable of so much more."

His confidence in me boosted my self-confidence, and I rang straight away. The form arrived the next day, and three days later, an interview was set with the Finance Director at their offices. Though I was excited about the possibility of change and growth in my career, Walthamstow had always conjured up a picture of run-down, dilapidated buildings, probably because I'd only ever been in that part of town on market days when everything was a mess. I was pleasantly surprised the day of my interview, when I found the company was based in a modern office block on the outskirts of Walthamstow, near the Seven Sisters underground station. I'd arrived with thirty minutes to spare, and I made the executive decision to go to reception directly, which turned out to be a smart one. The receptionist was a Chatty Cathy who didn't seem to think there was anything unprofessional about giving me a rundown of the other candidates. Between her answering the switchboard and greeting other visitors, I found out eight interviews had already been conducted, with one more to follow me.

As I waited, wondering how I'd measure up against my competitors, I decided I'd have to prove my worth. I flipped through the company literature to familiarise myself with the company and demonstrate that I'd done my homework. The subject matter was not at all thrilling, but the great thing when it comes to accounting is that figures are figures; I always had the opportunity to do what I love, while working in a wide variety of industries. In fact, I'd already worked for a clothing transport company, Rio Tinto Zinc, a Jewish jean manufacturer, and a meat wholesaler and retailer. I learned new skills with each move, and if I could only impress this upon Mr Kumar, maybe, just maybe, this would be the next rung on the ladder.

"I don't think the man this morning will have got the job," the receptionist smiled at me, twanging away in her cockney accent. "His suit looked creased, as if he'd slept in it, you know what I mean? Mr Kumar always dresses professionally, so that won't have gone down well. His wife is English, and she has good taste in clothes."

I smoothed my skirt and resisted the urge to ask questions, fearing that someone may catch me at it. The interview before mine overran its appointment, which is never a good sign; the interviewee must have impressed Mr Kumar enough to take time out of his day. With each tick of the clock, I grew more and more anxious about just how impressive my competition was. Then, two men entered reception – one tall, confident and well dressed in a light grey business suit and the other also smartly dressed and smiling. *This must be Mr Kumar*, I assumed.

"Thank you for the opportunity to get to know more about the position, Mr Kumar. I enjoyed our interview and hope I'll see you again soon." The two men shook hands then Mr Kumar immediately turned to me and presented his hand for a shake.

"Sorry to have kept you," he said. "Please, come this way."

I mumbled something about my wait being "no problem" and followed him out of the secretarial comfort zone and into the lion's den. Mr Kumar ushered me inside the rather unremarkable office and indicated which chair was mine. The office was on the ground floor, very basic with a single potted plant in the corner, two chairs, and a table.

"Make yourself comfortable," Mr Kumar said, handing me a document. "Here are a few more details about the position. I'd be interested in how you think you could make a difference within our company. Have a look and please excuse me for five minutes."

Despite having waited for nearly an hour, I was grateful for the extra few minutes to compose myself, especially with the intimidating image of my rival – the confident, well-dressed man – still vivid in my mind. I'd already started to question myself, my abilities, and my experience, so I forced myself to focus, instead, on the document before me, scanning phrases like "think outside the box", "excellent people skills", and "financially astute". Did I have any of these attributes? Was there a window in the room – an escape route? Before I could take any rash action, Brian's advice resounded in my mind, "Go into that interview knowing how good you are, knowing what you're capable of. We both know that's more than what you've already achieved, so be yourself but tell them you're eager to grow."

Mr Kumar returned and so did my confidence. His first question was a soft ball, "Can you tell me a little about yourself and your achievements to date?"

"Well, I was head girl at Royal Wanstead School, and though I left at the age of sixteen for family reasons and regret not having the opportunity for further education, I've given every job I've had since 101%. And, as my CV suggests, it's paid off to do so. I've received promotions at each company, and that's because I embrace new challenges and am always eager to learn and progress within the company."

I think Mr Kumar must have been waiting for me to pause for breath, because as soon as I did, he sat back in his chair, crossed his legs, and relaxed. *Uh oh,* I thought, not knowing whether his body language was good or bad. I shut my mouth, thinking I'd come off too arrogant. But then he said, "Thank you, Rosemary. It's refreshing after two days of hearing people list their qualifications by rote, to see someone with real enthusiasm before me." I smiled, but then he made that smile waiver. "Having said that, I am looking for someone who will be my number two in the accounts department, so the chosen candidate will need to command respect. Can you tell me about your people skills?"

I took a breath before answering, "When I was promoted into the role of office supervisor at Norwoods, a large part of my job was to manage a team of finance and admin staff, which wasn't as easy as it may sound; particularly because there was initially some resentment from two of the women who'd been there longer than me. I had to win them round and earn their respect, which I did. Of course, at times, I feel like I'm running a kindergarten, but they appreciate I have a job to do and I, in turn, respect them for their individual contribution to the team."

Mr Kumar seemed impressed with my professionalism and sincerity, so impressed that the interview lasted for nearly two hours. By the time it was over, I was exhausted. Mr Kumar – who had, at that point, suggested I call him Dev – walked me back to reception, shook my hand, and said, "I enjoyed our meeting very much. My secretary will be in touch with you, once we have a shortlist of candidates."

I fled the office in relief, coupled with a sense of accomplishment in selling myself well. I hoped Dev would buy what I was selling.

***

Brian was waiting up to hear about the interview, and when I arrived home, I described the highlights. When I arrived at the point where Dev and I had parted ways, I suddenly realised something that deflated my confidence.

"What is it?" Brian asked.

"I'm just thinking about what he said to me when we shook hands. He said his secretary would call me if I was short-listed. I didn't hear him say that to the man before me, which suggests he'd already been told he had a spot."

"From what you've told me," Brian replied, encouragingly, "I'm sure you'll get another interview."

And, as usual, he was right. My second interview was with Dev, the managing director, and the company secretary. The less formal format gave me the impression that it was a personality test more than anything. I knew the other two candidates were much better qualified – and they were men – , but would their personality types fit into an already male-dominated company as well as mine?

I felt more confident during this interview, and when Dev walked me to the door, he held my hand a bit past the point of comfort and said, "You've made it to the final stage of the hiring process. There are two of you now and, because you will be expected to travel with the job, it's important for me to see you in a non-work environment. Will this be okay with you?"

"Yes, of course," I answered. But on the drive home, my mind began to wander into unseemly hypothetical scenarios. I wondered if his request was unusual.

When I asked Brian what he thought, he said, "Sounds like you have a good chance of getting the job if it's down to your social skills. Just don't slurp your soup."

12

OFF TO A ROUGH START

My social skills didn't let me down. I got the job, and on the Saturday before I was due to start my new career, I woke up to find Brian standing at the foot of the bed with a cup of tea.

"What are you doing home?" I mumbled, not fully awake. "You didn't tell me you had the morning off."

"How about a 'morning sweetheart, thanks for the tea'?" he smiled, handing me the cup of tea and pretending to be hurt. "That's the greeting I was hoping for, cheeky face. Not the Spanish Inquisition!" I laughed and patted his side of the bed. "Oh no, I'm not getting in there with you. I know exactly what you're after, and there's no time for you to have your wicked way with me this morning."

"Honestly, you've got a one-track mind. I only wanted you to keep me warm while I drank my tea."

"We have no time for that either," Brian said again, with a flourish. "Pack your suitcase for the sun and sea!" He pulled his own out from the closet. "We're going to Majorca for a week!"

I almost choked on my tea. "Don't be silly. I start my new job on Monday, remember?"

"But didn't I tell you?" he was being mischievously mysterious again. "I called Dev as soon as you received the job offer. I told him you'd get off to a much better start if you could have a week's holiday first."

"Stop teasing me."

"He said it was a good idea and even congratulated me on being such a romantic. Told me he was more confident than ever that he'd made the right choice in hiring you, now that he knew you had a supportive husband. I didn't disillusion him on that point, by the way."

"Husband? Where did he get that idea?" I said, pretending to be repulsed, while really I was over the moon that Brian hadn't minded being referred to as my spouse. What he'd done propelled me well beyond the moon – a surprise vacation? What more could a girl ask for?

I immediately sprang out of bed to ready myself and pack a bag. "A week in Majorca on our own? What have I done to deserve— "

"Well, it was meant to be on our own," Brian cut me off, frowning. "I made the mistake of telling Mum all about it during the planning stages, and she booked a couple's holiday with Dad, alongside ours. Sorry, darling. If I'd ever imagined she'd do that, I wouldn't have said anything. The truth is I was so excited about surprising you, but I wasn't sure if I was over-stepping the mark – going over your head to talk to your new boss – so I thought I'd use them as a sounding board to make sure I wasn't crossing any boundaries."

He looked so contrite that I just hugged him, and with a big kiss, managed to feign complacency. "Don't be silly. I am *so* excited, and as long as you're not about to tell me they'll be sharing our room, what difference does it make? We'll have our own space and that's the important thing."

But, as I packed, I thought about Joan's motives. I found it strange that she felt it was okay to book the same holiday as us, without asking Brian first. She obviously didn't want to risk telling him, because she knew he would have advised against it. Joan and I had fallen into an easy truce. We got along fine, but I disliked the way she undermined Jim. It was none of my business, really; Jim accepted the position as underdog, and I didn't need to know why. But it still bothered me, and the way she treated me sometimes did as well. Determined that nothing spoil our holiday, I made a pact with myself not to rise to the bait if she decided to try and upset me.

When we arrived in Majorca, I found a modern hotel with a clean, comfortable room and a sea view waiting for me. Brian's parents' room was situated on the second floor and ours on the eighth. What a relief! Far enough away to mean there was less chance of getting an unexpected knock on the door at any time. Joan had a permanent and genuine smile on her face, which made me less suspicious of her. Brian and I had already discussed with her some of the activities, and her eyes lit up when she realised there was dancing in the evening.

"Mum is bound to try and monopolise me on the dance floor," Brian said with a laugh, "but don't be jealous."

"As long as you don't get jealous when some handsome young man asks me to dance. I saw a few handsome guys at check in who might want to whisk a neglected young lady onto the dance floor."

I detected a slight pause for thought before Brian got the last word in. "If that happens, say 'yes' for sure but don't tread on their toes." We were so in tune with each other that our happy banter set the scene for a fabulous holiday.

Dancing was our evening entertainment throughout the trip, and although Joan always hijacked Brian, I didn't mind; as long as he didn't neglect me, I was happy. Also, his mother's intervention meant none of the beautiful single ladies were taking my man for a spin, which would have awoken the green monster in me – a monster, I was happy to say, I'd kept buried for a time.

As I was watching Brian swing his mum around the dance floor, I heard a man to my left ask, "Would you like to dance?" I didn't think he was talking to me, but I turned to find a good-looking – albeit somewhat inebriated – golfer, leaning my way, his eyes locked on me.

"Y-yes," I stuttered, somewhat surprised and hesitant to agree to a dance. But why should Brian be the only one enjoying himself? The inebriated golfer pulled me to my feet, and we started to dance... I say "dance," but neither of us could, really. It didn't matter to me. Being asked to dance at all – and by a man who was rather handsome, to boot – boosted my ego. And my ego needed it. I wanted Brian to see that someone else had noticed me. In fact, as the golfer with two left feet attempted to twirl me, I asked myself, *Am I trying to make Brian jealous?* Probably. But he never did rise to the bait, and quite rightly.

And yet, I found myself, to some degree, wishing he would.

***

The following day I was sitting near the beach bar, when a group of golfers sat themselves down nearby. My dancing partner was among them, and he invited himself to sit down beside me.

"Where's your husband?" he asked.

"I haven't got a husband," the words spilled from my mouth, and I wondered why I'd admitted to it.

"Do you mean to tell me you're not even married to that guy?" he said in shock – a shock put on, no doubt, for effect. "I've missed my chance to win you over then. I leave for home today."

"Don't worry, there was no chance. I'm as good as married to Brian, and we're very happy."

In speaking to this smooth-talker, I was so grateful to be on holiday with Brian. I knew I was probably being made a fool of, as I was fairly certain the man was married himself and was looking for a bit of holiday philandering. *Not with me though*, I said to myself. *I'm not that sort of girl. Besides, I don't want anyone other than Brian.*

Whenever we were alone in our room, Brian relaxed completely, and it was so good to see him without the frown that had furrowed his brow on several occasions recently. Norwood's business was plummeting, and he knew he'd be out of a job soon, but he didn't talk about it much and so I let it lay.

On our last afternoon, I decided to seduce him, parading around in new sexy underwear. I pinned him to the bed and whispered, "You are the most wonderful man on the planet, you do know that, don't you? You always manage to surprise me, when I'm least expecting it, so I wanted to surprise you by acting like Lolita in the afternoon." Brian didn't need to say anything; it was evident it had.

Joan, Brian, Jim and me in Majorca

95

That evening, we were down late for dinner, and Joan was a tad annoyed. "You're late. Did you fall asleep?" she tried to keep her voice light.

"Rose couldn't find anything she wanted to wear," Brian lied. "You know what you ladies are like."

My blushes were saved, but the memories of Brian whispering, "I love you so much," stayed with me long after. I'm sure his love made me a better dancer that night.

***

The holiday was over far too quickly, and on the flight home, my mind turned to my new job. Was I fit for it? Could I actually handle all that the job entailed? What if the staff didn't like me? What if Dev was a difficult boss? So much negativity filled my mind, before I pulled myself together and turned to Brian for reassurance. He was fast asleep. *Never mind, I'll get my pep talk from him tonight,* I thought. *Tomorrow is the start of my new career.*

My first day at The Maintenance Company was a whirlwind of introductions, internal politics, and decisions; primarily, the colour of my new company car. I went with a turquoise blue Ford Cortina. This was the highlight of my day, and there were plenty of lows to outweigh it; I found myself in the thick of office politics and would have to choose carefully with whom I'd align myself. I went with Dev. He'd been the person who hired me and so, by default, he should be my primary ally... or so I thought.

Dev's chief antagonist, and therefore mine, was the company secretary. Initially, when I discovered he didn't like Dev, I wondered, *Is he racist?* I thought this because whenever an occasion to undermine Dev presented itself, he'd take advantage of it. Due to his inflammatory temperament, I knew we were bound to have a run-in. And, very soon, we did.

"May I get your autograph?" I asked one morning. I needed his signature for the deposit on a company car for a new manager.

When I presented him the cheque, he asked, rather abrasively, "Why can't we charge this to our usual credit account?"

"Well, because this manager wants a BMW, not a Ford," I explained. Ford was the preferred manufacturer for all company cars, and I knew he had already made an exception for this new hire; and yet, I could see he was about to fly off the handle. I was only the messenger for goodness sake.

"What is going on here!" he became suddenly apoplectic. "Why wasn't this discussed with me first? Only directors get a choice of car outside of company policy."

Although his anger was directed pointedly at me, somehow I remained calm. "I understand during the interview process, the candidate requested the same level of car as he had at his last company, and you approved this. Would you like me to check with Mr Kumar?" I didn't dare say 'Dev,' as I didn't want to further upset him; he didn't like the familiarity that had crept into the firm over the last few years.

"There's no way I would have…" he'd started to deny his complicity in the matter, when his memory kicked in. Red in the face and clearly flustered, he picked up the paperwork again where, flipping to the back of the job offer, he found the company car highlighted.

I decided to save his embarrassment. "I'm sorry, I should have pointed that out first."

"Er…" he grumbled, "don't worry about it. But next time, yes, point it out." He knew he hadn't handled the situation professionally and, thereafter, he treated me with more respect. I felt that I'd made my chief antagonist my ally.

***

I was three months in and, so far, I'd performed my job functions sufficiently well. But then came my first crisis. The company had a large number of overdue accounts, and one of my key measurements was how many days the debt averaged overall. With payment terms dictating leeway of '*thirty days at the end of month following the invoice date*', the debtor days should have ranged between forty on average and sixty at the latest, but I'd inherited a situation where many debtor payments were late by over 150 days, which was unacceptable. Before I spoke to Betty, who was responsible for credit control, I checked our company procedure for overdue invoices. I then crosschecked how Betty had been following these procedures, and what I found wasn't good. When I confronted her about her failure to adhere to company procedure, she made it crystal clear to me that she was an experienced credit controller and knew exactly what she was doing. In other words, I should mind my own business.

What she hadn't bargained for was my tenacity when it came to doing my job. I rewrote the policy to include the production of weekly cash flow projections, based on the debts outstanding, with a weekly update on Fridays to identify the amount of overdue payments that had actually been collected. As could be expected, her reports indicated that she overestimated and under collected. While her in-tray grew to overwhelming heights, my exasperation grew in tangent. I decided, again, not to skirt around the issue and, instead, to confront her directly.

"Betty, do you need help calling debtors?" I asked. "Your inbox seems rather full, and your reports are showing few collections."

"I've already chased the debt," she answered. "The money will be coming in soon."

"Well, I'll take over some of the calls anyway, so we can catch up."

Despite her reluctance to accept my help, I assisted in debt chasing and was appalled to find that, in many cases, Betty hadn't called the debtor companies at all and, moreover, had allowed them extended credit. When I discovered this, I couldn't let it lie.

"Betty, many of the companies I've called say they haven't spoken to you." I didn't want to humiliate her, but I had to be honest. On her end, I expected her to be embarrassed but didn't expect her to react as she did.

She stood up with a look of thunder on her face, picked up her tray and, with a flourish, threw the contents up to the ceiling. As all of the paperwork drifted to the floor, she brushed past me, arrived at the office door, turned back and, with tears running down her fiery cheeks, glared round the office and announced, "I'm done! You won't see me again. I can't stand it here any longer."

Everyone was stunned. The room went dead silent. Then, as if it had been rehearsed, the staff all bowed their heads in mourning and got on with their jobs.

I, on the other hand, was too close to the situation and needed time to compose myself before facing Dev, so I gathered the papers she'd scattered across the floor and returned the tray to Betty's desk. I then looked round at everyone and said in a shaky voice, "I'm sorry you had to witness that. I had no idea Betty would react in such a way. She was clearly struggling with her job, and I wish she'd spoken to me before it got to this point."

Everyone remained quiet for a moment then Tina said, "She told me she wasn't coping but asked me not to tell you. I wish I had now." I was grateful to Tina for speaking up. I could always count on her to call a spade a spade. She never had any problem representing the rest of the team.

"Never mind, it's probably for the best that Betty has gone home. I'll let you know what the situation is once I've spoken to Dev."

When I knocked on Dev's door, I found him unconcerned and completely oblivious to what had just happened in the office. Painstakingly, I explained everything – the reports, the inconsistencies between Betty's claims and her performance, and the episode that had just unfurled. I was relieved, and even a bit surprised, when he started to smile.

"I knew you were the right person for this job. I've wanted to replace Betty for a while now, but I was so swamped with work, there was never a good time. I should have just got a temporary worker in; I probably would've had better results. Can you tell personnel to write to her straight away? You'll then need to advertise for a replacement."

"I wonder if I can take on the role of credit controller and try to catch us up," I put in, boldly. "I'd like to get input from the team before rushing into hiring someone new. There's good potential amongst some of the girls, and it would boost morale if they could progress within the company."

Dev looked delighted at my initiative, "You have free rein to talk to everyone, with the caveat that you're not to promise anything without getting it approved first."

What could have been an awful day turned out to be one where I demonstrated my grit. I'd met my first crisis with panache and even resourcefulness. I walked out of the office that night with a smile on my face and a skip in my step.

***

Word about the "Betty incident" soon spread round to the rest of the company, and I was relieved I'd come out of it unscathed. Two of the managers even asked me to join them for the regular Friday lunchtime walk to the local pub.

"I hear you're causing quite a stir in the accounts department," one of them said. "It's about time something was done about collecting money in. Good for you."

At this point, I felt well and truly part of the company, and with personnel confirming I was now a permanent member of staff, I would positively do my utmost to revolutionise the internal workings of the department.

But not everything was rosy when it came to my new challenge. I arrived home late from work one day in May, and Brian sensed immediately that something was bothering me.

"What's the matter, honey? You look like you've got the weight of the world on your shoulders." He ushered me into the kitchen where he was in the middle of cooking dinner. "Sit yourself down, and tell me what's troubling you."

He had to beat it out of me before I would explain. "I need to travel with Dev to the Manchester depot and then down to Birmingham. This is the first time I'll be away overnight with him."

"And?"

"And I'm a bit... worried about it."

"Don't be silly," Brian smiled at me. "You knew this would be part of your job when you took it on. What are you concerned about?"

"I can't put my finger on it, really; but I just sense that Dev is going to make a pass at me, and I won't know how to handle it if he does. I've already asked Lynne to book my room on a separate floor, and she told me her instructions were to book adjoining rooms. Apparently, this is Dev's standing request... so what else am I to think?" When Brian was silent, I envisioned him ringing Dev and telling him to keep his hands off me, so I quickly added, "Please don't be overly concerned. I really like this job, and I can learn from these visits. I just need to know what to expect."

"Let's do this," Brian said after a moment, "I'll pretend I'm Dev and that I'm spending a night in the same hotel as a young staff member, one who I hope would like to climb the corporate ladder horizontally."

I laughed nervously, "Okay."

Brian dished out our dinner and set my plate before me then he filled two glasses with wine. "The first thing he'll do is make sure you're drinking. He'll likely push hard liquor on you, but you'll say you prefer wine. Dilute the effects of this by drinking lots of water throughout the evening. You can also top up your wine glass with water, so Dev thinks you're drinking more than you are. He will, no doubt, become inebriated, or at least act it, so you must be one step ahead of him."

I looked at Brian curiously. "You sound a bit too familiar with this..."

"I am!" he laughed. And at my look of shock, he added, "I'm only kidding. I've never done this in my life, but I can't say the same about some of my friends. You'd be surprised at how many promotions result from affairs of this sort."

Brian walked me through the whole hypothetical seduction, and with many questions and a lot of laughs, by the end of the night, I felt I could hold my own.

***

I tried to keep my mind from worrying about the potential impending sexual encounter by immersing myself in the management meeting at the Manchester depot. I found a lot of the discussion boring; repairing doors and windows isn't the most exciting subject matter. I came into my own when the discussion turned to financial matters and terms and conditions by explaining my ideas for a new debt collection system, one which would rely on everyone in the room doing their part, including the on-the-road engineers. The feedback was positive, and I got the go-ahead to implement it. All in all, the meeting had been productive, informative, and beneficial to me, and I was glad I'd been able to attend. When it finished, Dev and I drove to the hotel in Birmingham. Sure enough, we had adjoining rooms but, thankfully, they were not inter-communicating, as Lynne had said. In hindsight, I fleetingly wondered whether she'd been winding me up as a laugh but knew she would be on my side, she disliked Dev's antics as much as I did.

Once we'd split up, I hurried to ready myself for dinner. I wanted to get down to the bar before Dev, so I could order my own pre-dinner "cocktail". I never have been one for taking ages, since I don't wear makeup, so I was quick to shower and change and managed to beat Dev to the punch. I asked the barman for a non-alcoholic pina colada, saying I'd be drinking wine later and didn't want to get drunk too quickly. When Dev seated himself at the bar stool beside me and ordered a double gin and tonic, I grew more than nervous.

Brian couldn't have predicted Dev's behaviour more accurately. When we sat down to dinner, he filled my wine glass and was sure to keep it topped off throughout the evening. But I took Brian's advice and filled it with water as often as Dev looked away. If I'd really drank as much as Dev thought I had, I would indeed have been very tipsy, if not completely inebriated. But my tactics helped me maintain a pleasant level of tipsiness, enough to enable me to laugh at Dev's jokes, nod along in agreement, and be soberly present without appearing as though I didn't trust him enough to drink alongside him. My strategy also allowed me to excuse myself from the table on the basis that I'd drank too much and was feeling tired.

Dev followed me to my room but I was too quick for him. The key was in the lock, and I'd slipped inside before he had a chance to make his move. "Wait, Rosemary!" he called out. "We should have a night cap together."

"Sorry, Dev, it's been a long day. I'm really tired and need to get some sleep. Shall we meet downstairs for breakfast at eight o'clock?" He mumbled agreement, and I heard him struggling with the lock to his room.

Phew, mission accomplished, I thought as I readied myself for bed. Drifting off to sleep, I wondered if not putting out would hurt my career in the long run. I decided that if it did, then that was the price of self-respect.

***

Whilst my career did not go to shambles and, in fact, was on the up and up, Brian was becoming increasingly disillusioned with his. Norwoods' trading figures had gone south, and now that supermarkets were growing, selling more varied fresh meat products, he sensed that the company's old-fashioned approach would see to its demise. He'd tried to get them to diversify and modernise but to no avail, and now he was convinced his days were numbered. It was during our holiday in Majorca that we finally discussed his options and his dream of running his own business. We were both so relaxed, and Brian was happy and excited to talk about what the future might hold.

"I've been looking for jobs locally," Brian admitted, "but I've found nothing of interest. What would you do, Rose, if a business opportunity presented itself?"

"I'd review the business's prospects and be your conscience." I then teased, "My top priority would be that the business demonstrates good enough potential to allow you to keep me in the manner to which I've become accustomed."

Brian laughed but his features swiftly fell serious, a strange expression on his normally jovial face. He looked steadily at me. "Could you see yourself being part of the new venture, or would you rather continue your career? I know you love your job."

I thought about this for a while before responding practically, "I'd have to make that decision when the time comes. There are so many things to think about, and until the potential for you running your own business is a reality, I can't say how I might react. But one thing's for sure; I don't want our relationship to suffer. Then again, we're two intelligent people; I'm confident we'll make the right decision for the both of us."

13

A VENTURE ADVENTURE

Christmas came and went, and we found ourselves starting 1981 with only one income. Norwoods had made Brian redundant. The pressure was now on him to find a new challenge sooner rather than later. He scoured the local want ads but was more drawn to the businesses for sale. He registered with a national agency that dealt in the sale of hotels, restaurants, and shops. We'd agreed he'd do all of the initial investigative work, and I would only get involved when he found something intriguing. And finding something worthy of further investigation turned out to be a long, tiresome process. In fact, Brian had become quieter in the evenings, which was unusual and spoke to his frustration. I did my best to boost his confidence by encouraging him and showing an interest in his day-to-day, but the deadlock was draining for the both of us.

Then, during one of our weekly Wednesday night canasta games with our friends, Bob and Penny, Brian announced that he was hopeful about a certain potential opportunity. He didn't elaborate but it was clear he was excited, and I looked forward to the end of the game, so I could quiz him on our own time.

"Come on then, you little tease. Tell me what you've found that's put the smile I love so much back on your face."

"Maybe it's better I wait until I look at the business in person," he replied, smiling more broadly. "I don't want you to feel I'm leaving you out of the loop, but I also don't want to excite you over something that might never happen."

"Okay," I agreed, though he'd only made me more curious, "I can see where you're coming from. I'll let you decide when you want to bring me into the fold."

He kissed me, and I was so happy that he was happy. Our relationship had never once faltered, and I could sense our long-term future was soon to be cemented, and I'd finally have my happily ever after.

***

One day, at the end of January 1981, Brian called me at work. "I think this is it, Rose," he said, excitedly. "I feel as though we could make this project a real success, but I need your opinion. This is not just my project, it's ours."

I managed to get the next day off from work, and we were off. Brian always loved a bit of mystery, and as always, he kept me in the dark, so I could enjoy the surprise. We rose early and drove through London to the M3 towards Southampton, but just after Basingstoke, we took a left onto the A303 towards the southwest. He loved the West Country, and I remembered him saying he wished he could own a restaurant or hotel there. I kept guessing, though I knew he wouldn't let me ruin the surprise.

"Are we going to Devon?"

"No, not as far as that; we're going to a place near Stonehenge."

"At least tell me what type of business it is."

Brian just smiled; he was giving nothing away. We'd driven past Andover before I saw the signs for Amesbury, which was close to Stonehenge and would no doubt have frequent visitors. Brian must have been thinking the same and was quick to point this out to me. At last, I'd solved one of Brian's mysteries before the big reveal. Amesbury would be our destination, and as we reached the little town, we pulled up in a layby outside a Spar supermarket.

"Here we are," Brian said, happily. "Please don't be put off about the dilapidated, lacklustre premises. I have great plans for this place. What I need you to do is focus on what the owner has to say about the financial side of the business. Be your usual charming self, take notes, and leave the rest to me." He gave me the heads-up on the shop owner before we went in. "He's going through a divorce and seems totally disinterested in his own business, probably because he has to give half to his wife. Don't be put off by his indifference to anything you might ask."

I can't pretend I was wowed by his choice. The shop was on the outskirts of town and looked tired and run-down. But I reserved my judgment, put on a happy face, and followed Brian inside. A short, fair-haired man, wearing a white apron approached us.

"Aw, you again," the shop owner said with a smile when he saw Brian.

"I've brought my business partner this time," Brian replied. "Maybe I'll just leave it down to you to sell her on this place. What's your sales pitch?"

"Well…" the owner paused for effect then gestured around the shop, "it's a good size, and we sell everything you'd expect and more; newspapers, deli food, alcohol, groceries, cigarettes. It's done well for me over the past five years or so, this shop."

"So why are you selling?" I asked.

"To be honest, love, I'm going through a divorce, and I'd be happy to make a fresh start somewhere else. Simple as that. I must warn you, though, that the offer is hot, so if you really want the place, you'll have to act fast. Misselbrook & Weston, from Southampton, has shown an interest."

This appeared to be news to Brian. "We're competing with a corporate giant?" he asked, anxiously. "Can you tell me what's most important to you regarding the sale so that we might have a chance?"

"Well, if you and your partner, here, can come up with the money to buy the business faster than M & W, then it's all yours."

As we discussed the store on the way home, the prospect made Brian more motivated than I'd seen him for a long time. As a result, many of my questions and concerns remained unasked and therefore unanswered. I knew Brian would be able to improve the business and increase turnover, but it was down to me to make the figures work. I'd worry about the distance between Loughton and Amesbury once the project had legs.

My projections showed that if Brian could maintain the current weekly turnover at £6,000, increasing to £6,500 after six months and then to £7,000 by the start of the following year, we would have a viable business proposition to present to the bank. Brian went into overdrive and was determined to make a deal before M & W, tireless in his efforts to beat the big boys at their own game. He hand-delivered documents to our solicitors and to the owner's solicitors, knowing M & W had external and internal procedures to follow. Once the bank manager had reviewed the projections we presented to him, he fast-tracked our business loan, which was dependent on us putting our house up as security. Nothing was left to chance after we'd been approved and were given the green light. Brian's excitement and energy was infectious, but we still had a lot to talk about.

The night before D-Day, we sat down to discuss my list of concerns.

Brian would be following his dream; but in what ways and to what degree I would be affected, neither of us really knew.

"You know I'll support you with this new venture," I said. "I wouldn't have let it go this far if that wasn't the case. I'm just scared the business will become your focus, and I'll be the afterthought. Sorry if that sounds selfish, but how will our relationship remain strong when we're apart?"

Try as I might, I couldn't keep the tears from falling. Brian reached for me and held me tight. "Please don't be upset. I know it's not going to be utopia in the beginning, but we're a close unit. Nothing will change what we feel for each other." He hugged me tighter and rocked me back and forth. "Come on, cheer up! Think of all that free chocolate you'll be getting from the shop." I laughed. He always knew just what to say to put a smile on my face. "Everything depends upon whether or not we can sell the house quickly. Once we do, the cost of running the business will be less, as the bridging loan will be taken care of. Do you think you can stay working in Walthamstow, until we're making enough profit to move you south and find you another job?"

"I'll be making a much lower salary down south," I said.

"Yes, but by then the store will be lucrative enough to compensate for that. In the meantime, you can drive to Amesbury on Wednesdays after work and return early Thursday morning, and then down again Friday night for the weekend."

The trip was two hours, one-way. Daunting but, of course, untested. The proposed plan meant I'd only have three nights on my own, which didn't sound too bad. Slowly, I nodded in agreement.

"My first job will be to find us a place to live in Amesbury. Once I do, maybe I can settle Darren in." Darren had not been getting on well at home which had affected his schoolwork. He wanted to be with his dad. Although I had misgivings about having Darren under our wing full stop, I didn't want to add to the stress of all these changes by opposing the move, so I agreed. Time would tell if I'd regret it all.

***

In April 1981, we signed the legal documents and became the proud owners of a 2,500 square foot supermarket in Amesbury, Wiltshire. We visited our new venture, and I talked to the staff, noting who did what and when, in order to help calculate payroll, keep the books current, and help Brian manage. He was financially astute and knew where the profits would be made, but it was down to me to be record keeper. Reality set in: I now had two demanding fulltime jobs.

If I thought I'd been leading a busy life before, I soon realised I'd been mistaken. My time was now spent working, driving, or sleeping, but I embraced my new routine and looked forward to the day I'd move to Amesbury… which as it turned out, appeared to be sooner rather than later. We'd only just placed our Loughton property on the market, when an interested buyer put in an offer straight away. As we waited to exchange contracts, we chugged along with the new business, and Brian was getting to know the ins and outs of running a supermarket. He was even busier than me, as the shop required his attention from 5 a.m. to 7 p.m., after which he saw to the day's paperwork. He trained the smartest of the staff to look after the place on the rare occasion that he was out.

During our first week as owners, I entered the office at the back of the shop to find Brian and his dad talking about a pungent smell in the front of the storage area. "I think it might be coming from up there," Jim suggested from the doorway, pointing to some slightly stained square ceiling tiles. "Son, you should peer in the ceiling void and have a look."

"I was thinking the same," Brian agreed. "I'll wait until we close shop."

At the end of the day, he placed a stepladder beneath the tiles in question, climbed the ladder and, with a shove, lifted the tiles. What he found was enough to curl one's toes.

"Ach, disgusting!" we heard Brian shout from the front of the store. Joan and I were in the back office.

"What is it?" his mother called out.

"You don't want to know," Brian said. "You can thank your lucky stars you're not the one up here, sorting it out." We left him to his sorting, and when he entered the office, he was plugging his nose and pulling a face. "A pregnant rat," he said, pulling another face. "Dead." He then reached behind his back and threw a carry bag towards his mum, saying, "Here you go, Mum. Cook that for tea."

She screamed before noticing his laughing face, "You horror! I'll get you back for that."

Darren was in tow, laughing, "Gran, you always fall for Dad's tricks. You should know better by now."

Strange that a dead, pregnant rat had given us all a good laugh, but it was exactly what we needed in those tough first days of a starter business.

***

That night, when we were alone and happy about the progress we'd made, I told Brian, "You know, if you ever make an honest woman of me, my initials would spell 'RAT'. Do you think it's a sign?" He laughed, and I added, "I hope you won't keep me in the ceiling!"

"No, but I might keep you tied to the bedpost, so no one else can have you."

I needed to hear that; it meant he still wanted me to be part of his life. "I really miss you when I'm not with you, you know," I replied. "But you seem to have made a good start to the business."

Brian became suddenly animated, "Rose, you have no idea how much I can improve the store. I'm tired every night, but I know it's for a good reason. Ask me in another few weeks what the turnover is, and I think you'll be surprised." I cuddled into him, and he pulled me tighter to his side. "I can't do this without you. Please remember that. You're my motivation for working so hard."

He was my motivation too. In all honestly, my divorce had been finalised, so I was seriously considering our future. A wedding day was no longer legally off the table; I could now dream of it as a real possibility.

On my long drive back to work on Monday, I did just that; and I revisited Brian's words of devotion with a smile.

***

"I've decided the best way to boost our foot-fall is to introduce some loss leaders." Brian was so eager to propel the business forward, he'd resorted to speaking gibberish. We'd been discussing our priorities over the next few weeks, one of which was to raise the weekly takings for the store. He'd spent the first week visiting local competition, doing market research, and speaking to customers about changes they'd like to see made. So although I knew where he was heading, his new jargon still sounded like a foreign tongue to me.

"Okay, hang on a second. Remember who you're talking to, and remember I have no experience with retail. I assume that 'foot fall' means traffic in and out of the store, but what's a 'loss leader'?"

"Well," Brian began patiently, pacing the office, "I visit the wholesalers to make note of their special offers, and I decide which ones will sell the best in our shop. Then I buy that product in bulk. I check the Co-op price on the product, and I drop our price below theirs. That way, I'm still making a healthy profit per item, but I'm underselling them, our main competition. Even if it's only by five or ten pence, customers count every penny and appreciate the lower prices. If I do this early on, we'll foster customer loyalty around town. Also, it's rare for anyone shopping to buy just one item, so if they've come for the low-priced loss leader, they'll spend on other regular-priced products as well."

"What products are the best loss leaders then?" I could see how this should technically work, but I also wanted to make sure the numbers were there. I crosschecked the values as he spoke.

"Basics – like bread, sugar, baked beans, toilet rolls, dog and cat food. The majority of our customers are older pensioners. I know what's important to them, because I've asked them, so marking these items cheaply will drive them into our store. I've also bought a second-hand van, so we can offer a local home-delivery service. The old dears will love that! "

How right he was. By the end of the third week, Brian's implementation of these ideas had sent our business soaring, with a weekly turnover of over £9,000 – 50% more than our forecast! I was so proud of him and couldn't wait until I was beside him seven days a week, helping in his efforts to make a success of it.

***

Owning a supermarket is a seven-day-a-week venture. Brian and I had little alone time as we gave his dream wings, so it was a blessing when Darren went to stay with his mum for a week, and we had the house to ourselves. I'd like to say we caught up on lost time, but that was definitely not the case. We did manage a one-day break toward the end of the week, when Brian left his trainee, Simon, in charge and took me out to Marlborough, a picturesque town a forty-minute drive away. Though the trip was, for the most part, uneventful, the simple fact that I could hold his hand and have a conversation about something other than the price of eggs was enough to put a smile on my face.

Brian's initial marketing efforts continued to produce results, and if we maintained the level of turnover for the next three months, I'd be able to find a local job; hopefully, nothing as taxing as my current role. I was still seeing the computerisation project through to completion, and the new system was on track to be installed at the end of May. The key improvement to the system – postcode recognition software – would be innovative for the industry, providing the engineers with a list of jobs based on logistics. Brian and I agreed I'd stay on until The Maintenance Company had parallel run the systems for at least three months to ensure that any and all bugs had been ironed out.

Meanwhile, our Loughton house had been sold, and Brian was now looking for a local home in Amesbury that would check all the boxes. I'd already warned him I had no vision when it came to choosing property, so after he'd found a home he thought we'd love, he should have expected my initial apprehension, when we drove up a steep hill and pulled into a large driveway with a garden full of anything but trees and flowers. I thought he was pulling my leg. "What on earth is this place? The local rubbish dump?"

"Bear with me; wait until you see inside Spindlewood House before making up your mind." He proceeded around the corner and an enormous, red-bricked house came into view. It oozed character. Admittedly, the character it oozed was dilapidated and gooey, like the rest of the place... but, character, nonetheless.

"Okay," Brian said, putting the car in park, "I know this looks like it deserves knocking down and rebuilding, but as we walk round, I need you to look past the mess inside and just listen to my vision." He started to climb out of the car but paused, "I should tell you first that the house is owned by an eccentric old lady who lives here alone with at least twenty cats. Not a great smell to the place, but as she's unwell, she needs a quick sale. Her family wants her to move to Devon."

He hurried toward the house, and I trailed behind him, already dreading the tour. As I entered, the smell was so overpowering, I thought I'd vomit. Dirty saucers of cat food and milk were scattered everywhere, and the litter trays looked as though they'd been full for weeks. The owner of the house was a frail, old lady who seemed unaware of how the state of her home may put potential purchasers off. She led us into the house, chatting up her pussycat friends as each one appeared. When I was offered a cup of tea, I politely declined – I didn't want to be inside that house any longer than I had to. Brian could sense my tension, so he gave me a lightning tour round, and when we escaped the house, I was eternally grateful. I took a deep breath of fresh air.

"Are you serious, Brian?"

Brian looked apprehensive but didn't answer. Returning inside the house, he explained to the owner that we were in a hurry. From the yard, I heard him say we were interested and would be in touch again soon. I couldn't believe it but, then again, as I took a stroll around, out and away from the putrid smell, I could see why Brian liked the property. The views were stunning. You could see past the town, across to the little village of Boscombe Down, beside the River Avon, and the vastness of Salisbury Plain, which I knew was used by the military for manoeuvres. Brian returned to my side and glanced worriedly at me – probably due to my seeming disinterest and disgust… not entirely unfounded. He stood silently alongside me, as we took in the view.

"All right," I turned to him, laughing. "Now I see it."

Immediately, he fished out the estate agent's details and eagerly highlighted the pros. "Look at the price," he said, pointing it out for me. "It's ridiculously low for such a large property. It's been reduced due to the state of the place. But I promise you, if we buy this, spend money on getting it cleaned, fumigated, and remove all this rubbish, you'll be amazed at how big it really is inside. With a little design and a lick of paint, we'll have an amazing home in no time. Trust me."

Of course, I trusted him; I had no reason not to. Brian had lived eleven years longer than me and had so much more life experience. Nothing I had experienced in our two and a bit years together made me doubt him. Now I was growing excited to have a home we could call our own, one that neither of us had lived in before. We put in an offer, and it was accepted immediately on the basis of a quick sale. Now, it was all systems go.

***

On the 29th of July 1981, a royal wedding took the world by storm. Prince Charles had chosen a sweet and innocent young woman, Diana Spencer, to be his bride. Theirs was widely billed as a "fairytale wedding" or the "wedding of the century" and was watched by an estimated global TV audience of 750 million viewers. A national holiday marked the wedding in the United Kingdom but, as for me, I was glued to my desk… and not by choice. I would have loved to be part of the crowd lining the streets to watch the spectacle, but the new computer system was ready to go live, and I had to meet up with the Olivetti technician. Though I missed out on the "wedding of the century," when the system demonstrated success, I was at least free to ride off into the sunset with my own prince.

Brian needed to visit a new supplier near Mere, and he organised his Friday, so we could spend some time together. I sat in on the meeting and noticed a distinct difference between London and the southwest when it came to the pace of doing business. The southwest was much more laid back in their approach and demeanour, and the man we met was quick in offering to take us to a local country pub. I'm sure he noticed me and Brian glance at each other; it was obvious we wanted to be on our own, and we were both relieved when he quickly added, "I can only stay for one drink though. The missus has got our evening planned."

After a drink with the supplier, a drive through Mere's lovely market square, past a chiming town clock, and a delicious dinner at The George Inn, we realised we both had to get up early. The impending early morning seemed to have turned Brian into a racecar driver.

"Can't you slow down some?" I asked, grasping the arm of the door.

"Don't worry, darling. You know I used to be a professional driver. I know what I'm doing. Look, you see the lights from oncoming traffic at night, so it's easier to gauge when to pass – even more so than during the day." I hadn't thought about that before and paid attention for the rest of the journey. Sure enough, when the road was straight, Brian only overtook when distant lights shone or, better yet, none at all. We arrived home, safe and sound, and ready to fall into bed.

As I drifted off to sleep, I realised I was working too hard and might soon burn out. I wanted to have more days like this and be close to Brian again. With our mortgage approved and my major project at work successfully implemented, I could at last see a light at the end of the tunnel. To see that light brighten, soon I would have to start looking for a local job.

14

DREAMS & NIGHTMARES

Two weeks after our day out to Mere, I woke up early Monday morning to prepare for my drive to Walthamstow and was surprised to find Brian already awake. "Stay there," he stopped me getting out of bed. "Get some more sleep. I'm just off to the shop to sort out the newspapers then, once the staff are in, I'll be back to collect you. We're off out for the day." Just as I was about to respond, he anticipated what I was about to say, "Don't worry. I've cleared it with Dev; I told him you needed a day off after all the extra hours you've been putting in. You didn't even tell me you were working until past seven most nights."

"I was trying to get payments as up-to-date as I could before handing in my resignation," I mumbled. I don't think I convinced Brian; he knew the nights were too long without him.

"I'll be back before you have time to miss me," he kissed me goodbye. With that in mind, I easily sunk back into bed and slept soundly for another three heavenly hours. When Brian returned, I was up and dressed, ready for our excursion.

"Where are we going on this beautiful, sunny morning?" I asked, brightly. "I can't wait to get there, wherever it is."

In typical Brian style, he replied, "You'll have to wait and see. It'll be a magical mystery tour. But before you envision a trip over to France, I do need to be back to close up the shop, so don't get ahead of yourself."

We drove for nearly two hours to the tip of Dorset. A day at the seaside – we hadn't done that since our time in Loughton, when we'd go to Frinton in Essex on a Sunday morning. Those romantic beachy days floated through my memory, as he parked the car near the ocean. The days when we'd arrive early morning, eat breakfast in a quaint café, and be gone by noon when the beach was heaving with children and noise. Today, we found a traditional fish and chip shop, sat on the golden sand, and ate, after which, he took my hand, pulled me to my feet and said, "Come on, there'll be plenty of time for a snooze, but now we're going to walk off our lunch."

We climbed to the cliff-overlooking Swanage Bay and lay there, taking in the breathtaking view. The sky was clear, and we could see as far east as Dorchester and as far west as the Isle of Wight and Christchurch. Brian was relaxed for the first time in ages. The worry lines faded and laughter lines came to the fore. He worked so hard and sometimes I forgot that. When I was down and bemoaning my commute, I didn't often think about him slaving away from five in the morning until ten at night. Seeing him relaxed and wanting to spend time with me made me love him more than ever.

Pointing out the Isle of Wight, Brian said, "My parents just returned from a funeral there. Mom said there were too many flower arrangements sent – said, 'They must have cost a small fortune, and what a waste of money, really. I've heard they end up getting stolen and resold.'"

I laughed, "That's your mother, through and through."

"Actually, I tend to agree," Brian admitted. "When I die, I want to be cremated. I don't want any flowers. I don't see why florists should profit from a family's misfortune."

I reached out to him, "I'll try and remember that in forty years, when I'm planning your funeral."

He laughed, "What a thought – me, in forty years' time. I hope, by that point, we've both fulfilled our ambitions."

"You've started on yours – you own your own business. What other goals and dreams could you possibly have?"

"I still want to own a hotel or restaurant in Devon or Cornwall. If the success of the shop continues, we should be able to sell it for a decent profit and can then invest in a new venture."

"Hang on a second – you're not looking at selling quite yet, are you? Remember, we have a house purchase in the pipeline."

"Of course not, but as you know, I'm a dreamer. The house is my next project. I want us to enjoy it for a few years before we look at moving. And what about you? What do you want to do with your life, apart from spending it with me, of course?"

That put me on the spot. The truth was, *Brian* was my life. He was my dream and my future. Being with him was all that mattered to me. The last two years together had been the best of my life by light years. I didn't want to admit to Brian that he held my ambition in his hands, so I joked, "I know I make a great number two, so I'll be your right-hand man, of course. My dreams will remain on the backburner with the concession that you pay me well and give me lots of perks." I gave him a knowing look, and we both laughed.

"You've got a one-track mind, I'm pleased to say," he smiled, and we put the world to rights for a bit longer before heading back to the car for the long trek home. "We'll come back here at least once a year," Brian promised. "You agree? Today's been one of our best days together in a long time."

***

I was pleased when Brian asked his brother Michael, a semi-professional photographer, to visit the shop and take some official photographs. Which would be featured in Spar magazine. As he posed proudly outside the shop for the photo-shoot, he looked happy as a clam, smiling gaily, his eye shining. His name in lights at last!

Our shop in Amesbury

Brian happy and handsome

The next weekend in sunny August, my sister Marjorie, my brother-in-law, and their three children – nine-year-old Julie, six-year-old Michael, and three-year-old Angie – were coming to stay with us. They were a close couple, and he worshipped my sister, quite rightly; she was the nicest person I knew (other than Brian, of course).

After a day at Longleat safari park with the kids, we were all looking forward to our adult night out. We'd wrangled Simon, our trainee at the store, into babysitting and decided to have dinner at our favourite restaurant, The Antrobus Arms Hotel. On the way there, I recalled that wearing a seatbelt would soon be law. "'Clunk, click – every trip,'" I quoted the Jimmy Saville advert to Brian, making a point of putting mine on.

"I'll only start wearing one when the law passes," Brian laughed, "otherwise, I'm not about to make a habit of it."

Brian had become a notable local figure in the short time he'd been shop owner, and the manager of the hotel greeted us at the door. He seated us in the lounge, where we browsed through the menu.

"Aw, they have Duck à l'Orange; it's my favorite." I pointed it out to Marjorie on the menu, as I knew she liked it as well. "You must get this, Marjie. Delicious!"

"What wine would you like?" Brian asked. "I won't be drinking any, so keep that in mind."

"I can manage a share of a bottle of white. No problem."

"Don't go getting tipsy on us though," Brian remarked, "I can remember you getting giggly on grapefruit juice." He laughed, and we all joined in, but I wasn't going to let them think I was a lightweight.

"Grapefruit juice did progress to a martini and lemonade when I first left Mark, you know. Now white wine is my favourite, so bring it on."

Instead of drinking profusely, we caught up with each other's lives. They were interested in hearing about Brian's dream of a hotel or restaurant in the West Country, as they had lived near Weston-Super-Mare for a few years.

"We were really happy in Somerset," Marjorie said, turning to her husband for confirmation, which he offered with a big grin and nod of the head. "Angie had just been born. Rose, do you remember the babysitting evening we all laughed so much about?"

"Oh no! Please don't remind me. Brian will definitely have a different opinion of me if you regale him with that nonsense." I was laughing of course so that Brian would interrupt.

"Take no notice of her, Marjorie. I want to hear your version now, as Rose will no doubt leave out the best bits." She smiled.

"Well, this is what I remember but don't kick me under the table if I get it wrong, Sis. With three children under seven, and one only a few months old, it was never easy to find a babysitter. So we left Rose to babysit and went out for a rare evening together. The funniest thing happened just before we were leaving. Michael wanted a wee, so Rose went with him to the bathroom. It wasn't long before he came running out, squealing with laughter. 'I've just wee'd over Auntie Rosey,' he said, over and over again."

"Okay, okay, stop the laughing, you guys," I calmed everyone's amusement. "I didn't know I had to hold his little winkle for him, did I? I haven't had any children yet. Anyway, I'll now own up to the fact that I also took the plastic coating off the disposable nappy before putting it on Angie. And stop smirking – yes, it did leave these two to deal with a soggy bed when they got home."

It was well after ten o'clock before we made a move to go. On the ride home, Brian concentrated on driving while listening to the three of us chat about the children and laugh at their innumerable antics. The radio was on quietly, until we decided to join in with singing the *Kool and the Gang* single, 'Celebration', at the top of our voices. The chorus had just started when everything stopped.

***

The car stopped turning. *What on earth has happened?* Silence. Darkness. Momentary silence. Then my senses started to return. I heard the deafening sound of quiet moaning. *Who is hurt? What did we hit?* We were driving fast, but not too fast, and the road had been clear. No lights had shone at us in the dark of night. We'd been singing.

I sat quietly for a moment. *Am I hurt? What can I feel? Who is moaning? I have to get out of the car. My chest hurts. Someone is lying in the foot well on my feet. I must get of the car. But so must everyone else. No one is saying anything, only moaning. I'm okay. I am the strong one. I must help everyone.*

I heard Brian's voice, quiet, choked, distressed. He whispered, "Bloody hell, bloody hell."

"Don't swear, darling." I heard myself reprimand him. Brian never swore. "Are you okay?"

"Yes, all I've got is a broken leg."

"We must've hit something."

I took my seatbelt off. Someone was at my feet; the crash must have thrown my brother-in-law forward through the central reservation.

"Don't move. You're hurt, but I'll make sure we get some help." The seatbelt had bruised my shoulder, but I felt fine otherwise. No one said anything else. I was scared of the silence.

As I climbed out of the car, people were streaming from their own vehicles, and I could hear sirens. I was disorientated. I smelt petrol and saw a small car, crumpled beyond recognition. *No one could have survived in that car*, I thought. *It came out of nowhere.* We'd been driving in the middle lane of the A303 – a three-lane highway – but the lane had been clear. I'd seen no lights.

Someone took a gentle hold of my arm. "Are you okay? Can I help you?"

"No. Thank you, I'm okay. But Brian and the others need help." I rounded the Ford Granada to find the driver's side still intact. The front was smashed, but I couldn't make out much damage otherwise. I tried to open Brian's door, yanking the handle with all my strength, but it was stuck. "Can someone help me?" I asked, desperately. "I need to get Brian and Marjorie out of the car." I was concerned about the smell of petrol. What if the car caught fire? Just as I thought it, a fire engine appeared seemingly out of nowhere, and I recognised one of our customers amongst the firemen. I dashed toward him. "Help me, please! I can't get Brian out of the car."

"You need help yourself. Get in the ambulance. I'll look after Brian for you."

"No, I'm okay," I started to protest, but I was already being led to the ambulance only a few yards away.

"Lie down, miss," I heard someone command. I did as I was told but was relieved when, moments later, my brother-in-law was carried in and laid out on the bed beside me. He was holding his shoulder, shaking and groaning. They gave him something to ease the pain.

"Can you remember what happened?" a policewoman appeared by my side.

I shook my head. "Not really. But there were no lights. No head lights."

Suddenly, a rush of people were carrying Marjorie to the ambulance. "We need to lay her on the bed," one of the paramedics told me. "Can you sit at the bottom and hold her feet?" Marjorie was thrashing about and moaning terribly. I held her feet as best I could, while the paramedic worked on her, trying to ease her pain and ensure that she was as comfortable as possible. The doors to the ambulance were slammed shut, and we took off.

"Where are you taking us?" I asked.

"Salisbury Hospital," someone answered.

I then heard the paramedics exchanging words under their breath but couldn't hear what they were saying. And, suddenly, the ambulance stopped. I wondered why, but then a doctor climbed on board. I was still holding Marjorie's feet, which were still.

We took off again, and the sirens roared. We sped to Salisbury Hospital, where I was led from the ambulance into a hospital room. I was told to remove my clothes and put on a hospital gown. "Lie on the bed and wait here until the doctor comes," the nurse spoke distractedly.

"I'm okay. Can't I be with Brian? Where is he?"

"You'll have to wait here. Someone will be with you shortly." She hurried off. *What did that mean?* I wondered but followed her instructions, lying on the table for what seemed like ages. When no one was with me shortly, my anger flared along with my concern, but just as I was about to disobey my orders and go hunt someone down, the door opened. "I'm sorry, miss. Can I please have the details of those who were in the vehicle with you?"

"What details specifically?"

"Names, contact information, and telephone numbers of those who should be made aware of the accident."

I listed off the home numbers for my mum and Brian's mum. "I don't have my brother-in-law's information. You'll have to get it from him. If you don't mind, I'd like to call my mum and Brian's parents, myself."

The nurse ignored me in her rush out the door, giving me the distinct feeling that it didn't matter what I wanted. I needed help. I felt so alone and out of the loop. And where was Brian?

I climbed from the bed again and was heading towards the door, when I heard a sound that stopped me in my tracks: the sound of overwhelming grief. It wailed outside my room

"Nooooo!"

And in that moment, my world came crashing down. It hit me like cold water: I'd felt my sister die. When I was holding her feet in the ambulance, no one would admit to me that she had gone. My grief had been internalised up until I heard that tortured cry. My torture soon mingled with his. I heaved in, then I sobbed and sobbed, not pausing for air. I wanted to die. *It should have been me not her, not my beautiful kind-hearted sister.* I couldn't breathe; my chest was burning. What would I say to my brother-in-law? How could I look him in the eye when I'd lived while death took his love? He'd hate me for surviving. And Brian? How would Brian be able to live with himself?

I have to go to him, I thought. *I have to go to Brian. I don't want him to be alone.*

I left the room to search Brian out but instead found my brother-in-law in a wheelchair with his arm strapped up. When he saw me, he cried, "What am I going to do, Rosey? I can't live without her!"

I tried to console him and myself. But what could I say? There were no words. Speechless, I sat on the chair next to him, and let him cling to me. After a while, I forced myself to be the voice of reason, "We have to call Mum and your parents. Someone needs to look after the children."

He became even more distraught. "What am I going to do, Rosey?" he repeated. "I can't cope on my own."

"We'll get through this," I tried to reassure him, though I wasn't sure myself. But he was inconsolable. I detached myself from him, saying, "Try to rest. I'll go find a telephone. We need to do one thing at a time."

I also needed to find someone who would tell me where Brian was. I had to find him as soon as possible, so he would know the crash was, in no way, his fault. There had been no headlights. We were in the dark. And I was in the dark, now. I had a sense of foreboding. No one would tell me a damn word.

Instead, they showed me to a room with a telephone, "M-mum," I managed to stammer, "there's been an accident. I need you to drive down straight away and help with the children. Mum, can you come?" I didn't tell her Marjorie was gone, because it was a five-hour drive, and I wanted her to arrive safely.

"Oh my god, of course I'll leave now, and I'll ask Paul to come as well. How are the others? Is Marjorie okay?"

"They're hurt," I said, "but I don't know… The hospital's very busy, Mum. I'll ring off now, as I need to call other people. Drive safely and don't worry." I felt guilty for hiding the truth, but what useful purpose could it have served? *Mum's lost her daughter,* I thought, *the wrong one. It should have been me.*

I asked anyone who looked as though they might know how Brian was, I still couldn't convince anyone to tell me anything. At last, a nurse told me he'd been taken to the operating theatre. "But you must return to your hospital room. You need to be seen by a doctor."

Reluctantly, I returned to my room, infuriated. Everyone was refusing to tell me how Brian was doing. As I waited, my fury grew. Finally, when the door swung open, I was shocked to see Brian's mum and dad standing, slump-shouldered, in front of me. At the sight of them, I realised why I'd been kept in the dark – I wasn't related to Brian. In the eyes of the hospital, I may as well have been a whore he'd picked up on the street that night; that's how insignificant I was. A pain more powerful than physical pain pierced my heart.

Brian's parents were both in tears as they approached. Joan took me in her arms and hugged me tight. "How did it happen, Rose? Brian was such a careful driver." Before I could say anything, she added, "Don't worry, we'll still be here for you."

I hadn't accepted it yet, but with her words, the penny dropped. "What do you mean? Where's Brian?" As soon as I spoke, I understood. He was dead. My handsome prince had ridden off into the sunset without me.

Joan was mortified. "My god, haven't they told you? I am so sorry; I assumed you would've been the first to know."

I crumbled. "I want to die," I repeated my earlier thoughts, this time aloud. "Please, let me die."

Jim, who hadn't said a word, came toward me and whispered in my ear, "You know, Rose, he loved you dearly and was planning to marry you in September at Salisbury registry office."

I shook my head. That was Brian for you. Full of surprises.

15

THE AFTERMATH

Eventually, I was put to bed. I woke up the next morning to the rushing and murmuring of a hospital ward. Nurses dispensing tablets, porters delivering the breakfast trolley, patients calling for nurses. And moaning, lots of moaning. Someone told me I'd been placed on the same ward as a young girl, badly injured in a car crash. *Our car crash?* I wondered. I never did find out.

I'd tried to eat, but my breakfast sat untouched on its tray. I was force-feeding myself a bite of toast, when I glanced up to find a police officer approaching. "Sorry to disturb you, Mrs Webster, but I've come to take a statement from you." He took out pad and pen. "Can you tell me what happened?"

"We were driving down the A303. We weren't speeding. And, suddenly, things went black. I didn't see any lights," I emphasised. "There were no lights."

"You didn't see any, or there were none?" he asked again, patiently.

I searched my memory. "Both," I said. "I didn't see any, because there were none. Just before everything went black, Brian steered the car to the left. The other vehicle must have hit his side of the car full on. Another car pulling a trailer prevented him from moving into the inside lane. He had nowhere to go."

The police officer finished scribbling my statement, shut his notebook, and leaned forward in his seat. "Your vehicle was travelling north, down a hill in the middle lane of the A303 at about seventy miles per hour. The other vehicle was travelling south in the same lane at a similar speed. The accident happened, because the nose of both cars faced downward, hence no lights were seen. It was unfortunate timing." The officer paused, as tears rolled down my cheeks. I tried to make sense of what he'd just said. "It's an accident black-spot. Mark Phillips, Princess Anne's husband, recently had an accident there as well."

This last comment made my blood boil. *Does he think that will make me feel better?* I felt like screaming at him but, through my tears, I kept calm enough to question him, "Why hasn't something been done about it then? How can two cars be allowed to overtake and be traveling in the same lane at the same time?" Without a word, he shook his head and shrugged. "Did anyone from the other car die?" He shook his head again. "How can anyone in that small car have survived a head-on collision?" I asked, incredulously. "Their car was a crumpled mess; our Ford Granada looked intact."

"We were surprised too. The collision impact was at least 130 miles per hour. The driver's seat of your car came off its runners and ricocheted into the rear passenger. There will be an investigation, of course." Two lives lost, because the car seat malfunctioned and the Ministry of Transport hadn't done a thing about a dangerous stretch of road. Two lives lost and many more ruined.

***

I learned later that the impact of the car seat had severed Marjorie's aorta, while the seat's rebound had propelled Brian forward and ruptured his liver. *With two white lines, they would be alive,* I kept thinking. *Double white lines, indicating no overtaking, and two souls would have remained on this earth.* I couldn't get out of my head all afternoon. *Who is responsible? Someone has to be responsible.* For some reason, I felt justice would produce some semblance of closure. But even holding the culprit's feet to the fire wouldn't have brought Brian and Marjorie back.

I managed to coerce the hospital staff into letting me in to see my brother-in-law, who'd been given his own room. He had his arm in a sling, and cuts and bruises on his body. He looked so forlorn, I almost regretted bothering him. I didn't know what to say to make him feel better. "I should be going home later today," I made an earnest effort. "I'll make sure the children are okay. Do you want them to know what's happened, or would you prefer to tell them yourself?"

He shook his head, avoiding my look. "I want to tell them. Hopefully they'll let me out tomorrow." We sat there for a moment in silence, and then he said, "I have no idea what I'm going to say to them, Rosey."

We didn't talk about the accident. I wondered if he blamed Brian. I wanted him to know it wasn't Brian's fault. I wanted to tell him about the accident black-spot. I wanted to tell him about the car seat malfunctioning. But I couldn't bring myself to talk about any of it. Knowing probably wouldn't have changed much for him either. Nothing said or known would return his wife to his arms.

***

Brian's mum and dad came to collect me that afternoon. Fifteen minutes into the journey, I realised Joan was driving a different route to our usual one.

"Where are we going?" I asked. I wanted to get home to see the children.

Jim turned to me, "We didn't want to drive on the same road, Rose. You need to be ready for that, and we felt it was too soon."

I smiled weakly. I would need to be ready. And I was not. Not nearly. All I could think about was returning my life to something that at least appeared ordinary. The shop was still there. It would still have to be run. I would have to do it. I wondered if the staff had come in this morning. I wondered if they'd closed shop for the day. As if he'd read my mind, Jim said, "Don't worry about the shop; your brother, Paul, is helping Simon and the staff. Joan and I will help too. You need to get yourself 100% well again."

I tried my hardest to control my emotions as I asked, "How are the boys taking the news? Are they still at their mum's?" Jim nodded. I imagine he had to hold back his tears too.

I didn't ask any more questions, apart from silent ones. Every last cliché of a question that might unravel in such a time of loss unravelled all round my head. *Why is life so cruel? Why them, not me? Why anyone at all?* And then the relentless flashback, replaying the event, every excruciating second – one minute, four happy adults had been singing at the top of their voices and then, with a crash and a shatter of glass, fate lent a hand, taking two away forever. My mind replayed it a million times over. My brother-in-law had lost his wife and I had lost my beloved sister and the man I loved, the man with whom I'd planned to spend the rest of my life. Five children had lost a parent. Three parents had lost a child.

If I had died instead of Marjorie, only five lives would have been deeply affected, instead of ten. My brother-in-law, Marjorie and their children could have returned to their home and carried on with their lives. I couldn't make sense of any of this. The only answer was that Marjorie and Brian were needed by a higher power. Although my mind determined this – determined it only in order to save my sanity – my heart could not. *How will I ever be able to let them go?*

***

Time heals all wounds, but my time wouldn't wait for those wounds to heal. Practicality brought me back to the present – my life had been in flux *before* the crash, with one foot in Loughton and one in Amesbury – and now, more than ever, I needed to stand firmly in one place. So I was forced to return to reality, yet unhealed.

I decided I should plant both feet in Loughton, where I had a job and a life. Running the shop on my own was too much of a risk. And renovating that house? Out of the question. As soon as I could pull myself together, I became the strong one. I did what I always do when there are things to be done: I went into overdrive. I had people to call, funerals to arrange, the shop to manage until it was sold. And the new house? I'd have to pull out of the agreement. For once I was glad that solicitors take an age to exchange contracts. And as for work, I hadn't called them yet, but I knew they would be sympathetic and give me the time I needed.

Meanwhile, the three children had prepared a play for their Dad, to be presented when he was released from the hospital. They knew Mummy wouldn't be coming home. The elder two, Julie and Michael, probably understood, but Angie was too young. We all smiled and clapped at the play's finale, but the pain we were all experiencing was heartbreaking.

***

When everyone left Amesbury to return home, I felt alone on more levels than one. I was surrounded by people but may as well have been on another planet, absent of life. Customers at the shop seemed to be torn between two minds: wanting to leave me alone and not bring up the accident and wishing to offer up their condolences. I didn't know which I preferred, myself. When

127

they did the former, I felt isolated; when they did the latter, it was all I could do to keep myself from falling apart.

One morning, I was serving behind the counter when the fireman I'd spoken to at the scene of the accident strode into the shop. His eyes searched the store and found me directly, and he approached. "Can I speak with you?" I left the staff to run the front of the store and led him into the office, offering him a cup of coffee, which he accepted. He sat down across from me, looking somewhat embarrassed. "First, I must apologise for not coming sooner. I wanted to see you, but I couldn't face you. I know how you must be feeling and didn't want to add to your pain. Having said that, I'm hoping what I've got to tell you will be helpful in processing your grief." I was glad when he took a long draught of his coffee, as it give me a chance to mentally prepare. For what, I wasn't sure; but I knew that, far from relieving my grief, whatever he had to tell me would harshen it. He continued, "When I was cutting Brian out of the car, he was conscious. He was in a lot of pain and thought he'd broken his leg."

I gasped, "I remember now –he said that to me." No wonder I'd been in shock when I'd finally been told he'd died. I'd thought he'd only broken a limb.

The fireman continued, "It was obvious to me he was badly injured. But he wanted to tell me something. He spoke clearly, although he was in a lot of pain. He asked me if everyone was all right, and I nodded. He then asked about you specifically. He said to tell you that he loved you and to ask if you'd keep the shop going while he got better. Then he said, 'Tell her I'm sorry.'"

My God, sorry for what? For the crash – the crash that wasn't his fault?

I felt drained. Even when he was dying, Brian had clarity of thought, and selfless thought, at that; he was thinking of all of us rather than himself. I know he loved me that was never in doubt. *But what have I got now?* I grasped desperately at straws. *No Brian, no love, no life.*

***

"When I die, I want to be cremated," Brian had told me only weeks earlier. "I don't want any flowers. I don't see why florists should profit from a family's misfortune."

I'd told Brian's parents about our talk on the cliff at Swanage, and we honoured his wishes. We laid only a pair of roses on Brian's coffin – a red one from me, a yellow one from Joan & Jim. The service was simple, and the curtain closed round the coffin, signifying the end of his life on this earth. I was strong, but my brother-in-law was inconsolable. I understood his tears were mainly for Marjorie, but I sensed they were also for me; I knew he felt my loss, as I did his.

Marjorie's funeral was a stark contrast to Brian's. Whereas Brian had the two modest roses laid atop his coffin, hers looked like a florist shop, a rainbow of bouquets adding colour to what was a black day for those closest to her. The small local church of St. Andrews was packed full of close relatives and friends. Nothing had prepared me for the crowds, but I suppose I should have known. Marjorie had been a well-loved Sunday school teacher there and well loved by all who were blessed enough to cross paths with her. My brother-in-law was the strong one this time, keeping his stiff upper lip through the service, while I weakened, an emotional wreck, dissolving into torrents of tears. I'd spent the time between the crash and the funeral looking after everything and everyone else. I hadn't properly grieved for my sister, my best friend in the world. And now the funeral had officially cemented the fact that she was gone.

"Would you walk up to the graveside with me and the children?" My brother-in-law asked, pulling me aside when we'd returned to his house. He gathered up the children, and the five of us left the house.

***

Once everyone had gone, life normalised. Paul stayed behind to run the shop, and I was grateful to him for stepping in when I most needed him. I called Misselbrook & Weston – our initial competition when we'd bought the shop – and told them my story. They understood, and I knew it would be a quick sale. When the offer came through, it was a lot more than we'd paid for the business only sixteen weeks earlier, but I couldn't have cared less about the money. All I wanted was for the commute from Loughton to Amesbury to end. It was making me feel worse than I already did, and I hated being in Amesbury, despite kind words from the customers. I'd been going down the dangerous road of "ifs" – *If we hadn't bought the shop, we never would've been here in Amesbury. If we hadn't been in Amesbury, we wouldn't have driven down that stretch of road. If we hadn't driven down that road, Brian and Marjorie would still be here.* This road of "ifs" was just about as dangerous as the one we'd driven down that night. The one that led to darkness.

I was certain I wasn't the only one going down the same dark road as me – *if only this, if only that*. My brother-in-law and I found comfort in each other, two lost souls coping with tragedy. He did have something to hold onto that I didn't: his children. Not only did they save him, but knowing that he was responsible for three young lives must have forced him to get out of bed every morning. Thank heaven for the children. They knew their mum had gone to be with Jesus and accepted that their lives had changed. They trusted their dad to make everything okay again, and so he didn't fall apart. He coped. He lived for those kids.

I did too. My life now revolved around work and visits with Marjorie's family. I went up as often as I could. We reminisced about the time he came to collect me from boarding school, when I was fifteen. All the girls had stared at him from the windows. We didn't see the male species very often, after all. He'd driven me home to Durham, and we'd never stopped talking. He'd been one of the few people who'd written to me regularly when I was at school, and I now realised how important that initial friendship was. With our shared tragedy, that friendship had been rekindled.

***

When returning home on the train from one of my visits, I was reading *The World is Full of Married Men,* a typical girlie book which had been making the rounds amongst my friends, when something happened that shocked me. The novel by Jackie Collins was hardly a literary masterpiece, but it was easy reading and kept my mind off my grief. The last two weeks had been full on. I actually looked forward to four hours of escapism on the train, without any demands on my time. And so I delved into the sex and debauchery of *Married Men* and left the world behind.

The shock came when I found myself aroused by a scene in the book. My face went bright red. I scanned the carriage to see if anyone was watching me. How could I be turned on by this smut or by anything, really? Brian wasn't here anymore, and I certainly wasn't interested in other men. Nor should I be. Nor would I be ever again. I felt ashamed.

Then I recalled a conversation we'd had in Swanage. After Brian had told me he didn't want flowers at his funeral, he'd said, "You'll find someone new to love after I go." When I began to protest, he continued, "Listen – you and I have a wonderful relationship and an electric sex life. You'll need that again. It's how God made us – to love and desire – and there's no way you'll want to be without someone who makes you feel alive. No one will ever fill my shoes, I know. I'm a one off," he grinned, "but you will need someone. Trust me, you will. And that'll be okay."

"You're wrong," I'd answered, defiantly. "I wouldn't even want to be alive if you were gone. But I suppose I'll be at least sixty when you're in your seventies, so our sex life will probably have dwindled a bit by then."

We'd laughed and imagined what the other would look like in thirty years' time. But here I was, not a few weeks' older, and he'd gone leaving me a widow without a ring. And, even worse, he'd been right. My sexual needs were already going unfulfilled, and I missed Brian the more for it.

I looked round the train carriage again to see if anyone was watching. Of course they weren't. I was alone with my own desires and my dirty little book. So I carried on reading.

**

At the inquest on Brian's death, it was clear he'd not been drinking over the legal limit, which I'd known already, but it was important to me that everyone else knew as well. A verdict of Accidental Death was recorded for both Brian and Marjorie. The police had told me that they'd gone back to the scene of the accident and timed how long car lights vanished in the dip of the road. It was a few seconds – but a long time when a car is being driven at seventy miles an hour. Though our accident may have saved future drivers on the A303 after the road become a dual carriageway, the fact that my loss was everyone else's gain was no comfort.

The months seemed to rush by in a blur. October came and went, with no secret birthday. Brian's tradition had gone forever. I found a lovely new home in Woodford Green, and before I moved, the girls at work persuaded me to celebrate with them in Loughton one last time. I agreed, on the basis that they got me good and drunk. I'd never been drunk in my life and still hadn't developed a taste for alcohol, but I thought, *Now, more than ever, would be the time to try.*

Lynne took control of the proceedings. There were only six of us, and she was by far the most outspoken. "The rules of the game tonight are there are no rules, other than the fact that you cannot refuse to drink whatever is put in front of you." The look on my face must have said it all. "Come on, now. Remember our mission is to get you drunk – and drunk, you *will* be, if you do as you're told and don't ask what's inside the glass."

This was met by a chorus of "hear, hear" all around.

They were right, of course. This had been my idea, and I decided to embrace the moment and just do it.

"So what am I waiting for then?" This was met by a loud whoop of delight.

"Bring it on!" someone shouted at the bar staff. I didn't have to wait long before a tall glass appeared in front of me, containing multi-coloured layers of alcohol. With this, came a straw... and not just any straw – a spiral straw, which meant I had to suck extra hard in order for the liquid to make its way through the many spirals en route to my mouth. I just went for it. I joined in all the fun and games, until I was well on my way to not knowing what day it was. The only thing I refused to do was play strip poker in a public place. But they were probably kidding anyway. Maybe.

By the time the evening was over, I felt awful. The taxi dropped me off at home, and I nearly had to crawl to the door. I lay on my bed, while the room spun round and round. When I started seeing double, I knew I was going to be sick. I barely managed to make it to the bathroom, and I wretched in the toilet for what must have been days. At some point, I passed out and woke up feeling nearly as dreadful as I had the night previous. *Why would people do this to themselves?* I thought. *I feel as though I'm at the brink of death's door, begging for the Devil to let me in. Maybe I have alcohol poisoning?* All I knew was I'd never, ever in my life get drunk again.

Despite the fact that I'd lain at the gates of hell all night, I decided I had to go into work. The engineering manager was picking me up. He'd taken a shine to me, and I knew he'd do anything for me. He was happily married, but he felt protective towards me in a fatherly way. He'd been so pleased when the chairman had offered me his villa in Lanzarote. My brother-in-law and I had decided to take the kids there for Christmas. Darren, too, wanted to join us, which pleased me; I didn't want us to drift apart.

I wasn't really in the mood for talking on that short drive to the office but made an effort, since he'd gone out of way to collect me. "What's your view on excessive drinking?" I asked him.

He laughed, "So they really did get you well and truly oiled then?"

"Put it this way, if I don't ever see another drink again, I'll be happy."

Darren with my sister Joan at a family reunion in France

***

The children arrived at my house the following day eager for our trip, which would begin with a plane ride the next morning. On the way up the stairs that night, I tripped and gave myself a black eye – no, I hadn't been drinking. And so, we were off to a stupid and clumsy start to our holiday.

That night, I tucked Angie in bed and read her a short story, after which she looked up at me quizzically. I thought she was admiring my black eye, until she asked, "Auntie Rosey, is it tomorrow we are going on the aeroplane?"

"Yes."

"And will we be flying above the clouds?"

"Yes."

"Will we see Mummy up there, because she's an angel now?"

A shiver ran down my spine, and I didn't know if I would manage to hold myself together. I felt like bursting into tears, but instead, I just cuddled her and kissed her forehead. "You go to sleep now, and morning will soon be here. We're going to have so much fun in the sun." She fell asleep, dreaming of angels.

***

The sun was shining in Lanzarote, and the villa offered plenty of open space for Darren, Julie, Michael and Angie to enjoy their playtime. I hoped the trip would help me forget that awful August night. New scenery, new memories, a new adventure to replace the old memories that were much too painful to bear. The new memories, however, were not much better.

The black eye my clumsiness had graciously bestowed on me gave everyone the impression that I was with a wife-beater. All who spoke to us assumed my brother-in-law was my husband, and after double-taking in my injury, they'd turn back to give him a dirty look. The assumption was so blatant; I thought it necessary to explain to people that I'd tripped *up* the stairs, though I'm sure not many believed me. The situation was awkward for all involved, but I felt especially bad for him, since he wouldn't hurt a fly.

I tried to be upbeat for the others, and I thought I was doing a pretty good job. Inside though I couldn't stop my memories from flooding in – Brian's smiling face, his surprises, and his ability to make me feel loved and wanted. I'd never before understood what a broken heart would feel like, but I did now.

I didn't realise my mood was palpable, until Angie came over to me and took my hand. "Come on, Auntie Rosey," she said determinedly, giving me a tug.

"Where are we going?"

"We're going to the shops."

"What for? It's Christmas Day."

"To buy you a new Uncle Brian, so you can be happy again." Though I put on a brave face, my heart stopped for a second. All I wanted to do was crawl into bed and cry.

So I did that. I went into the bedroom and cried until I couldn't cry anymore. I just wanted life to return to me, unchanged, happy, and with a future I could fathom, a future with Brian. It was slowly – very slowly – sinking in that life would never be the same again. I tried my best to look happy and relaxed for the rest of the holiday and enjoyed having the children around me. I owed it to them to show them that life goes on.

Lanzarote for Christmas – Julie, me, Angie and Michael

16

THE RECOVERY

The rest of the holiday was a haze. Although the children enjoyed themselves, which was the primary objective, it had wrecked me. Mainly, because my time there had made me realise I was not okay. Not in the slightest. I was so not okay that when I stepped off the plane at Gatwick, for some bizarre reason, I expected Brian to meet me at Arrivals. He'd be standing there, a huge smile on his face, welcoming me home. He'd never been dead; he just wanted to surprise me. Brian had always enjoyed a good surprise.

When I turned the corner, heart racing, my scattered mind expecting him and my eyes scanning the crowd, of course he wasn't there. And the defeat of my imagination sunk me deeper and deeper into a depression that propelled me through the motions of living without any inner life, apart from despair. Outwardly, I may not have seemed any different. Inside I was dying. I had yet to become suicidal, but I didn't want to be alive.

One Saturday morning, I left the house with my handbag and no conscious destination in mind. Two hours later, I was staring at the Departures board at Paddington railway station. I didn't know how I came to be there and had no idea what I was doing. Confused, I opened my bag and saw I had my purse and chequebook, but the other items surprised me: Brian's photo and a pair of knickers. I furrowed my brow and wondered what I'd been thinking. But suddenly I knew what I had to do. Run away. Run away from the constant reminders of Brian and inquiries into how I was holding up. Run away from my non-life. Run away from the pitying looks.

I focused on the Departures board. *Penzance,* I read – that was far enough away, and I had friends there who would leave me in peace, who wouldn't ask me any more of these tortuous questions. Jim and Pam. I didn't have my address book, but Jim was a policeman, so I put a call through to the Camborne police station. A man answered.

"Hello, is that Jim?" I inquired. The man wasn't Jim, but he was on duty, and I was put through to him.

"Jim Pearce speaking. How can I help you?"

I immediately started to cry, but somehow I managed to make him understand who I was.

"Rose, just get on the next train here. Pam and I will meet you at the station. Are you okay to do that?"

I nodded into the phone. "Yes."

***

It was nearly midnight when I arrived in Camborne. I knew Pam and Jim from my days working at Norwoods. They'd been friendly acquaintances with Brian and must have guessed what I was going through. They took me to their small bungalow, and the spare room was ready for me. Pam made me a hot drink and gave me some pills to take.

"These will help you sleep," she said. "You'll need decent sleep to get yourself feeling better."

She was absolutely right. I didn't leave that room for three days. Pam fed and watered me and gave me sleeping tablets. I don't remember dreaming or waking, although I do remember Pam had to remind me to occasionally eat, drink, and go to the bathroom. If she'd told me I hadn't done any of those things, I would have believed her, as I couldn't recall anything. When I eventually resurfaced, I felt like I could face the world again for the first time in what seemed like ages. But one step at a time.

"Rose, how do you feel about coming shopping with me today?" Pam knew I disliked shopping, but she wanted to test the water and see if I was ready for the outside world again.

"Well, I can certainly do with some fresh air, even though it looks freezing out there," I replied with a wry smile. "Shopping, eh? As long as you'll take me to a store where I can get some clothes, I'm up for it."

Pam laughed, "Of course, I'd actually forgotten you arrived with only one pair of knickers and have been wearing my pyjamas ever since you arrived. Clothes shopping it is then. Food shopping too – I can't have you fading away."

After the first successful outing, Pam started to invite friends round and talked to me about the past again, the good and the bad, and then the future too.

"I know I need to think about my job, but I'm not ready yet and am not sure I can face everyone. There are so many loose ends to tidy up, and I have to get back to help with the children." It wasn't until these words came out of my mouth that I realised I hadn't spoken to anyone since I ran away. "Pam, can I use your phone? I really should let them know I'm okay."

"Just treat this as your home until you're ready to move on," Pam answered, generously.

I hugged her. I knew I'd done the right thing, running away to friends I barely knew. I'd been savvy enough to know they'd be sympathetic without mollycoddling me. Kind, but firm. With their help, I grew stronger, and after two weeks, I thought I should probably let people know I was still alive. When I'd left for Camborne, I'd had the presence of mind to call my brother, John, who I was living with at the time, and he'd been nothing but supportive. I called him again and asked him to let the family know where I was.

"When will you be coming home? Do you know yet?" John asked, before realising he shouldn't have. "No pressure, of course," he recovered quickly, "just come back when you feel ready. We miss you and are looking forward to seeing you."

I wasn't ready yet. "I think it will probably be in another two weeks, but I'll let you know."

My next call was to Cliff and Sue in Barnstaple. I'd moved on from not wanting to talk about Brian to wanting to laugh and cry with his friends. They'd loved Brian immensely, and it was important to me to be close to people who had known him well. Sue sounded delighted to hear from me and invited me to stay.

"I have to warn you that I'm not sure if I'll be good company," I told her, "but I'm feeling a lot better than I was two weeks ago. If you're okay with an open-ended arrangement, I would love to stay."

"Just get yourself over here, and we can take each day as it comes," she paused. "We miss Brian too, so I think we're likely to shed more than a few tears over a glass of wine."

"That's obligatory, Sue. I want to laugh and cry and know I have friends that won't forget us. We were so happy, and I need to remember that to keep myself going."

Next on my list of recovery was to write a letter of resignation to my boss. They wouldn't want a nutcase back working, so I'd save them the trouble of finding a safe way to fire me by resigning.

After that, I called Mum. She was a bit teary but understood exactly what I'd been going through. She'd lost Dad when he was forty-eight, and she was forty-five. "I wish I'd done what you've done instead of going off the rails. I'm sure my life would have been very different."

Remembering this reinforced my future plans. I'd spend the rest of my life on my own. I'd never go off the rails again. I'd get back to normalcy. And now that I was stronger, I felt it was time.

***

When I returned home after being away for four weeks, I found a letter from Dev informing me that my resignation had not been accepted, and I should return to work as soon as I felt ready. I was relieved. My job was something I loved and knew I was good at, so returning to it would help me get my old self back.

On my first day back, I sat in my office, and as each member of staff arrived, I thought about each of their lives. Everyone had problems to deal with – some were struggling financially, others had relationship issues, still others had children to worry about and contend with. Some, even if they didn't realise it, struggled to do their jobs. I accepted that I had a decision to make: I could either wallow in self-pity or pull myself up by my bootstraps and get on with living. This decision altered my life's course. I decided to live every day as if it was my last and enacting this motto determined my future success and my mind-set for all the days to come.

***

In March 1980, Lynn and Bob, two of my best friends, brought a son into the world and named him Russell. I was invited to Russell's christening in April 1982, and some of my old colleagues from Norwoods were there. Lynn pulled me away from catching up and introduced me to someone I didn't recognise.

'This is Bob Bruce, you met him when he tagged along with us to your party in 1978 at your house in Loughton just before you and Mark split up,' she said, forcing us into an awkward coupling. Bob looked six feet tall and had an athletic build but very little hair. "So…" Bob began. "How long have you known Lynn and the other Bob and how come you don't remember me?"

"Sorry, Bob, I am useless at remembering people. Lynn and I worked together for two years at Norwoods. You?"

"Over ten years. There's a group of us who've known each other for a while, and we always meet up at Christmas and in the summer for a barbecue."

He was quick to let me know he'd lost his hair in his early twenties, saying, "It didn't really bother me, and as I haven't been able to find it again, I just got used to it." I laughed. The fact that he didn't take himself too seriously reminded me of Brian. "I can't imagine you let many things bother you, do you?" I didn't wait for an answer, "You certainly seem comfortable in your own skin, and so you should. You're in great company."

"I have to confess," Bob said, nodding toward the new baby being paraded around, "I haven't had much experience with babies and none with parenthood. What about you?"

"I'm one of seven children. My two sisters had six children between them, and my brother, John, has three daughters, so I've occasionally had to babysit. I can't say I'm very good at it though."

Bob smiled. "I think Lynn and Bob are ready for parenthood. I'll just keep my fingers crossed they don't ask me to babysit."

I was pleased I'd managed to hold a conversation with a single guy without feeling guilty. Bob was easy-going and had a great sense of humour. Chatting with him made me feel there was a chance I could move on.

***

Dev had been replaced with an incompetent finance director and working at the firm quickly lost its appeal. When my reservations about the man were ignored, I resigned. They ended up recruiting four people to fill my position and replaced the manager not long after, when they realised my reservations were not unfounded and, in fact, were right on the money.

I searched for a local job without worrying about the salary. A firm of chartered accountants, called Haslers, was close by and looking for applicants. After I was hired, I soon discovered the job was less challenging than I needed or wanted. I wasn't being stretched enough. If I were going to stay there, I'd have to make it more interesting. So I started daydreaming about Bob Bruce.

One evening, when I was watching TV with my brother John and his girlfriend, I turned to him out-of-the-blue and asked, "John, if you were a man, would you mind me calling to ask you out for dinner?"

The look of indignation on his face was laughable. "What do you mean 'IF I was a man?' What am I then, a girlie?"

"No, you're just my brother."

"Well, if you were a woman, I wouldn't mind. Why do you ask?"

"I want to invite Bob to join us for dinner and go out for a night on the town.

"That's a great idea," John replied, clearly excited at the prospect of his sister moving on.

With John's advice in tow, I plucked up the courage and was delighted when Bob accepted the invite. John and his girlfriend and my brother Roger and his girlfriend were all coming to dinner, and now Bob and me. I'd asked Marjorie's husband to come and was sure I could find a nice young lady to join us to make it a table of eight.

I'd chosen a Greek restaurant newly opened in Wanstead, not only for its good reviews, but because Greek restaurants are lively, noisy, and great fun. I didn't want any embarrassing silences.

It was absolutely the right choice. The eight of us got along from the get-go. We allowed the restaurant to choose the food, and the table was never short of delicious morsels to tempt us, such as tzatziki, dolmades, Greek salad, and pita bread; this was followed by moussaka (a favourite of mine), marinated lamb kebabs with rosemary (very apt, I thought) and more and more to come.

For the men, I'm sure the highlight was the dancing girls. Not one of them was shy about attaching pound notes to their skimpy costumes. Roger's girlfriend didn't appreciate this, as it was not the done thing, as far as she was concerned. We all broke china plates, as was custom, and the highlight for me was the slow dancing with Bob. Being up close with someone new seemed so natural; so natural that I felt a tinge of guilt when I thought of Brian. But only until I recalled what he'd told me. "You will need someone. Trust me, you will. And that'll be okay."

Bob stayed the night, sleeping in the lounge, where I'd made two beds up.

I had vacated my room so that the other guests could have proper beds. Bob and I talked to the small hours of the morning, before I, at last, succumbed to sleep with a smile on my face. By the time Bob left after breakfast the next day, he'd been accepted as part of our family.

***

Bob had brought love back into my life, and I decided to start living again. My brother-in-law had also found a new love at a Gingerbread meeting for single parents, who looked so like Marjorie, it was uncanny. She was delightful. She had four children and, despite personal hardship, was always laughing and making others feel good. Not long after, they moved in together with the seven children, and Bob and I visited them whenever we could. The children called him Bobby Brewster, and he loved it all as much as I did.

On our first holiday to Malta, which came the month after that first dinner, I taught Bob how to play backgammon. He was a quick learner and seemed to love the game as much as I did. Our relationship developed and we enjoyed having meals out, especially with Lynn & Bob who lived not too far away. I was so thankful that they had introduced the two of us, and that I had been able to move on with my life.

Lynn's Bob, me, my Bob, Lynn having fun

The following May, we went on a three-week holiday to the United States and Canada, which took in the West Coast, San Francisco, Alcatraz, Disneyworld, Lake Tahoe, Yosemite National Park, Las Vegas, the Grand Canyon, and at last, New York. The whirlwind trip covered a lot of ground, but New York was my favourite.

After taking a helicopter ride over the city, we went out to a Lebanese restaurant in Brooklyn Heights. On the ride, Bob struck up a conversation with the taxi driver.

"Where are you guys from?" the driver enquired.

"England. You?"

"Argentina." In the back seat, Bob squeezed my hand, and we looked at each other nervously. England was currently at war with Argentina over the Falkland Islands. Bob only released his grip when the driver grinned, "Don't worry, I don't agree with anything that's happening. I won't drop you off in Harlem."

The last leg of our trip, we travelled to Montreal to see my friend Josée, who had booked us an upmarket B&B to stay in. It was nothing like we expected, more like a stately home than a house. Just after checking in, I became distraught when I couldn't find my bag with all my valuables. Josée arrived just as I was panicking.

"My god, Josée, I must have left my bag in the taxi! What can I do?'

"Do you know the nationality of the driver?"

I shook my head. "He looked foreign. Dark skinned, maybe Indian?"

Bob put his hand on my shoulder, "Don't let's panic just yet. We have a phone number here." He produced the cab receipt, and Josée took it upon herself to call the number, while Bob gave me a cuddle and said endearingly, "Don't worry, scatterbrain." If I hadn't been so scared, I would have kissed him, but all I could do was search my mind for the bag's last known location.

Within thirty minutes of Josée's phone call, the driver was back. He had the bag in his hands, a compassionate grin on his face. "Ma'am, I think you left this?" he handed it to me, and I gave him the same fare money again, thanking him profusely for his help. We were all grateful the drama had subsided. I never thought I'd see that bag and its contents again.

"Thank goodness for honest taxi drivers in Montreal! This is going to be a good trip after all!" I enthused, over the moon with my luck. "Let's go party!"

Dining in style on our amazing holiday

Bob hit it off with Josée immediately, and she was the perfect tour guide for the few days we were in the city. I was sad to leave Josée so soon after arriving, but I was also looking forward to a romantic last night with Bob at Niagara Falls.

I half hoped Bob would whisk me off to get married by Elvis in Vegas, but I knew we weren't to be. He always made me feel so good when we were alone together, I suppose it wasn't surprising that I wanted the relationship to last forever. But we never really talked about the long term. Although he'd never been married, Bob had been in a long-term relationship prior to ours. He was a typical man – didn't like talking about love and the future – and I certainly didn't want to scare him off by forcing a conversation. Instead, I decided just to bide my time in the hope that my irresistible personality and charm would win him over.

***

It turned out that Bob could easily resist my personality and charm. Whilst we got on really well, he guessed that I was looking to replace Brian, and I wasn't the person he saw himself with forever. When he broke up with me three months after our trip, I just let him go, heartbroken but not enough to make a fool of myself. I was taken aback when he called a few weeks later, and we got back together, picking up where we'd left off. But it wasn't long before we were at odds again. And in Paris, of all places.

Paris was a present for his birthday, and during our first romantic meal of the weekend, I felt compelled to ask, "Bob, you've no intention of staying with me, have you?"

"No," his response was flat and quick. Although it didn't come as a complete shock, it did kill the romance. This time, the message was crystal clear; I accepted that Bob wanted to move on. He must have been relieved when, not long after Paris, a shift in my career gave our relationship its final blow.

One of Haslers clients was Hogan Systems, a banking software company based in Regent Street, London. Richard Warren, the MD, was impressed with some work I'd done for them and offered me the position of Finance & Admin Manager at Hogan. I didn't hesitate to accept. When I told Bob I'd be working in Woking in Surrey, he knew I had accepted the relationship was over. He'd already fallen for someone in his office, whom he would eventually marry. However, we never did fall out with each other and remain friends. After all, you can never have too many of those.

On the 1st January1984, I started in my position at Hogan alongside twenty other new employees. Within two weeks, I was on my first quarterly trip to Dallas to spend time with the finance department and learn the accounting requirements for the UK. This was a time when women were not often considered for managerial positions, and many an over exuberant salesman would go away with a flea in his ear when he'd ask me if he could talk to my boss only to discover I had none. I considered myself extremely lucky to have been chosen for this position, especially as managing in the corporate world was still 90% male-dominated. I knew I was good at my job, and being single allowed me to work as many hours as was necessary to stay on top.

I couldn't believe my luck when I found what could only be described as a dream home. An eighteenth century cottage in Horsell just ten minutes drive from the office, beautifully decorated with oak beams, low ceilings and a garden full of flower beds and an immaculately tended lawn. During my first viewing I was surprised when I recognised the owner's face, however, I couldn't remember his name.

"Welcome to my home, please take your time looking round and I will be right here to answer any questions you may have." As I walked down

Jim enjoying my new garden

I loved Pine Tree Lodge

two small steps into the long elegant sitting room I soon realised that the cottage belonged to Don Revie who had been England's football manager. That didn't influence my decision to buy the cottage, but it did impress potential boyfriends.

I embraced the American way of doing business, which was far more decadent than the uptight customary British routine. Many an evening, I'd be invited out for a company dinner, where money was no object and fun and laughter was mandatory. I had really fallen on my feet, loved being a successful woman in a man's world, and by the end of 1984, I felt on top of the world. My grief was behind me. I couldn't wait to see what the future had in store.

17

LIFE GOES ON

1985 got off to a great start. My position as finance and administration manager in the UK meant I became acquainted with everyone quickly, and I soon found there were some real characters amongst the lot, one of whom was Colin Bensley. He was a project manager who reported to the technical manager. He also had a reputation for being the company clown. He was the life and soul of any social event, but he was viewed as a difficult employee, doing things his way rather than being a "yes" man. I never saw this side of him, myself; I only heard the annoyance in his boss's voice, when Colin had, once again, spoken out of turn to a customer, promising them something he couldn't deliver.

Colin started visiting my office on a regular basis to have a chat. What he lacked in good looks, he more than made up for in personality, and somehow we always managed to bring the conversation around to his personal life. "I'm divorced and have a four-year-old son, Brendan," he confided early on, "but my ex-wife still plays an active role in Brendan's life. She looks after him on Wednesday evenings and Saturdays."

"That's a good thing for Brendan," I tried to appear interested, though I wasn't sure where this was leading or whether or not I wanted it to lead anywhere. Colin was no oil painting. He was overweight, wore thick glasses and, regardless, I wasn't on the lookout for romance with a Hogan employee. But Colin wasn't prepared to let me overlook him. He was persistent.

"I love my son and would do anything for him, but I admit I'm a bit lonely at times. I hope to someday meet someone who'll fit into our life."

Reading between the lines, I could tell he was leading up to asking me out on a date. I wasn't sure if I wanted to go out with him. On further reflection, and probably because he'd mentioned his son, I found myself re-evaluating Colin. Sure, he wasn't everyone's cup of tea, but he did have a wicked smile and was much more gregarious than anyone I'd ever dated. I wondered what the other managers would think if I started dating a colleague.

One day, when I was feeling particularly sorry for myself and felt sick and tired of being single, Colin strolled in and fulfilled my premonition. "Would you like to go out for a meal?" I hated being alone, and as I didn't have anything interesting going on in my personal life, I agreed.

***

Colin came to collect me from Pine Tree Lodge, and I could tell he was suitably impressed with my eighteenth century cottage. He'd heard about it from people at work, but this was his first invitation inside – albeit, for not more than five minutes, while I finished getting ready. He drove me to a restaurant a few miles away, which he said was one of his and Brendan's favourites.

"I'm sure you'll like it as much as we do. All I ask is that you choose whatever you want. Please go all out. I want you to enjoy the evening as much as I know I'm going to."

"I'm looking forward to it," I lied. I'd actually thought about cancelling. I'd started to get collywobbles over whether I was doing the right thing. My job was important to me, and I was obviously concerned about going out with Colin, otherwise I would have told someone about the date. But I'd told no one.

No expense was spared on the meal, but Colin made it clear that his spoiling me would be a rarity. "One of the reasons I asked you out is because you're in the same financial bracket as me," he told me as an opener. My face fell, and when he realised his *faux pas*, he attempted a recovery, "You also fit my ideal profile for a date."

I rose from my chair, "Well, that wasn't very flattering." The expression on his face was priceless. I laughed, "I'm only going to the bathroom." When I returned and sat down again, I said, "So what does your ideal profile for a date look like?" I took my time straightening my napkin on my knee before looking at him. He appeared suitably chastised and started apologising, but I cut him to the chase. "I wasn't aware anyone knew my financial standing.

I'm not even sure that I do, as money isn't important to me. So let's change the subject. Tell me more about Brendan."

At the end of the evening, when he dropped me off, Colin reached across and kissed me lightly on the lips and said, "I've enjoyed your company very much. I hope we can do this again sometime soon."

"I'll check my diary for next week." *Check my diary?* I thought to myself. *That's a bit of a joke, really. I'm free and clear as far as the eye can see.* But I wasn't about to tell *him* that. "Thanks for dinner," I dashed inside and shut the gate, before he could ask to come in for a nightcap. I had mixed feelings about this man and didn't know what to think.

***

After a few more dinner dates, I still didn't have any strong feelings either way, but Colin was keen for me to meet Brendan, the ace up his sleeve. They came to Pine Tree Lodge one Sunday and Brendan was shy, reluctant to join his Dad in the lounge where there were three strangers waiting for him. Instead he played quietly with his cars in the hallway. He sprung to life though when his dad said, "Shall we take Rose to Chessington Zoo?"

He nodded, "Will the others come as well?"

"No, that is Rose's brother and his wife and they have to go back to London."

A look of relief showed in his face. "Okay let's go then before it get's too late."

When we arrived at the entrance to the zoo, Colin batted at his pockets. "I think I've forgotten my wallet," he mumbled, embarrassedly.

"Don't worry, my treat." I hadn't assumed he would pay and had my purse at hand.

Brendan was a delight and, no longer shy, as we walked along, he showed me what he was made of, kicking snow at me to see my reaction. Without a word, I joined in. Colin hung back, watching the dynamic between the two of us. Only when Brendan slipped on the snow did he charge forward to pick him up.

"Dad, stop it! I'm okay. I'm not a baby anymore; I'm nearly five." Brendan dusted the snow from his trousers and stood indignantly, pulling faces at Colin. He then pulled a face at me, as if I'd made a retort, "I *am* at school, you know."

"Well, I can see you're a big boy already. What do you like best about school?" Brendan chattered away about his classes, friends, and teachers over the rest of the walk around the zoo. He also pointed out his favourite animals, and by the time we left that day, the two of us had formed a bond for sure.

When Colin drove me home, I was a bit more reluctant to get out of the car. "Goodnight, young man," I said to Brendan. "I hope I see you again soon."

"Bye, bye," he mumbled with a yawn.

"It's past his bedtime. I should get him home," Colin put in. "Thanks for a lovely afternoon. You've been a big hit with Brendan. He already adores you."

After that, our dates became more frequent. I started to stay over when Brendan's mum was looking after him, and Colin would stay over at my place as well. On one of these occasions, we made love on a beautiful silk rug I'd bought in Hong Kong.

"I have to tell you something," he said afterwards, chuckling a little. "I have an outstanding bet with colleagues in the technical department about whether or not I'd sleep with you on this very rug. Georgina told me about you buying it in Hong Kong. I guess I won."

A cloud came over me. I felt extremely irritated and degraded, not only because of the bet, but for the fact that Colin had been discussing me with our office colleagues at all. Where was this relationship heading? What was I getting out of it? Sometimes I felt totally at one with Colin, and other times – like this one – I felt I was just a means to an end for him. He didn't make me feel like Brian had… or even Bob, come to that. *So why don't I break it off?* I thought. And before long, the answer was clear: it wasn't Colin I was after. I was becoming more and more attached to Brendan.

***

During a week away to Tenerife with one of the girls in the office, I realised I missed Colin and Brendan's company. My travel companion was lovesick for a new man in her life, and we did little more than fantasise about our new or imaginary partners. Colin missed me while I was away as well, and upon my return, wasted no time in suggesting we become an official couple and move in together. I'd evidently passed whatever tests he'd set for me, especially since Brendan and I got on like a house on fire. If we were going to live as a family, we'd have to sell both our properties and buy a house together – a huge step, I knew, but as I hadn't enjoyed my solitary confinement since Bob and I had split, a readymade family was too tempting an offer to pass up. After discussing it, we decided to wait until the spring before putting our houses on the market and looking for a home.

Colleagues at Hogan were now aware that Colin and I were an item and so we occasionally got invited to join in with social events. When the invitation came from Georgina asking us to go to her Hen Party, Colin was really exuberant. He knew it was difficult for me sometimes in the office, and he had tried really hard to be his calm, enthusiastic, funny self rather than being too extrovert.

'This will be great fun, we must go. Georgina and I always have good banter when we are together.'

I don't know what possessed me to agree to wear the clothes Colin picked out for me. I was dressed in a lime green suit – the colour brought back schoolgirl memories. Colin had a baby pink pullover on – pink had become popular amongst the men for some reason. It wasn't until I saw the photos that I realised that we looked like Kermit the Frog and Miss Piggy from the Muppets.

It was a great night out as Colin had predicted and it was clear we had been accepted as a couple. This was what I needed to convince myself that we should move in together.

If my personal life was on the up and up, the sky was the limit for my work life. I loved working at Hogan, primarily because Richard inspired everyone and achieved a management style that perfectly balanced hard work with fun. The results spoke for themselves; from nothing, the company had grown to £10 million in two years. Imagine our shock when we were called into a meeting and informed that he was leaving to work in Dallas. The powers that be had decided the company needed a managing director with more experience in running businesses in the UK and Europe. We were all devastated. A new MD, George Grainger, had been appointed, and he wasted no time in getting to know his team. Some of us were singled out to take part in expensive training courses. I was one of those people.

Hogan enrolled me in a three-week residential course, and I can't pretend I wasn't daunted by the prospect. In fact, I was scared out of my wits and dreading it. Having had no education since I left school at sixteen, I didn't know what to expect and, even worse, I wasn't sure I would meet the standard required.

When I booked into my room on the Sunday before training started, the attendant said, "You're the first ever female to attend this senior management course. Congratulations!" I laughed nervously. Though I knew he'd meant it as a compliment, being "first woman" didn't help my nerves. I was relieved to find that most of the attendees were also nervous.

When asked to introduce myself, I said, "My name is Rosemary, and I'm Finance and Admin manager for a US Banking Software Company." Then with a grin, I added, "I've just been informed I'm the only female on this course, so I hope you guys will be gentle with me." This broke the ice and, one by one, we got to know a bit about each other.

As I'd expected, the course was difficult and covered all aspects of business, including finance, marketing, sales, and people skills. We worked in teams as well as individually and received one-to-one feedback on our progress. I found the marketing tasks most demanding. I'm not creative and felt even less so when I was paired up with the youngest – and by far, the best-looking – man on the course, who just so happened to major in sales and marketing. He proved to be a good delegator, and having acknowledged my people skills, tasked me with acquiring public opinions about our new alcoholic beverage from students not on our course. I received lots of great feedback on the pink-orange beverage, and my work paid off. On the last day of the course, I was voted an "Honorary Chap"! During an era where female managers were still a rarity, this didn't come as a surprise. I liked being a trendsetter in business... I certainly wasn't one anywhere else.

While I was away at my course, Brendan and Colin were on holiday for a week in Greece. There, Colin wrote me a nine-page handwritten letter, which was both confusing and full of love and affection:

"This holiday has made me realise 150% that you are all I now desire in every way. I love you so much... Please forgive me for upsetting you and making you cry. Please help me to ensure it does not happen again. We must discuss things to the nth degree if necessary, to avoid repercussions of that unhappy day... As you know I shall always feel guilty about Brendan and will always go over-the-top about giving him a good life... I have one request, I expect you to still have a lot of love for Brian, but I ask you not to display any photos of him..."

What I took away from the letter was that I'd become the second most important person in the world to Colin, Brendan being the first, of course. The rage I saw when he made me cry over nothing concerned me, but not enough to halt the fast train journey I had started with my two new best friends. At Colin's request, I put Brian's picture away, though I knew this man would never replace the love of my life that, even after four years, was never far from my thoughts.

***

When Colin told me he'd found the perfect home for us, I wasn't expecting a seven-bed detached house on one of the most desirable roads in Esher, but that's what I got. Littleworth Common Road was a five-minute walk from Sandown Racecourse and a ten-minute walk to town. Not content with one large property purchase, we also bought a newly furnished two-bedroom timeshare apartment called the Montagu Suite at Rhinefield House in the New Forest. How I'd managed to go from a council house background to owning a mansion and a timeshare was beyond me. I didn't dwell on it, but I did feel like I'd been transported overnight into another social class.

Colin had left Hogan and was working as a consultant. His leaving was such a relief, because I didn't feel comfortable dating someone from the office who didn't conform. Colin had a way of upsetting both bosses and colleagues, and I think he probably realised he was in danger of being fired. Despite his ineptitude when it came to being a team player, he was an extremely talented business analyst, and before long, he was given a project to work on. Whilst I had the steady income and was climbing the corporate ladder, I seemed to attract men who liked to be self-employed.

In September, I climbed another rung: I was promoted to Associate Director for Finance and Admin. A press release was published in the *Financial Times* and the *IT Press* with our photographs, which I showed to as many people as I could. I was proud all my hard work and long hours had finally paid off.

The Esher house was great for entertaining. We had many dinner parties, and on a few occasions, Tony Pidgley, the property entrepreneur who started Berkeley Homes, and his wife, Ruby, showed up in their Rolls Royce, leaving their chauffeur to wait in the car. A chauffer's job, of course, but if my mum was staying with us, she 'd always invite him in to have a coffee with her. We'd also sometimes organise a day at the races. With Sandown Racecourse so near, we'd ask everyone to dress as though they were attending the Royal Ascot, with the men in suits and the ladies in

Our Esher home – Colin's the gardener

The beaver with his Dad in our garden

posh frocks and hats. On more than one occasion, admiring onlookers inquired if we were 'famous people'.

I should have known the fun and games wouldn't last. They came to an end when Colin grew bored of consulting and decided he wanted something more challenging that would generate more income. What better than a180-acre farm in West Sussex, complete with a rundown sixteenth century farmhouse? Colin didn't tell me anything about it until the day he drove Brendan and me to view the property, which was situated between Crawley and Rusper at The Mount.

"The site is called Mount Farm," Colin told me as he led me on a tour of the property before adding firmly. "I've worked out a business plan. This is what I want to do." A far cry from Brian's approach to introducing me to the Spar Supermarket we so briefly shared.

"Seems like a huge project to be taking on," I replied, "and it's way outside of anything I've experienced." Really, I thought it made the supermarket look like a tired little corner shop.

"I made a success of that smallholding I had." Colin had the project with his first wife, and he'd boasted about this smallholding on several occasions. "I can cope with this it's the same kind of project but on a larger scale."

I had no reason to doubt him. He'd been successful in his various schemes and loved a good challenge. So I moved on to another practical query. "What's the cost? Will we need a larger mortgage?"

"We'll receive a good profit on our Esher house," Colin insisted. "We won't need to increase the mortgage significantly to buy the farm. Besides, the move will be best for all of us. Think of how amazing this home will look, once it's renovated. And Brendan will be free to roam and have adventures in his own outdoor playground. And think of the dog…" I'd wondered why he hadn't put up a fight when, after months of begging Colin, he'd suddenly given into the purchase of a golden retriever puppy who we named Cindy; he'd had this farm in mind, the perfect lure for any dog lover. "You'll have the opportunity to live in a magnificent farmhouse in the country, and I'll be hard at work improving the property and increasing our net worth." He finished his pitch with a puff of the chest, and against my better judgment, I allowed myself to be persuaded. Before I knew it, we'd exchanged contracts on Mount Farm in October, 1987.

18

HAVING A HEYDAY

Colin was right about one thing: Brendan loved the freedom of the farm. He and Cindy enjoyed exploring their new home, and it wasn't long before Colin let me choose a second puppy – a red-setter-coloured golden retriever named Goldie. Colin's, best friends Clive and Karen, would often bring their children along whenever they'd visit, and all three of the kids had great adventures with the dogs, climbing into the hay lofts and playing hide-and-seek. Gerald, the farm manager, directed Colin in the prioritisation of farming projects. The land took as much work as the house, resulting in a conflict of interests; Colin was keen to prioritise the outdoor work but knew he'd first have to move me and Brendan to the farm fulltime.

In fact, Colin had altogether underestimated the amount of time and intensity this type of work required, and he began to take it out on Brendan and me. In a flash, he'd turn into a controlling monster. He'd shout at us – or anyone who happened to be around, for that matter – as soon as something wasn't going his way.

"Colin, I am really concerned about the cost of renovating the farmhouse and the land. Are you sure you have the financial side of it under control?" I asked one afternoon. I should have known better.

"For God's sake, stop querying every penny I'm spending, will you? It's getting on my nerves. What do you know about this type of project? Can't you see what I'm trying to do here?"

"I can but—"

"No 'buts,' you idiot. Just accept I know better than you do, and keep out of the way."

He wouldn't listen to me about anything, and our finances were starting to get out of control. Now, even he must have been questioning his decisions, although he wouldn't voice self-doubt. I was tired of my opinion carrying no weight and sick of being yelled at for no reason at all. Seemingly, he didn't need me for a thing. So I put that to the test. I left him.

I drove Brendan to school as usual and went to work. Two hours before Brendan needed picking up from school, I called Colin.

"Colin… I'm not coming home. You'll need to collect Brendan."

"What – why?" Colin was flabbergasted and couldn't absorb what I was saying.

"I've had enough of it."

"What have I done that's so terrible? I'm sorry if my shouting was out of order; I was just having a bad day. Please come home. I need you," he paused before adding, "and Brendan needs you more than I do. We can talk this through and resolve things."

Colin had found my pressure point. I'd grown to love Brendan so much; I couldn't leave him. Colin was right – Brendan did need me, and so did Cindy and Goldie. *So did Colin, really,* I thought, *if only he'd realise it properly.* And so, I weighed the bad times with the good. Colin's moods were so fickle; I felt I was on a rollercoaster, emotionally driven up and down at nausea-inducing speeds. *When he's good, he's very, very good,* I said to myself, *but when he's bad, he's horrid.* Unfortunately, I had yet to see how horrid he could really be. And so I returned home that night.

***

While all of this personal upheaval unravelled, my work life was no easier. I had been project managing a new office building for Hogan, working far too many hours, and becoming thoroughly run down. I could no longer cope with the pressure and knew I had to do something about it.

I marched into the MD's office, fully armed with all the projects I had on. In a prelude to my resignation, I said, "There's no way one person can complete this workload. It's too much." Then I gave some recommendations on what was required to run the department more effectively and efficiently. "You need to have a fulltime human resources manager and a building manager. The company has tripled in size since I began, and no one seems to have noticed I'm drowning under the workload."

"Your workload *is* excessive," my MD admitted, taking me aback. "Your hard work and dedication to the company is duly noted. We wouldn't want you to resign or feel exhausted from overwork. Please look for a personal assistant and an office manager to help you."

I walked out of there with my head held high, feeling that a huge burden had been lifted from my shoulders. I should have tackled this issue ages ago, but at last, some of my work stress lifted... even as the stress of my home life gradually compounded.

***

One of our first farm projects was haymaking. Colin's dad, Ben, drove one of the tractors with a trailer attached to put the hay in. Gerald, our farm manager, was in charge (as much as Colin would let him be) and directed the whole operation.

As Ben's trailer was being loaded with the sweet-smelling, golden hay, nothing could entice Brendan more. "Dad, may I please ride on the hay bales!" he begged.

Colin was quiet for a moment. He was so protective of Brendan in day-to-day life, but he saw the farm as an opportunity for him to experience new things. "Yes," he granted his permission, "but only if Rosey will ride up there with you."

Climbing to the top of a hay trailer, eighteen feet high, was not high on my agenda; but of course, I'd do it for Brendan. And so, I manoeuvred my way up with a lot of help and laughter from Colin and Ben, and Brendan climbed up after me. When we were both safely at the top, I was pleased I'd made the effort. Our land stretched as far as the eye could see: 180 acres of it, all of which we owned. It was the first time I'd taken it all in from such a height, and the expanse made a profound impression upon me.

But the impression was quickly toppled. Literally. As we approached the barn, Ben turned the tractor onto the gravel, and the hay started to slide. "Stay put!" I told Brendan, and forever after, I wished I'd heeded my own advice. In the process of trying to save the hay from falling, I fell with it. Tumbling a hard eighteen feet to the ground, I cried out and immediately nursed my throbbing left arm.

Colin rounded the corner a moment later. When he saw me lying on the ground, he grabbed my injured arm and said, "What are you sitting down there for? There's a lot more work to be done yet."

I screamed in agony, and Ben shouted at Colin, "Leave her alone!" Colin appeared totally bemused; he hadn't seen me fall off the trailer.

"I really wish I was skiving," I gritted my teeth, angry tears trailing down my cheeks, "but I think I've broken my arm. How am I going to get to work?"

Ben drove me to Crawley Hospital, and on the way, Marjorie flooded my memory. When we were children, Marjorie and I had chores, of course, and our main job was to do the dishes. Mum worked all day for a lady in a big house, so the dinner dishes piled onto the breakfast load, to be done by Marjorie and me, all at once at the end of the day. One afternoon, Marjorie arrived home with her arm in plaster. My heart sank. I knew Marjorie couldn't avoid an accident, but I resented her; I'd no longer have help washing up every night. However, Marjorie's absenteeism from chores was short-lived. Mum grew suspicious when she didn't have any hospital appointments. She threatened she'd go to the school and investigate what happened. Only then did Marjorie confess that some of her school friends had applied plaster-of-Paris very convincingly. I was so mad at her, but Dad thought it was hilarious. Of course, he did; Marjorie had always been his favourite, so she received no punishment.

Through the pain of my throbbing arm, I smiled at the memory, while waiting to have my X-ray done. The X-ray showed that my arm was well and truly broken. The doctor applied plaster – real plaster – and I was told the cast would need to stay on for at least three months. On our way back to the farm, I asked Ben, "What do you think Colin will say when he sees this?" I gestured at my cast.

Ben knew better than anyone that Colin was not the most sympathetic of people. "I'll have a word with him," he stressed. "It was an accident; it's not your fault."

But when we returned to the farm, we were both surprised to find Colin was full of remorse for yanking my arm. "You only did it to get out of the washing up," he joked.

I laughed, "No, that was my sister did that," and I proceeded to tell him my memory of Marjorie. He gently pulled me to him, avoiding my left arm, and kissed me passionately.

"I really am sorry. You do believe me, don't you?" I nodded. "Brendan's gone to bed, but he was very upset. Will you go and check he's okay? And give him a kiss even if he's asleep."

Forgive the outfit – love the dogs

I'd intended to do that anyway, so I made my way upstairs. Even through our squabbling, I always believed Colin was a good parent. And he was fun to be around when he was calm and unstressed. "When he is good, he is very good…" I didn't finish my thought, as I didn't want to go to bed thinking he was horrid. I never wanted to focus on the negative. And he was only horrid occasionally. Right?

***

When Hogan found out about my broken arm, they realised I wouldn't be able to drive to work and arranged for a chauffeur to transport Brendan and me on our daily routes. I don't know many employers who would have done that. Still, the atmosphere at Hogan had changed for the worse. Oh, how I wished Richard was back at Hogan UK. Working with George was not easy or pleasant. He sidelined me one day, saying, "I just wanted to inform you that I intend to hire a qualified Finance Director." This was the position I was effectively performing.

Little did he know, I had people with seniority on my side. I'd continued to travel to Dallas every quarter and was always made to feel welcomed there. The US team recognised me as a conscientious and more than competent financial mind, and when the CFO heard what was happening in the UK, he immediately called me. "I'm sorry about what's going on over there," he said. "We've decided to make a few changes. You'll no longer be reporting to George; instead, you'll report to the Vice President for Business Management in Dallas."

I was pleasantly surprised. "What will I be reporting?"

"You'll be given specific projects for the US and asked to comment on the financials produced by the new UK finance director. Basically, you'll be monitoring expenditure."

Despite the fact that I was no longer his direct underling, George would still hand me newspaper or magazine cuttings containing new business ideas or models and order research done on the contents to be reported back to him. I knew it was a power play. He never gave me deadlines for any of these tasks, and after completing the first few I could tell he was just paying lip service to me when I delivered the information. Nothing was ever followed up. His power play became moot after I marked a special drawer "GG" for use only when he handed me his busy-work.

But worse still, George seemed to want to cut me down a peg at every opportunity that swung his way. One day in the spring of 1986, the company was planning for a staff incentive trip in the Caribbean. The trip was primarily for sales achievement, but the staff also voted for a non-sales person to accompany the team on the coveted holiday. When the HR manager told me I'd won, I was thrilled to bits. However, my delight was short-lived, after George called me into his office. "I'm sorry to do this, Rosemary, but I've overruled the vote. The Tech Department has worked very hard this year, and they need some accolades. I'm sending a software technician instead." He was not one bit sorry, and I saw right through his façade. I never forgave him.

***

Not long after this, I ended up in hospital for eleven days. No, I wasn't in a major accident, and I hadn't caught some dreadful disease. I just wanted to have a baby and couldn't conceive. They discovered that I had severe endometriosis. Though medicine has advanced to the point that the surgery for endometriosis is now considered "minimally invasive," in 1987, the operation left a four-inch scar, three inches below my belly button. For some reason, I agreed to be a human guinea pig, with student doctors loitering over me, while I answered any question thrown my way. Embarrassment aside, there was a silver lining: I was told the operation had been a success, and I'd be pregnant within six months. Well, I wasn't. And with so much going on in our lives, I'm not sure why I was surprised.

One morning I got a lovely surprise. After I had dropped Brendan off at school I looked through my rear view mirror and saw him chasing the car. I pulled over, wound the window down and heard him calling, "Mum, Mum, stop, stop." I thought I would cry, this was the first time he had called me mum and it made my heart swell. "I left my bag in the car," he panted, out of breath from running. "Thanks, I would have been in trouble. See you later." Off he went, not realising how much his words had meant to me.

Hogan had started to falter. The heady days of unlimited expense accounts and multi-million pound deals had come to an end. Perhaps because of this, I was awarded "Sales Person of the Year" at the annual kick-off meeting. They cited my role in the Midland Bank (now HSBC) contract as the reason for my recognition, when really all I'd done was assist the negotiations. The gesture – awarding someone in the financial department for salesmanship – was intended to jolt the sales team from their hibernation, in the hopes that they'd perform better.

As 1987 was drawing to a close and the Financial Director began the budget process for 1988, I took a call from my US manager. "What I have to tell you is confidential," he said. "You must be discreet." I agreed, wondering what would come next… though I thought I might already know. "Dallas wants you to work on a budget scenario for the UK, reducing staff numbers by a minimum of ten people. You're then to put together proposals on how the company would operate going forward."

Yikes, I thought. *Ten peoples' livelihoods in my hands?* A big challenge but one I thrived on; I was always at my best when challenged.

That very same day, our Sales Director, also approached me confidentially. "Rosemary, can you do a budget plan for me? One that excludes George?" he asked. "I've heard through the grapevine that George's plan excludes me, so I know my job is on the line."

After a lot of work and many reiterations, the US office went with their plan. I had to organise a meeting on a Sunday in March to which all of the remaining managers were called. The business plan for 1988 was presented, and in the end, thirteen people had been let go. That Monday became known internally as "The Night of the Long Knives". The new MD, who was from Dallas, was introduced that night as well. Thereafter, I reported to him and was rewarded for my efforts by being promoted to Deputy Managing Director, with my main remit to indoctrinate him into the European way of doing business.

***

Back at the farm, Colin had spent a fortune on farm equipment, including a tractor with a quadrophonic stereo system. He with Brendan by his side would tend the fields at weekend, and with help from Clive on the property, they were making progress. Our farmhouse had been renovated and at last I could see Colin's hard work and his vision, but I didn't feel he appreciated my contribution – endless hours at Hogan to bring in a regular salary, and never-ending jobs on the farm. Clive, Karen, and their two little girls visited most weekends, which meant Brendan had playmates, while I was relegated to chief cook and bottle washer and never had time to relax. I didn't dare, otherwise Colin would find me something horrible to do.

He'd decided to take advantage of a new farming initiative called 'Set-aside,' a scheme designed to reduce the production of arable crops by setting aside 20% of the land used for agricultural production, in return for annual compensation payments. Colin wanted to rear sheep and cattle, so the scheme suited his needs and the rest of the household's. Both Brendan and I loved the animals. We were happy to join in during lambing season and feed the calves their milk when they came to us just a few weeks old. We favoured one particular chestnut brown cow, and Brendan named her Angie after my niece. The calf soon understood she'd been singled out for special treatment and would come up to the gate to meet us upon our approach.

The farm was taking shape but there was little time for socialising other than with Clive and Karen. Brendan's Mum drove to the farm every Saturday and took Brendan out for the day and on one of these occasions we were shocked to get a call from the Crawley police. They said that Brendan had been found putting money into a games machine in the lobby of the local bingo hall. It transpired that she had left him while she went into the Ladies toilets to take drugs. Colin was outraged and told her that she was not seeing Brendan anymore and that, furthermore, he was taking the car back that we had given her for the express purpose of the visits. It was left to me to drive her home that day and she only saw her son once more and that was a disaster. I had thought it would be a good idea for him to be able to give his mum a Christmas present and I got Colin to agree it was okay. When she opened the door to her flat it was clear she was stoned; she took one look at us both and slammed the door in our faces. Brendan had wiped this from his mind until twenty-seven years later when I started writing my story and we were reminiscing.

With the farmhouse nearly finished, we could actually start enjoying it and have friends by for a visit. We decided to celebrate Colin's thirty-ninth birthday early. I designed party invitations and wrote the following poem, entitled 'The Lords, Ladies and Tarts Party':

'On July 1st this very year
Gentlefolk will come from far and near
To what? To where? I hear you say
What is happening on that Saturday?

'Tis the annual bash at The Mount Farm
Where folk get merry, but come to no harm!
There'll be wine to sup and nibbles to eat
And listen chaps, you're in for a treat!

The tarts are to come with suspenders in place
Ladies will wear jewels, satin and lace.
Lords will wear dinner jackets and black tie,
And fun will be had until morning draws nigh!

Bring your tents and stay the night.
Breakfast will be served at first light!
Come one, come all and have some laughs
With Rosey, Colin, Dogs, Sheep and Calves!'

Our guests wrote some witty responses and duly came dressed up embracing the theme for the party.

RSVP - Yes,
we'll be there at the
Mount
As Lord and Lady (or
was it a Count ?)
To enjoy the bash in
both fields and
ditches
To see all the Ladies and
tarty dressed stitches.
Suitably clad we will
surely be
But don't dare ask for
our family tree!

from
Lord + Lady Owen
of Maidenhead

Cheryl showed us her artistic and poetic skills

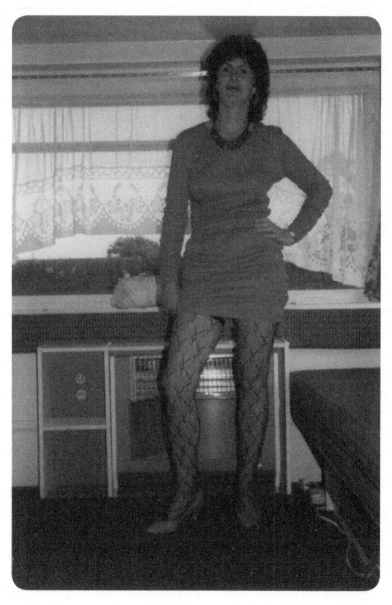

A Tart it had to be!

What a cake – just imagine the biscuit crumbs!

We also had a vicar or two, and several brought their tents to stay overnight. No expense was spared to make the evening the best social event we'd ever hosted, and our friends appreciated the opportunity to have a good drink without having to drive home. The cake I'd had made for Colin was designed as a farmyard, and partway through the evening, I noticed someone had crumbled up a chocolate biscuit beneath the cows' backsides.

The music played nonstop, and anyone thinking they could get away without dancing was mistaken. We did the conga around the tennis court and garden, and more than one couple decided the night was right for romance. The neighbours hadn't been invited, but we had no noise complaints, so it didn't get quite *that* rowdy. Colin enjoyed himself and appreciated being the centre of attention. I was thrilled when he stopped the music and changed it to a smoochy one, declaring, "This song is for Rose, the love of my life, and the most forgiving girl on this planet. Thank you, darling, for putting this birthday bash together for me."

***

Proud Mum with her seven babies

To me, this was the beginning of a wonderful period in our relationship. My only regret was I hadn't become pregnant. This incompleteness was highlighted when our dog, Cindy, was mated with another pedigree golden retriever. Once the delivery date neared, I'd invited my sister, Joan, and Mum to help with midwifery duties, taking turns sitting with Cindy throughout the night in two-hour shifts. When my turn came, I traipsed downstairs, and Joan said excitedly, "She's waiting for you to be here!" Sure enough, the first of seven puppies was delivered within two minutes of my arrival. The delivery was the most moving moment of my life. I loved both of our dogs so much and realised they'd become my baby substitute.

During our first proper Christmas in Mount Farmhouse, Brendan had just started to learn the piano, which he wasn't too keen on. "C'mon, Brendan," I put on my best air of persuasion. "We can organise a little carol concert for your dad, grandparents, and Cora."

"I don't want to," he huffed, reluctant at first; but once we'd started planning, and he began practicing, he grew excited about performing for everyone on Christmas Eve. The night of the performance finally arrived, and the biggest showstopper was a song I wrote, which we sang to the tune of 'While Shepherds Watched Their Flocks by Night'.

'While the Bensley's washed their socks by night
All seated round the tub
Nanny Cora on her broom came down
And they begin to scrub.

Fear not said she, for Colin's feet
Will smell much nicer soon
And Granddad will be merry and bright
After having a whiskey or two.

Auntie Val has made the Christmas pud
And Cora's iced the cake
Dogs and puppies must behave themselves
And not keep us awake

We hope you have enjoyed this song
And will come back next year
Brendan and Mum hope you have fun
Best wishes and good cheer.'

Each of the references to family members was received with gales of laughter. Brendan shone as a musician and was thrilled to perform. Even more thrilling, perhaps, was his enormous red and white stretchable stocking made by his mum. It was extraordinary, and no matter what size his main present was each year, the stocking was never full. On Christmas morning, he thoroughly enjoyed pulling out present after present, and this year was no exception.

With a roaring log fire in the inglenook fireplace, the mouth-watering smell of lunch cooking in the kitchen, and plenty of alcohol to keep the adults happy, this is what I'd envisaged our farmhouse would one day be: harmony and happiness. The two entwined during that happy Christmas, putting all of our trials and tribulations on the farm into perspective.

***

In February, Colin announced he was taking me away for a few days, not flying off somewhere exotic, but driving in a campervan of all things. The trip was over Valentine's Day, and I wondered if Colin was planning something romantic along the way. Despite our ups and downs and Colin's mood swings, we had learned to live happily together, so I knew what my answer would be.

The night before Valentine's Day, Colin drove the van into a small country house hotel near Barnstaple, where he booked us in for the night. At three in the morning, we were woken by the fire alarm. We lay in bed for a minute or two, hoping it would stop, but it split our ears until we were deaf. We quickly dressed and rushed downstairs, following the signs for the fire exit. When we were outside, I cuddled into Colin and whispered, "We should've been sensible and grabbed our duvet." He was unusually quiet, and I wondered what was going through his mind. Before I could ask, the fire was deemed a false alarm, and we were soon swept inside again.

With such drama, we returned to our room, wide-awake. I noticed Colin appeared nervous and distracted; his movements were jittery. I realised why he was being so strange, when he went down on one knee and asked, "Will you marry me?"

Though the proposal wasn't quite what I had envisioned, it was heartfelt and real. "Yes, I'll marry you," I said without hesitation. I had expected this… not during the aftermath of a fire alarm perhaps, but I knew it was on the cards. Colin had been a different person, since I flexed my muscles, questioning the financial side of the project. He'd begun to show me more respect and was much more loving. *Why wouldn't I marry him?* I now thought.

***

One thing was still missing from my life: a baby. I talked to Colin about trying IVF. I was thirty-six years old, and the six-month mark since my operation had long passed. My window was narrowing. Despite the cost, we started the treatment at the Harley Street Fertility Clinic in London. Tests showed my eggs and Colin's sperm were healthy, making us feel quietly confident that the treatment would be successful. The drugs and injections were unpleasant, and the procedure was the only thing I could think about, but if we could get pregnant, I knew it would be worth the pain and anxiety.

Eventually the lining of my womb was ready, and the time was right for me to go to the clinic late one evening. They gave me the trigger injection HCG that starts the eggs' maturation process, thirty-six hours after which they would collect the eggs. The same day, Colin would produce a semen sample. He wasn't looking forward to it, but he knew how important this was to me. He was also excited about the prospect of being a dad again. The fertilised eggs would then be implanted into my womb. That's when the waiting game would begin.

When I arrived for the implant, the nurse met with me. The look on her face sent my heart plummeting. "I'm sorry to tell you this, but though both of your specimens are healthy, your partner's sperm cannot fertilise your eggs." My mouth went dry, and I felt as though I couldn't move. "Your case is very rare. One in several million."

I couldn't believe it. The nurse was sympathetic, but my pain was beyond sympathy. When she left my room, I rose and paced in a daze, distraught. I didn't know how I was going to break the news to Colin. I had a pain in my heart so intense, I just wanted to curl up and die. I left the clinic and sat in Regent's Park for what seemed like hours. *Why me? What have I done to deserve this? My two sisters had only to look at their husbands to get pregnant. Aren't I good enough to be a mum?*

Once I'd calmed myself down and stopped the downward spiral of self-pity, I realised how selfish I was being. I had Brendan. He might not be my natural child, but I was his mum; he loved me and I loved him. I had my dogs and my home and a job I loved. I had Colin.

I pulled myself together and called Colin to break the news. After a mutually numbed silence, I attempted to put a positive spin on our situation. "I can now concentrate on the wedding plans and give all my love and attention to you and Brendan," I said through my tears. We never spoke about IVF again.

19

THE HONEYMOON PHASE IS OVER

As if to remind me what a lucky person I was, the next day I received a once in a lifetime invitation. Part of my job was to arrange permits and visas for Americans to work on our complicated banking systems, and the gentleman I always dealt with was retiring. He asked me if I'd like to attend the Queen's Garden Party at Buckingham Palace. Of course I did, and though my last name wasn't official yet, the invitation to the party was the first I'd ever received addressed to "Mrs Rosemary Bensley."

Shortly after receiving the invitation, there was drama at Hogan. I'd been on the interview committee for our new European Managing Director, and no candidate had stood out yet. One morning, while the process was in full swing, I walked into the office and without a second's delay the receptionist turned to greet me, followed quickly by news she guessed would upset me, "What do you think of your new boss?"

My heart sank. Without a word to me, Hogan's president had given the job to a thirty-year-old, blue-eyed boy from Dallas, and I knew I'd take the brunt of this decision. The boy's inexperience meant a larger workload and intensive training, and I didn't want the added pressure. I went straight to my office in a huff and called Colin.

"They've hired a kid, Colin, and without involving me in the decision or even telling me about the appointment. I'm so angry right now. I don't really want to leave, but I think this is indicative of how the company is going to be run in the future."

"Don't say something you'll regret," he replied. "Come home, and we'll figure it out."

By the time I arrived home, he'd typed out my resignation for me; I amended the wording to ensure I would be guaranteed a good pay-off and returned to the office to deliver the letter. My boss was happy to agree to pay me six months' salary, which he told me I deserved. So that was that. Seven good years at Hogan, ended unhappily and abruptly. But the timing couldn't have been better; I could now concentrate on the family for a change and get on with the wedding plans.

***

With me out of work, Colin decided it was best to start spending like a king. He bought four new cars – a Ford each for our parents, a Range Rover for himself, and guess what I got? A bright red Ford Escort Estate. A bit of a downgrade, after I'd just had my company car – a Jaguar XJ6 – taken away, but Colin assured me it would be very practical. *Great*, I thought. *Just like me.*

Summer brought several weddings in quick succession, the highlight of which was of course our own. The wedding was held at the Methodist Church in Sandhurst, Surrey. The ceremony was poorly timed, as it happened to be on the same day Marks & Spencer opened a superstore nearby, causing traffic and chaos. Everyone was running late, including the wedding party.

My four bridesmaids were two of my nieces, Julie and Angie, and Clive and Karen's daughters, Susan and Katie. They all wore handmade, dusky pink dresses with ivory bows, while I wore an ivory dress, with its fitted top and flowing skirt accentuating my figure. I felt like a goddess.

Despite the fact that we were running late, when we arrived at the church, we were asked to drive around again, since traffic was holding up a great many guests. Fiona was one of the latecomers, and she was horrified when she realised that, in her haste, she'd left her driving shoes on. Fiona was always impeccably dressed even in casual clothing, so I told her it made me smile. Unlike my first wedding to Mark, Julie sang only the hymns and not 'Winnie The Pooh'.

At the reception in Penny Hill Park, nine-year-old Brendan's speech was the most endearing. "I was told that, as best man, it would be my job to toast the bridesmaids," he said. "The idea horrified me. That is, until I realised it didn't mean they'd actually be toasted," he held up an electric toaster to make the point. He stole the show in his light grey, tailor-made Austin Reed, which matched his Dad's and Granddad's.

Thanks Jo for helping me choose my dress

Beautiful bridesmaids Angie & Julie with Susan & Katie in the front

Colin with his Dad and Brendan his best man

The deed is done – happy days

My speech made reference to absent friends, referring to Brian and Marjorie of course. There were several missing faces that had declined our wedding invitation because of Colin's behaviour in the past. Losing friends at the expense of Colin saddened me, and with a ring now binding us, I was soon to find myself even further alienated.

***

The next day friends and family waved us off from Waterloo Station as we started our trip on the Venice Simplon –Orient Express heading for one of the most romantic floating cities on earth. The rough crossing at the change of transport at the Channel made everyone ill. *Not a good omen for our honeymoon*, I thought. But we decided not to let seasickness spoil our fun. We boarded the luxury train in Paris, and we made the most of every moment. As soon as we'd been shown to our cabin, taken in the dazzle of the walls with their ten coats of varnish and the art deco floral-and-leaf patterned wallpaper, and laughed at the fact that we had bunk beds on our honeymoon, we changed for dinner and headed to the restaurant car.

After washing down our delicious dinner with expensive champagne, our interest turned to the piano bar, where we heard uproarious laughter. I looked through the door and saw the carriage was tiny, and only two couples and the pianist occupied the room. I wasn't even sure there would be room for us. I caught the eye of one of the women, an elegant older lady dressed in a silver gown. "Come and join us," she called out. "We can squeeze up." We were beckoned in and made to feel welcome. We introduced ourselves to the two other couples, who were downing champagne.

"We're celebrating our twenty-fifth Wedding Anniversary," one of the couples told us.

"And we've escaped Australia for the time being to try and rekindle our marriage," the other couple said, openly. "This trip will either make or break us. But don't let that scare you away."

We spent the next two hours roaring with laughter while getting nicely tipsy. Our honeymoon could not have gotten off to a better start.

***

We awakened the next morning to snuggle in the same bunk together after sleeping apart overnight. Once we realised we were on our honeymoon, of course one thing led to another. While in the middle of things, we pulled to a stop at some random station, and looking up from our lovemaking, we realised we hadn't drawn the curtains. Outside the cabin window stood a platform full of commuters, looking in. Colin flung the curtain shut, and we laughed and laughed. What did we care? We would never see them again.

When we arrived in Venice, the magic of our journey – with all its laughter and transient scenery of mountains, chalets nestled in valleys, and sheep grazing beneath the pine trees – vanished with Colin's change in mood.

"Darling, let's ride the gondola!" I exclaimed, thrilled to be in romantic Venice.

After inquiring with the gondolier about prices and engaging in a somewhat hostile back-and-forth, Colin returned to my side and grunted, "We're not doing the gondola, Rose. It's a waste of money."

The spendthrift has suddenly become a penny-pincher? I thought. I've never liked wasting money, but surely the gondola was a must for a honeymoon couple in Venice. "Please, it's not that much money in the grand scheme of things. You've been talking for ages about taking the gondola. I thought it was something you wanted to do?"

"I don't want to spend a small fortune on it," he grumbled. "It's really something for lovers in their first throws of love. That's not us, is it?" I looked aghast, and he covered his tracks a bit. "Come on, let's not bother with it. The price is exorbitant. Besides, there's so much to see in the few days we have here."

Am I so wrong to want romance on my honeymoon? I asked myself; then instead of drowning in confusion, I decided to ask him instead, not expecting an explosion of anger in response. "What have I done that's so wrong?"

"Go on the gondola, if it's the last thing you want to do this holiday! For God's sake, you are so ungrateful."

I started to well up. *Why did I marry I this man?* I thought, miserably. *He'll never change.*

Whether Colin read my mind or just realised in time that he was out of order, I don't know. But the next time I turned around, he was negotiating prices with a gondolier, and when we were off, the gondolier began to sing 'Just One Cornetto'. Colin had asked him to sing it, just to see me smile. *Okay,* I smiled in an instant, *maybe he isn't such a monster after all.*

***

The Buckingham Palace Garden Party made returning home easy. The sun was shining on the day, and Karen had lent me a stunning royal blue dress to impress the royals. Colin was dressed in a traditional top hat and tails, while Ben acted as chauffeur. He was also our designated photographer, although he wasn't allowed any closer than the palace gates (as it happened though, it didn't matter, since the chemist ended up losing the film). We were led from the large courtyard and directed to the gardens, which were already full of guests milling around. It was a wonderful sunny day and the grounds were magnificent, stretching further than the eye could see.

I saw the royal family up close; in fact, at one point, I was stood only six feet away from Princess Diana. She was as elegant as I expected her to be and animated when she spoke to the chosen few that got to shake her hand. I also watched Audrey from Coronation Street sing 'I'm so Pretty' while twirling around in her party frock, which was a delight for me. I was a Coronation Street fan, taking after my mum who had watched every episode since 1960. "The day could not have been any better," I told Ben when he collected us several hours later at the palace gates. Before long, I was asleep but not before I told myself that it wasn't a dream.

***

I started job hunting once the honeymoon period was over and I was feeling my brain was being under-utilised. It wasn't long before I'd found my mark. In accordance with the National Health Service and Community Act of 1990, under which health care providers could become independent of health authority control, Kingston Hospital needed to recruit people with accounting skills to implement new financial systems. With my background, I fitted the bill.

However, when compared to the innovative commercial companies I'd worked for in the past, the NHS was a dinosaur. Implementing the new financial system took a lot of patience (and patients) before the system would demonstrate financially security. I worked as hard as ever, but I could see I was fighting a losing battle, and one thing I always thrived on was success. So when six months later, I had a call from the former CFO of Hogan Systems, a weight lifted from my shoulders.

"Would you consider joining the UK office of the Harris Adacom group?" he asked. "It's an innovative IT hardware company. I'm now their CFO, and I need someone to take on a consultant role for European Finance. I'd really like you to consider joining me."

"How many subsidiaries does the company have? Where are they located? Is there a job description I can review? What are you offering for a daily rate?" I reeled off question after question, the last answer of which, I could hardly believe. I'd be paid more in one quarter than I was paid annually by the hospital. It was a no-brainer.

My consulting role at Harris Adacom involved producing financial plans with local finance managers in the UK, France, Germany, Spain, the Netherlands and Belgium. Each country had its own rules and regulations, and I was constantly traveling to meet with the prospective company heads. The travel was exhausting and the work, more so. Bearing in mind each country's different set of financial laws, I was asked to design a forecasting model to encompass the nuances of the operation, which enabled the head office to gather a consolidated view of Europe, after which I'd review the financials and recommend efficient ways to increase profit.

Colin appreciated the money I was bringing in, but he didn't appreciate my being gone all the time; while I, on the other hand, loved the time on my own, far and away from Colin's controlling nature, which had grown more constricting as of late. "Why do you have to go to France overnight?" he'd ask. "Can't you get it done – there and back – in a day?" I had to justify every trip to Colin. *For goodness sake*, I thought, *my job is keeping us afloat. Why can't he just accept it comes at a cost?* His wish was granted, when after consulting for six months, I became the Finance Director for the UK office, which meant less travelling and more home time.

Regardless, the role required me to travel occasionally, and I was asked by the new European managing director to spend three weeks in Holland working on the European financials. My heart sank. How was Colin going to take this?

As soon as I arrived home that night, I plastered on a crestfallen expression and said, "You'll never guess what I've been asked to do now."

"Come on then, spit it out," Colin responded. "You're clearly worried about telling me, so it can't be good."

"They want me to take three weeks in Holland going over the European financials," I mumbled.

To my bewilderment, Colin's face lit up, "Well, let's turn it into a family adventure then. Brendan's on school holidays, and I don't need to be here all the time. What are the dates?"

True to his word, he planned a three-week vacation at Centre Parks, which was only a thirty-five-minute drive from the Head Office. On the second day, as I was getting ready to leave, he said, "When you come home tonight, you'll find the two of us here," he pointed to a small swimming pool. "It's more exclusive, and although we have to pay to get in, you'll enjoy the peace and quiet after a hard day's work."

I like this new Colin, I thought, as I drove to work. *He's genuinely interested in making me happy on this trip.*

After a long day at work, I was looking forward to relaxing by the pool. I turned up in my swimsuit, only to look around and find the swimmers all naked. This swimming area was exclusively for nudists. Being that I was never an exhibitionist, I found it all very embarrassing. I could sense Brendan did too. *How silly was I to think Colin wanted to make me happy?* I thought. *What is he playing at?*

He repeated this routine every night of our trip, and I was too timid to argue. I didn't want to deal with drama, and at least the nudity kept Colin from shouting at Brendan and me. *Let him have his holiday,* I thought. *I'll keep my head in a book and hope no one's looking.*

Interest rates brought me back to the reality of life funding a farm with very little income. They'd increased steadily, nearly doubling from over 8% to where our mortgage was over a staggering 18%, and so I grew worried about our financial situation. With all the borrowing we'd done, we now had an overdraft of £600,000, and the quarterly interest was more than my annual net salary. The situation was making me physically ill, and I just couldn't let it continue.

"Unless we start to clear the loan," I sat Colin down, "I won't be staying around to see everything we've spent our time building come crumbling down."

"Oh, don't be dramatic, Rose," Colin tried to make light of the situation, when deep down, he knew I was right. After a time, he said, "All right then, we'll sell some of the land off in lots." After receiving further advice, he suggested, "We should market the house as well as the land and see what interest we get. Let's market 140 acres in twelve different lots and leave the other forty acres as part of the house offering."

***

Colin was intent on finding another project, and I knew the worst thing for me would be to have him sitting around with nothing to occupy his time. He always dreamed big – secretly, I think he wanted to be king of the castle – and so he travelled the UK searching for new properties. He took Brendan and me with him whenever he could. We looked at mansions with at least ten acres of land, we looked at Holy Island in Scotland with highland cattle and horses, and we looked at a Scottish castle where the owners had their own pew at the local church.

In no time at all, we had great response to the land sales; we sold land and a small lake to a local fishing club, we sold land to gypsies, we sold land to a famous fashion designer for his mistress to keep her horses on, we sold land to locals, and we sold land to an electronics company. The last had to be seen to be believed. Colin was the one who saw it, and he was completely fired up when I arrived home from work. He couldn't wait to tell me what had transpired in the space of a few hours.

"Company executives arranged to meet our lawyer on site," he told me. "They turned up in two cars, with lawyers and secretaries, and announced that they wanted the transaction agreed upon and completed today. These business men in their suits traipsed the land in Hunter Wellington boots." Colin laughed. "It was a sight, let me tell you."

The land was important to the company, because they had a tower in one field at the bottom of our property, which they used to beam signals to a small wooden hut in a field near the top of our land. Our lawyer explained that the firm was carrying out important tests that were part of a study, which is why the deal was the most profitable. We received more than double the original asking price. And thank goodness for that, because now we were financially stable once again. For a while.

***

We looked at a mansion in Denbighshire, North Wales, called Llantysilio Hall. This was the one project where even I could see the potential – grand architecture and stunning grounds, extending far and wide, with peacocks running about… how much more magical can it get? We fell in love with the Hall, and Colin, Brendan and I spent his summer holidays backwards and forward assessing the opportunity to turn it into timeshares. All we needed was a buyer for the remaining forty acres and the farmhouse at Mount Farm to be sold and we were in business.

Colin suddenly became dead-set on getting Brendan into Edgarley Hall, Glastonbury – the prep school for Millfield School. Doing so was not easy. Despite the hefty fees, many parents wanted a top-notch education for their children. Candidates were also required to undergo an all-day interview process and pass an entrance exam. Brendan was not particularly academic, and he didn't do well enough to make the cut. For most parents, a rejection letter would have been the end of it. But Colin would not accept rejection and decided to do everything within his power to get Brendan into that school.

One of Brendan's best friends from Parkside, who'd started at Edgarley that year, just so happened to be the son of one of the Millfield School governors. Colin called him and explained Brendan's situation, "Is there anything that can be done? It would be great for your son to have a friend there, I'm sure." It's not what you know, it's who you know, as they say; soon enough, we received a letter of acceptance. Brendan started boarding at Edgarley in September 1991.

Brendan looking smart in his new uniform

Colin's interest in Llantysilio Hall waned as no buyer materialised for the farmhouse, and knew our time would be better spent on other work needing done at the farm. Though we came close to a deal, gradually we faced the fact that we were unlikely to complete the purchase, which was a shame, but it simply wasn't meant to be.

Colin's focus then turned to searching for a new venture in the West Country, since Brendan was now at school in Somerset. Never mind that my commute to work would be torturous. When I'd say anything about it, Colin would just shrug his shoulders and reply, "We'll cross that bridge when we come to it." No surprise there. I was being made to feel superfluous to Colin's needs and desires.

Despite how superfluous I felt, I was beyond thrilled that Brendan loved boarding at Edgarley, and I looked forward to his letters, phone calls, and of course our visits to see him. We would drive down on a Saturday morning to watch him play sports and then we'd take him out somewhere special. I was also enjoying the challenge of learning about a new industry at work. IT networking was where technology was heading and where Harris Adacom wanted to make its mark. I worked long hours, and with Brendan away at school and the farm work dwindling, Colin had also started to feel redundant and had grown increasingly moody. The slightest thing could set him off.

***

One weekend when Brendan was home, Colin mentioned over breakfast that the last of the cows were being collected, including Angie, our beloved pet. The farmer had promised she wouldn't be slaughtered and would be kept on his farm with some of his favourite livestock.

After breakfast, Colin said to Brendan, "Get dressed straight away and go to the field to say goodbye to Angie." In the meantime, I got on with the household chores and completely forgot about the time. That is, until Colin came charging into the kitchen with a face as black as thunder.

"Where have you been?" he asked, livid.

"Here, of course, doing the washing." I couldn't even think what was the matter.

"You didn't send Brendan down to the field to say goodbye? You didn't care to say goodbye to Angie, yourself? You are a selfish, uncaring hypocrite, making out you love animals and Brendan, when all you care about is yourself."

Angie the cow

I hadn't noticed he was holding one of my special bone china ornaments in his hand, until it hit me in the face. I screamed and couldn't believe what had just happened, what he'd done. I looked at him for a moment, full of rage, and then I raced out of the kitchen, grabbed my handbag and car keys, and drove off without looking back.

I'd never experienced violence from him like this, and I wasn't going to accept it now. I didn't know where I was going or should go. I was crying and shaking and needed to find somewhere to pull over, so I could clean up the blood. But not until I was a world away from Colin.

I'd driven in the direction of the office, but I immediately altered my course. I needed to talk with someone who would be sympathetic but not too critical, and I decided Linda would be the best person. She lived in Chilbolton, about an hour-and-a-half from the farm. When I arrived on her doorstep, dried blood at my temple, she was mortified.

"What on earth has happened to your face? Did Colin do this to you?" She instinctively knew Colin had caused the damage above my eye, which was already turning itself black. At Linda's wedding in Denmark not long before, Colin and Linda's husband, had had a falling out, because the night before the wedding, Colin had accused him of not treating Linda properly. We no longer saw each other often, and she – like all my other friends and relatives – had no idea what I was going through at home. "Let's go for a walk, so you can talk openly," she said, closing the door behind her. As we strode down the lane, she insisted, "Tell me what happened."

I first told her about the most recent incident with Angie, the cow, and then spent the next two hours filling her in about Colin's moods and how he'd become so controlling lately; so controlling that he even went so far as to stop me from seeing my girlfriends. Once I started, I couldn't stop talking, which made me realise I'd had no one to confide in. Colin's horrendous treatment of others and myself had alienated me from everyone, including my sister Joan, many friends, and everyone dear to me. Every time I visited someone who Colin didn't approve, I had to pretend I was going to see someone else, making me feel like I was having an affair without a man. Fiona was the one he disliked most, but the one I saw whenever I could, which wasn't often enough.

After hailing Linda with this downpour of troubles, she hardly raised a brow. Her lack of surprise indicated she'd dealt with similar men in her past. "Has he ever physically abused you before?" she asked.

"No, no. This is the first time. He's never shown any signs of physical violence against me or Brendan… as far as I know."

"This might be a one-off," Linda replied. "He might just be upset about seeing all his cows go."

"I'm sure that's what it is." I don't know why I'd already started to justify Colin's actions, even though at that point, I could have murdered him. After chatting a bit longer with Linda, I felt consoled. I knew she would understand and offer me words of wisdom without being unnecessarily sympathetic, and that's how it had been. As we parted ways, I added, "I promise I'll keep in touch. And I'll let you know if anything like today ever happens again."

Next on my list of counsel was Colin's Dad. I decided I would call in to see him and Val. I knew Ben would be horrified when he saw my face, but I felt he had a right to know what had happened. As soon as he opened the door, he exclaimed, "What's happened to your eye? Did Colin do that?"

Though his reaction surprised me, Ben added, "Colin called me when you went missing. He assumed you came here. He told me some of what happened… but clearly not all."

I explained the events leading up to the assault and said, "Honestly, Ben, I could understand him being upset about the cow, but Brendan wasn't bothered about going down to the field. The truth is I didn't want to force him, because I didn't want either of us to be upset. You know what I'm like with animals." Ben nodded in understanding, seemingly appalled by his son's violence.

After talking it out with Ben, I called Colin. "I don't understand why I reacted that way," he admitted in a voice of remorse. "I just want you to come home, so I can make everything alright. I'm so sorry. I never meant for the ornament to hit you. Please come home. Brendan is feeling bad, because he thinks this is his fault. Come home for his sake if not mine." Yet again, he was using Brendan as a way to manipulate me. I could see that clear as day, and yet I loved Brendan so much, I was willing to be manipulated.

When I arrived home, they both greeted me as if I'd been gone for weeks. They spoilt me for the rest of the weekend, and as busy life again interceded, the horrific incident was soon forgotten or, at least, swept under a rug, as horrific incidents so often are.

20

CHARLTON HOUSE & ROYAL GUESTS

Christmas 1991 showed me another side of Colin, a side I did not wish to see. Colin was always strict with Brendan, yet I'd always considered him a good parent. Many times, he told him off far more harshly than fitted the crime, but this particular Christmas, he was more than just snarky; he was downright cruel.

"Hold up a minute," Colin hollered at Brendan a few days before the holiday. "Aren't you forgetting something?"

Brendan's eyebrows shot up to meet his hairline, his jaw went taut with apprehension, his eyes round with fear. His first school report from Edgarley was less than satisfactory, and he knew his father would be cross, so little Brendan had hidden it under the cushion of the piano stool. Unfortunately for him, one of the other parents had asked Colin whether he was pleased with Brendan's report. Colin just assumed Brendan had forgotten to give it to him.

"Simon's mum asked me about your report today. Did the dog eat it?"

Without hesitation, Brendan dissolved into tears, and before the interrogation had even begun, the poor kid confessed. Colin went berserk, shouting like a madman; his face grew red as a furnace, and steam veritably billowed from his ears. He smacked sweet Brendan across the backside and sent him to his room, where he was imprisoned until Christmas, a teetering mountain of schoolwork as punishment.

During these episodes of tension and rage, my motherly instinct was to rush over to Brendan to cradle and defend him, but I was forbidden from doing so. Brendan and I each suffered in the same way but our bond was never in question. My job was to sit back and feel the lash of Brendan's pain in absolute silence. But while I thought the whipping would pass in time for Christmas Day, the worst was still to come.

When I traipsed downstairs on Christmas morning, I saw Brendan reaching underneath the enormous tree, searching for his presents. Beside him was his big red sack – empty apart from his school report. When Brendan looked up at me, big alligator tears stood in his eyes, and being that Colin was nowhere near, I rushed to give him a hug.

"What's wrong?" I asked.

"The only thing Santa left me is my school report," he answered in a choked voice. I couldn't believe it; surely Colin couldn't do this to his darling child.

On my last trip to Dallas in the summer, I'd bought four large Transformers, which were all the rage at the time. I couldn't wait to see the look on Brendan's face when he opened the present and found not just one, but four of these action figures for battling. Unfortunately, I never got that pleasure. Colin's cruelty extended to my gifts as well and did not reach its tether in the evening, as I expected it would; instead, it would outlast every last drop of mulled wine and every needle in the carpet.

"You can't keep other people's presents from Brendan," I told Colin defiantly when we were alone. "I bought him those toys, and he'll get to enjoy them." I did manage to persuade him to allow Brendan one gift eventually, but I still wish I'd done more. It had become clear to me that, in this relationship I was not the strong one. At work I was a powerhouse, but at home I was as quiet as silent night, avoiding any and all confrontation. Colin's outbursts were not frequent enough for me to be concerned for Brendan's safety or mine but I hated myself for not being stronger. When Brendan witnessed him shouting and kicking me hard repeatedly, for no good reason other than I had been out playing with Cindy & Goldie, he told me he wished his dad wouldn't treat me like that.

***

Early in 1992, we dropped Brendan at school and drove twenty minutes into Shepton Mallett, booking ourselves into Charlton House, a country house hotel on the outskirts of the small town. One of the parents from the school had recommended it, and when we arrived, we were surprised to be greeted by the owner, Cath. We had a pleasant evening chatting with her, and the next day on our drive home, Colin said, "I get the feeling that Cath is not totally enamoured with the hotel and would like to get out of the business."

"Where do you get that idea?" I asked.

"Well, she talked a lot about never having intended to work fulltime in the hotel. Clearly, she's tired of it." She'd mentioned that she and her husband, George, had originally been in a partnership with another couple with whom they'd fallen out.

"Do you really think –"

"Just let me give Cath a call to see if my intuition is correct. If it is, we should explore the possibility of buying."

"I'm not sure running a hotel and maintaining the high AA and RAC standards required is in our ballpark. It does look like long hours and hard work." I may just as well have papered the wall. Colin never heard me anyway.

The only time I'd ever even thought about owning a hotel was when Brian and I discussed it on the cliffs at Swanage. I felt sad we'd never been given the opportunity to see the idea through. But I didn't want to see the idea through with Colin. Colin was nothing like Brian; his increasingly frequent tantrums concerned me, and I thought it unlikely that he had the temperament to run a hotel. At this point, my opinion didn't matter, as this was not any more likely to progress than any of the other feelers he'd put out there. But I should have been vocal, because progress it did.

Colin's intuition had been correct; the owners were looking for an out, and soon I found myself being led by George on a tour round the hotel. He proudly pointed out how he'd renovated each room, and when I went through the books, I was surprised at how profitable the hotel had been in the current climate. *With economies on spending and more marketing*, I thought, *we could be sitting on a goldmine*. Out of all the projects I'd ever been part of, this one captured my imagination the most, and more importantly, I could see my role in making it a success.

We talked to Cath and George about the idea of swapping Mount Farm for the hotel, and they agreed to come view our home. Cath fell in love with the house, and George loved the land, the outbuildings, especially the walled garden. The exchange was quick and easy and soon we were the proud owners of Charlton House – a nineteen-bedroom hotel with seven acres of garden, a stream, a tennis court, a swimming pool, and a sauna.

The Mount Farm near Rusper

Charlton House in Shepton Mallett

***

At last, Colin was lord of the manor. He'd have the run of the operation from Monday through Friday, while I'd supervise at weekends, manage weddings, and ensure the bookkeeping was done properly. Colin ruled the roost and was the perfect host. Guests loved the fact that the owners had a table in the dining room and joined them in the bar. Though our hotel's exterior was all polish and veneer, behind the scenes, we could have been rehearsing a scene from Fawlty Towers, complete with a rat running round the bar, Colin shouting at the kitchen staff, the chef throwing tantrums, and our own Manuel from Spain. Tempers did clash, but the atmosphere was mostly positive, and the staff appreciated the time, effort, and money we were putting into the hotel to make it successful.

I soon found I, too, was in my element. Not only did I love interacting with the guests and entertaining, I also implemented a new accounting system and trained two of the receptionists to proficiency. We now had current financial data at our fingertips, which was something the previous owners never had. Even my mum would help out in the office when she visited. The only downside to this new gig was the five-hour round trip commute to my job. FIVE HOURS. My day began at 5 a.m. when I'd wake for a swim then catch the early morning train from Castle Cary or Bath to Reading and transfer to Winnersh Triangle. The daily commute ensured that by Friday, I was completely drained. Yet, I was supposed to be sprightly and on my game for my weekend work as host of the hotel.

Luckily, the hotel brought the sprightliness out in me. The energy of the place was contagious, with rich or famous people coming to stay or dine on occasion, including Jeremy Beadle, Van Morrison, Michael Eavis (the organiser of the Glastonbury Festival), Gillian Taylforth (Kathy Beale in Eastenders), Jeremy Guscott, and Charlie Watts. At the time of Charlie Watts' visit, Brendan was into playing drums, and so we were thrilled to tell him about our famous drumming guest. His reaction was not at all the one we were hoping for.

"Who's Charlie Watts?"

We gaped at him until Colin informed him, "He's the drummer of the Rolling Stones."

"Who are the Rolling Stones?" Our faces were priceless.

No matter, the guests were endless; lords and ladies, weddings and events, short stays and long. In our first month there, I organised a wedding between a local girl and an Irish rugby player. The majority of the party guests were Irish, and after gallons of Guinness had been consumed, the noise was deafening. All sorts of shenanigans were going on. Our staff reported that some couples were creating even more heat and sweat in the sauna than usual, and others were swopping partners. Wearing clothes was seemingly optional, and most preferred the naked option. I certainly didn't want to swim in the pool the next morning. But no harm done, apart from one broken vase and stains on the carpet.

The excitement was also endless. One Saturday morning, we had a call from Edgarley Hall asking us if we would clear the hotel of guests between noon and two o'clock. King Hussein and Queen Noor of Jordan wanted to visit the hotel with their son. Fortunately our guests were always out being tourists at that time of day, so we confirmed the clearance. We watched as the local roads were all shut down and our royal guests arrived with eight enormous bodyguards. They quickly inspected the ground floor before the king and queen were permitted entrance. Two guards stood at attention at the bottom of our staircase the entire visit.

The king and queen were delightful and chatted to us, as if we were old friends. They were dressed just like anyone else would be, no crowns or tiaras, just stylish day-wear, though no doubt hand-made.

"Your hotel is just what we hoped we'd find near the school. It's quaint and very nicely decorated," the king said. "Is your son enjoying his schooling at Edgarley?"

Colin piped up immediately, "Oh yes, your Royal Highness. He's really progressed, especially when it comes to sports, which he never liked before. We also discovered he has a musical ear, and he now plays in the school concerts."

I knew Colin would talk the king's ear off, so I politely interrupted, "Brendan really surprised us the first time we heard him play percussion, as he didn't enjoy learning the piano at all."

"How would you like a ginger beer?" Colin asked their son. He accepted it with a broad grin; no doubt he thought he was very grown up with a beer in his hand.

We provided a light lunch of sandwiches and salad, and when it was time for our royal guests to leave, one of the bodyguards approached us and asked, "How much is the bill?"

Both Colin and I answered in unison, as if we'd rehearsed, "Nothing, it's been our pleasure and honour to serve the king and queen." Regardless, after everyone had left, we found two fifty-pound notes under the plate as we were clearing everything away.

***

I should have known Colin's diplomatic temperament and social competence wouldn't last. One night, we had a call from the office of Frank Warren, the renowned boxing promoter. "Could we book the entire hotel – all of the rooms – for ITV interviewers, Jim Rosenthal and Gary Newbon, and other important staff?"

We committed to the booking, after which we discovered the guests would be involved in the Frank Bruno comeback fight against Rodolfo Marin from Puerto Rico in February. The fight was being held at the Bath and West Showground, and we were the nearest country house hotel. Since Bruno had dealt a knockout punch in the first round against Jesse Ferguson the previous year, this fight was sure to gain publicity. Every one of the hotel's staff, including me, was highly anticipating the entourage.

The night before the fight, I was in the hall of the hotel, when I picked up on a heated telephone conversation from the other room. Colin was shouting into the receiver, "If you can't be here by 11 p.m. then don't bother arriving until tomorrow morning! Our doors will be locked at eleven on the dot."

"I don't think you realise who you're talking to. My name is Gary Newbon, and I'm someone big in ITV."

Quick as a flash, Colin retorted, "And I don't think you know who *you're* talking to. My name is Colin Bensley, and I am someone big in Charlton House. The doors are locked at 11 p.m."

I rushed over and wrenched the phone from Colin. "I'm so sorry," I apologised. "We're a family-run hotel and do have our own rules. If you can promise me you'll arrive no later than midnight, I'll certainly wait up for you."

"I'm truly sorry about this," Gary seemed entirely apologetic. He added politely, "Thank you. I'll make sure I'm no later than that."

"Here you go again, Mrs Do-gooder," Colin snapped, once I'd hung up the phone. "I thought you were complaining you were tired?"

"I may be tired, but not tired enough to ruin our chance to have the ITV crew stay."

"Okay, I take your point." *That makes a change,* I thought. "I'm off to bed," he continued, "so good luck with your egotistical guest."

When Colin and Gary shook hands the next morning, mutual respect was instant and they acted like they'd become the best of friends during Gary's stay, which was as brief as the fight, with Bruno again securing a win in the first round. Brendan and Colin had been thrilled at having the opportunity to go to see the fight. They had front row seats and heard every exciting moment but were disappointed it wasn't a longer fight. Little did I know, Colin had many rounds to go.

***

"Edgarley has always stood by its founder's ethos of attempting to discover and nurture whatever talent a young person has," Brendan's school declared; and the declaration was justified in Brendan's case. They'd fostered his natural musical and athletic talents until he shone. Whenever I attended a rugby game or a concert, where he played the theme to *Star Wars* on the marimba or showed off his A-game on the field, his talent made my life brighter. The last time I'd heard him play an instrument was the piano at home, and he'd hated it. And now he was one of the stars of the concert. He also demonstrated speed and athleticism, representing the school in the hurdles, for which he held the county record. In 1993, Brendan was accepted into Millfield School.

As life marched on, the running of the hotel consumed so much of our time that not being able to see old friends and family was taking its toll on me. Not only that, but the business had started to suffer a loss of customers.

"You're not pulling your weight," Colin would complain, seeming not to notice I had more than a fulltime job. He'd convinced himself I really wasn't doing my fair share to the point that one night, when I returned home from work at 8 p.m. he said, "Why am I doing everything, while you're off enjoying a life of leisure? You know what – my day is over. I'm going to go entertain myself. The hotel is all yours until the last guest goes to bed."

No discussion. Nothing. This was the way of things from then, onward. The minute I returned home from my fulltime job, I was to immediately thrown into the next. This meant I was sometimes on my feet until one o'clock in the morning, only to have to rise four hours later to ready myself for work. Cindy and Goldie were my only company, and they kept me sane. It didn't matter how my workday had gone or what mood Colin decided to be in when I walked in the door. Seeing my two dogs sitting in the office waiting for me to arrive, happy as can be, with their tails wagging and drool dribbling, enabled me to cope. I never fought back or dissented, because all I wanted was for Colin to be satisfied. I certainly didn't want a repeat of the flying ornament episode. A rosy garden is all I wished for. But I suppose even roses have thorns.

***

I made the decision to keep on the right side of Colin's mood swings which ended up paying dividends when he unexpectedly surprised Brendan and me. He booked us on a QE2 cruise across the Atlantic to New York on our own. I kept waiting for the sting in the tale. Was he going to suddenly produce a third ticket and come along? Or had he truly decided I'd worked hard enough to earn a break? The latter, it seemed, as Colin was sweet and kind before we set sail. This would be Brendan's first trip overseas without his dad, and he looked forward to enjoying some freedom. I was Brendan's playmate for the duration of the cruise, and since we had similar temperaments, I knew the holiday would be delightful.

"Get dressed, we're going to the casino," I said one night to Brendan's surprise. He was only fourteen, but when he dressed up in his dinner jacket for the formal dinners, he could pass for at least eighteen. Neither of us gambled of course. We enjoyed each other's company and had great fun playing on-deck sports, like quoits and mini-golf.

In the formal dining room, most guests still dressed up in their finery, and silver-service waiters attended to our every need. Brendan and I were sat at a table with six other guests, all of whom were American. They loved our English accents and were sure to include Brendan and me in the conversation.

"Well, young man, have you joined the on-board teenager club?" one of the older gentlemen asked. *Uh oh,* I thought. Colin had told Brendan he must join the club to find new friends and make the most of all the activities, so now Brendan might think this man was a spy, reporting back to his dad.

"I haven't, because I prefer to have my own exercise regime," Brendan piped up, much to my surprise. "I run around the top deck every morning and really love seeing the dolphins swimming in front of the ship. I'd also rather hang out with Mum," he grinned and turned to me, "because even though she's not sporty, she does play deck quoits very well."

When Brendan and I returned to the cabin, we chatted so easily. We laughed about how different our trip would have been had his dad come along. Brendan rarely spoke to me about Colin when we were home, probably because he knew I wouldn't have said much for fear of being overheard. But here we were free to speak. And so we did.

"Do you think Dad is going to be cross when he finds out I didn't do as he instructed?" he gazed at me with a little fear in his eyes.

"Not after we show him how much we've missed him not being here," I winked, "and you can tell him how your fitness has improved by doing your own exercise routine."

"And yours, he won't believe we won a prize. It might only be a T-Shirt but I am very proud of both of us."

"Tomorrow, we'll buy him that expensive-looking desk set we saw in the gift shop. I know he'll like that."

"Good idea, and I'll look for something else in New York that I can say I chose specially for him."

With each day, our bond grew stronger, and I knew I had made the right decision to put up with Colin's tantrums in return for having this wonderful young man in my life. The five days on board seemed to vanish, and when the ship approached New York in the early morning, the extraordinary sight was far better than we'd imagined.

On our last night in New York, I asked Brendan, "So did you enjoy the Big Apple?"

"Yes," he said then after a pause, "but I enjoyed the cruise more."

I'd enjoyed the cruise as well, and deep down, I knew it was because Colin hadn't been there to cast our joy overboard. I would not have relished being on that ship with him for five days, as his temper was never far from the surface. And soon, very soon, I would drown in it.

21

BLARING THE HORN

I only wish the buzz and success of the hotel could have lasted, but for whatever reason, in two years' time, Colin had grown tired of the day-to-day and had started to let standards slip. We no longer had a fulltime chef, and he often donned the chef's hat for breakfasts. He also chose to start upsetting more and more people, including guests, the staff, and the suppliers. This had a detrimental effect on the economic viability of the hotel, and of course, on Brendan and me.

We both knew we were in trouble when from out of nowhere Colin screamed out "Brendan, where are you? Come here NOW and bring your mother with you." 'Here' was the landing between our bedroom and Brendan's. We knew better than to speak before being spoken to.

"Have you forgotten something?" We both looked at each other and I spoke, "I can't think of anything important. What's on your mind?" He was irate and screaming at the top of his voice, "You are both selfish and don't expect me to join in with anything today." While he was shouting he was writing on the inside of the landing door in large letters the words 'THINK, THINK, THINK'. That was to be a reminder every time we left our apartment. We looked suitably chastised and kept out of his way and by bedtime Colin's rage had subsided, as it often did.

As Charlton House was seeing a downturn in business, so was Harris Adacom. The IT market had changed drastically, and whilst the UK had changed course to meet the challenges of the new marketplace, the rest of the Harris Adacom group had lagged behind. During this extremely stressful and exhausting period, Colin was not being supportive. This shouldn't have been a surprise, but somehow I'd hoped he would rise to the occasion. In fact, he'd done the opposite and seemed out to destroy my career.

This became apparent when the international directors were attending a group meeting in Winnersh, and he arrived at 6 p.m. to pick me up. Instead of waiting patiently for the meeting to wrap up, he slammed on the horn of his Range Rover and left it blaring until I went down to talk to him. I had never been so embarrassed professionally. I apologised to the chairman and said I would sort out the problem. Sick to my stomach, I traipsed down the stairs, knowing I'd be confronted by one of Colin's rages. He'd just been to meet his dad and Val, and I guessed that the visit had not gone to plan.

"Colin, stop that awful noise. You'll damage your eardrums." I gave a weak smile, attempting to lighten the mood. But it only made him roar the louder.

"You are such a liar!" he shouted, red in the face and looking like he could kill me. "You promised me you'd be ready by six, and its ten minutes past!"

"I won't—"

"No excuses – just get your things now!" he glared menacingly, and I knew there was no point in looking for some way to appease him. "If you're not back down here in ten minutes, I'll be gone, and I don't think Cindy and Goldie will like seeing me like this, will they?"

I had already turned away, my heart thumping out of my chest, and as soon as I entered the building, a colleague who I could see had heard the exchange outside greeted me. "Mike asked me to let you know the meeting is ending and that he remembers you saying you had to leave by six o'clock."

"Can you thank him for me, and tell him I will catch up with him first thing in the morning?" I was trembling with embarrassment and anger.

This episode was only the beginning of the deterioration of our relationship; it further proved to me he was interested in what he wanted and nothing else. I was there to mould myself around his moods, his decisions, and his life and never, ever the other way round. But even if he'd decided to give up on his job, I hadn't given up on mine. I would not let him take that away from me. At least I was making money, whereas the hotel was now losing it, thanks to his disinterest.

***

Later that same week, Colin had collected me from work, and we were driving on the M4 motorway to Bath when, after a coffee stop, he said, "I'm tired. Take over the driving for me?"

Not half as tired as I am, I thought. He'd been up to see his dad and Val again and obviously something had soured his mood. I knew better than to ask, but I also knew I'd receive the blunt end of it. And sure enough…

"For God's sake, stop driving like an old woman!" he hollered.

"I'm doing just over seventy miles an hour. What speed do you want me to go?" Suddenly, he reached over and yanked on the steering wheel, making it impossible for me to control the car. I took my foot off the accelerator and screamed, "STOP, COLIN! STOP!"

All I could do was brake and hope other drivers kept clear of our swerve.

"You stop!" Colin shouted at me. "Pull over."

Once he'd let go of the wheel, I pulled onto the hard shoulder. He stormed over to the driver's side and yanked me out of the car. The rest of the ride was silent fuming on both ends. By the time we arrived at the hotel, he had calmed down, but my thoughts were seething. *He almost got us both killed.* I wasn't sure how much more of this I could take.

***

Not long after Colin's road rage, I visited the company's bankers in London; the senior manager surprised me by putting forward a proposition. "Would you be in interested in doing a management buyout with two of your directors?" It was not the question I had expected when I visited the company's bankers in London for a routine meeting. They complimented me as they explained their rationale. "We only have praise for the UK operation, but the group is in danger of collapsing. We have every confidence in the three of you, and would support you financially if you wanted to carry on the business and form a new company."

When I mentioned our conversation to the MD and sales director, interest was ignited, and we decided to proceed with negotiations. "I suggest I continue to be the main negotiator with the bank, whilst you both carry on relationship-building. We have to keep all of this confidential until the bank and legal side of the takeover is complete. Liquidators will be involved, and the three of us will have to work long hours if we're going to pull this off."

"What will Colin have to say about that?" I was asked, the car horn still blaring in our ears.

"I've already spoken to him, and he's going to fully support me." If either of them had any doubts about this, they didn't make them known. I had my own doubts – particularly, concerning whether or not the bank would fund us, but I just couldn't let this opportunity slip through my fingertips.

After many months, a new company was formed, called HAL (UK) Limited. With the bank's backing, we started to trade. Our suppliers agreed to us settling outstanding debts in IT networking, which was the part of the business we wanted to continue, and business continued. After the initial few months of enthusiasm and settling into our new offices, introducing a new accounting system, and marketing like madmen, the future looked promising. Our loyal staff retrained into the necessary positions, and our customers started to buy from us again.

Colin – having not been particularly supportive during this process, despite asserting he would be – at last seemed to be embracing the situation. I'd even become a source of pride. Many a time I'd walk in on a conversation between Colin and someone, where he'd be gushing, "Rosemary is now Finance Director of her own business. I'm very proud of her." He'd even sent me a beautiful bouquet of flowers during the office move. However, his thoughtfulness wore a bit thin after a few months, when I realised he'd just put a standing order in with the florist.

And yet, he made no allowances for the extra pressure I was under at the office. The minute I tried to relax at home, he'd holler at me and call me lazy. I couldn't even take fifteen minutes out to read a book without being accused of shirking and not pulling my weight. Despite the stress at the office, going to work was an escape. I looked forward to shutting our home's heavy oak door behind me each day and driving away. Away from Colin.

***

Our sales and support people were intelligent and understood IT Networking. Within our first year, through the efforts of the technical team and Anna, who was an amazing sales negotiator, HAL was nominated for an IT Industry Award for innovation.

Unfortunately, being "innovative" often means you're ahead of the times, and the same was true in our case; whilst we could interest and intrigue customers, only a few would take the plunge and be pioneers with us. Cash flow eventually suffered, and the MD and Sales Director never saw eye-to-eye. The Sales Director had no answers as to how we could improve sales and after a while, his life must have become too much, because he left the company. Soon after that the MD also recognised the overheads were too high and stepped down. I became MD. My first order of business was to delay payments and keep the company afloat whilst simultaneously looking for a business partner. And in my other life, I had to deal with Colin.

Colin had finally got what he wanted – an enormous family home. The hotel was now running as an occasional B&B, and he'd converted one of the downstairs rooms into a kitchen and dining area with a wonderful red, double oven Aga – a total waste of money as far as I was concerned. He'd turned the main dining room into our lounge and the smaller one into a snooker room, with a full-size snooker table. Not for guest use, of course, but for Brendan and Colin. Brendan now had his own two-bedroom apartment, while Colin and I had the best bedroom in the hotel, overlooking the gardens at the back. And although it may seem as though I should have been thrilled, I was miserable and fed up with having to wear a brave face in front of everyone. Although Colin had become unbearable, he couldn't see it himself. Yet still I tried.

Colin's birthday was in July and my mum and I went into Wells to shop for him. My mum bought him a shirt, although I know she didn't want to buy him anything at all. I bought him several presents, including three bone china mugs depicting farm scenes in our new kitchen colours, red and yellow. He'd always been impossible to buy for, so I was beyond pleased when I found them, as it would show him I'd gone to the trouble of searching for something personal. I thought he'd be over the moon.

When he opened his presents on his birthday, he didn't say anything, not one thank you, no expression other than complete and absolute indifference.

"I hope you like the mugs, in particular," I said. "I took a lot of trouble to find something you'd like." If I was expecting enthusiasm or a hug, I was disappointed. I made excuses for him, and as I drove to work, I told myself he would thank me when I returned home. But that night, he said nothing. After we'd gone to bed, I arose to use the toilet and must have woken him. Suddenly, he barged into the bathroom, red-faced and angry. I was sitting on the toilet and jumped in my seat. The verbal abuse that shot from his mouth had to be heard to be believed.

"You are so inconsiderate," he hollered. "You never take any trouble over my presents. It's like you don't even care about me!" He slammed me just above my left breast, so hard it took my breath away.

Retaliation would have been futile, so I just sat there until he left the room. When I was sure he was asleep, I climbed back into bed. If I were to go to another room, I'd only have made him angrier. I still couldn't wrap my mind around how he could change from normal everyday husband to this monster without provocation. If I thought sleep would change him back, I was sorely mistaken.

In the morning, he grabbed one of the mugs and threw it at the wall and then cut up the shirt my mum had brought him. I'd grown used to being blamed for everything, but I didn't want to grow used to erratic violence and abuse. I didn't tell anybody though; I was too embarrassed. The bruises wouldn't show. He'd delivered the punches where they could easily be covered up. And so, I continued on as though nothing had ever happened.

***

Colin took Brendan away for a week on the Norfolk Broads during summer holiday, and I was delighted. Our B&B customers were being looked after by our housekeeper, so Colin's absence gave me time to fully concentrate on HAL. The company was not doing great; I'd gone through a redundancy programme, so I invited the staff to the hotel for an overnight brainstorming session. During the first day, we came up with several strategies to move forward, and the atmosphere amongst the staff was harmonious. Everyone believed in the success of the company, and we were all determined to pull together and make it work. The next day launched with the same enthusiasm, and we were in the middle of discussing the strategic planning ideas when, horror of horrors, I saw Colin's Range Rover pull up outside.

"Can everyone please carry on, while I go speak to my husband?" I said before racing outside to meet him.

"What's going on here?" Colin asked, as though he'd finally caught me doing God knows what.

"We're just having a conference here, Colin. HAL has paid for the facilities."

Before I could stop him, Colin barged past me, opened the door, and screamed at the top of his voice, "Everyone out! NOW! Pack your things and go!" My staff knew Colin was a difficult man and wasted no time in doing what they were told. Once they'd gone, Colin continued to berate me. "You are such a calculating bitch! Taking advantage of my time away to enjoy yourself, is that what this is?" I said not a word; there was no point. He never heard me when he was hell bent to holler until my ears bled. "You know what? As punishment, I'm going to buy myself a motorbike, and you, Brendan, get a moped." Brendan was standing just inside the door, looking scared, wishing the earth would open up so he didn't have to witness his Dad berate me. He didn't dare glance my way for fear of Colin seeing him. Now I understood what this fit was about; we'd recently agreed we didn't have the money for extravagant presents, so this faux rage was his way around that. Again, *his* way. He got exactly what he wanted.

Cindy and Goldie cowered in the corner of the office, shaking with fear, no doubt wondering when Colin's rage would be directed at them. We'd all been on the wrong side of Colin's anger, and they wanted to make sure they were out of the way. But when everything was free and clear, they cuddled up to me, as I cried, showing me they cared. They made me feel wanted, and they needed me as well. Even if no one else did.

***

Time marched on, and Colin's hostility ebbed and flowed. During an ebb, I broached the subject of cash flow. "Despite all our efforts," I told him, "HAL is not doing well, and I've had to take a pay cut." I deliberately didn't suggest that we put the hotel on the market, hoping he'd come up with it on his own. If I'd learned one thing where men were concerned, it was to let them think they'd come up with the ideas first.

"We should sell the hotel," he replied. "And you know, Rose, I'm sorry for my behaviour over the past few weeks. I put it down to the stress of this property and knowing your job isn't secure."

I breathed an internal sigh of relief and was surprised I'd even somehow rung an apology out of him without trying. "The value of the property is unlikely to be anywhere near what it was worth when we bought it," I said.

"Even with the renovation we've carried out?"

I nodded. "Still, financially, our position is positive. We'll need to realise at least £550,000 on the property to enable us to move forward."

"That should give us a sizeable deposit for our next house," Colin replied.

The word "house" was music to my ears. Perhaps Colin had realised we needed a break from the constant pressure of his projects. He even added, "Our next home will be near to where you work. No need for you to spend five hours of each working day traveling."

***

Our house/hotel hadn't been on the market long before Roger Saul, the owner of a design company called Mulberry, put in an offer and wanted a quick sale. We couldn't believe our luck. Charlton House Hotel was sold to Kilver Court Properties Limited on the 5th November 1996, for £575,000 so we reached our goal, thank goodness. Colin handled the sale, while I soldiered on at HAL.

We were now discussing a merger with another company, which is what I'd been praying for, as we couldn't survive on our own. I didn't count my chickens though; I knew how difficult it was to progress these matters and "heads of terms" hadn't yet been agreed upon.

Colin was busy organising the clearance of the hotel and looking for a temporary home for us. We also had a new addition to the family, a Newfoundland puppy. Tiny and soft, adorable, we named her Cuddles and she settled straight in but it was clear she was Colin's dog. He couldn't resist spending money, and before I knew it, not only did we have a new four-bedroom house in Glastonbury but also a warehouse unit to store all our excess furniture. On top of that, he bought a second-hand white van to transport everything. But I didn't argue. I didn't want to rock the boat; Colin was back to being his old self, and life was calm at home. But not at work.

In the autumn of 1996, the MD of a digital telephone company contacted me and explained he wanted to get into the IT networking business. We discussed merging the two companies. It seemed like a marriage made in heaven, and it didn't take long to agree the "heads of terms" between the two companies. Although the terms were not ideal, we weren't in a position to negotiate; we were rapidly running out of cash. My main concern was that all of the existing staff would be taken on under the TUPE rules, carrying their length of service with HAL forward into their new employment. I was to be the new operations manager. By the timetable agreed, we'd have everything completed by early December, and I was beginning to think that 1997 would be a good year. Optimism has always been my fatal flaw.

Two weeks before the deal was due to be signed, I was pulled to one side by my future boss. "Having again reviewed HAL's figures, I propose that you allow HAL to go into liquidation, after which I will negotiate with the liquidators to buy the assets." This is referred to in business as a "Phoenix from the Ashes" deal, meaning that from nothing, a miraculous recovery is made. I was devastated but knew I didn't have a choice.

"Can you confirm that everyone will still be taken on?"

"Yes, they'll be treated fairly," he agreed. The employees were all reconciled to the demise of HAL, and whilst they were grateful to have a job, they didn't like how their soon-to-be MD had handled matters. Disgust turned to anger when, within two weeks of taking them all on, he cherry-picked those he wanted to keep and fired the rest. Right before Christmas. Even though I'd been told to turn up for work on the 2nd of January, I was also eventually informed I wouldn't be employed after all.

To say Colin was angry was an understatement. Livid and breathing fire, he ranted down the phone at the MD's wife who happened to answer the phone and then turned to me. "Call our lawyers!" he shouted, absolutely furious. "We're starting a legal case against that imbecile."

"It's not worth the time, trouble, and emotional toll," I tried to reason with him. "Let's forget it and move on."

But Colin ignored me, as usual, and went ahead. A long drawn-out, costly legal battle commenced. Though I eventually won the court case in 1999 and received £40,000, justice was thin on the ground. £40,000 didn't even cover the legal fees.

***

With neither of us having a "proper" job, I found myself, for the first time in my life, signing on at the local unemployment office. This was necessary because of the court case; I had to demonstrate I was unemployed and looking for work. It was soul crushing. Having no formal qualifications, I knew I was unlikely to score an interview for a Financial Director position. The only chance I'd have would be if someone knew my capabilities or me.

Finally, I received an offer for a Financial Manager role in Devon. I told Colin about it, happy to have found something, even if it didn't pay much.

"What's the salary?" he asked.

"£16,000 per annum," I answered.

Colin sprang to his feet and threw up his hands, "Is that all you're worth? You might as well give up looking for work, altogether. Are you honestly telling me that you – Mrs Ex-MD – can only get an office girl's position now? You've got to be out of your head."

"But Colin, you're the one who said you wanted to downsize and get me out of the rat race, remember?"

"Oh, so you took that to mean you don't have to use your brain anymore?"

"Well, what are you going to be doing then?" I was spitting feathers and so angry. I should have known better than to ignite more verbal abuse, but I thought, *I've been to hell and back over the demise of HAL and then here my husband is, kicking me when I'm down.*

"Don't you dare question what I'm going to be doing."

As he berated and belittled me, I felt so low, I thought about leaving him for good. Instead, I wrote him a letter. I gave a copy of it to my friend, Cheryl, and asked her to keep it in the event that I divorced Colin. The letter explained the effect his difficult behaviour was having on me.

You treat me like I am worthless and never contribute anything. My self-esteem is so low, all I do is cry. I think you forget that I've been financially supporting your projects, and yes, I know that you've increased our net worth, but look at the hotel's loss. Do you ever question yourself? Do you ever question what effect your moody and callous behaviour has on Brendan, never mind on me? I think you need to take a good hard look at yourself. If I'm so worthless, then you're better off without me.'

After reading the letter, Colin was subdued. "I hadn't realised you felt this way," he said. "Thank you for staying for Brendan. You know, I don't mean to shout and don't even realise I'm doing it. I promise I'll try really hard to stop if you try not to upset me."

What cheek! I thought. "I never, ever set out to upset you, so how is that supposed to work?"

He must have taken that on board, because the next three months went by without incident. In fact, we were better than we'd ever been.

***

Despite our financial uncertainty, we attended the Caravan and Camping Show in Olympia and bought ourselves a brand new Kon-Tiki Motorhome, one of the first models to have a full shower room on board. Whilst at the time the motorhome seemed like an extravagance, it turned out to be one of the best investments we'd ever made. The van provided plenty of room to take the dogs, and we strapped Brendan's moped to the back for transportation around campsites.

In May of 1997, Colin and I drove our new motorhome north to join in the family festivities for my brother John's fiftieth and also my sister-in-law Lynne's fortieth. We were one of the first couples to arrive, and after parking the campervan in the lot, we headed into the hotel for Lynne's birthday bash. Apart from Roger and Lynne's name cards, which were already placed on the main table, the plan was open seating. As I found my seat and set down my bag, Colin lifted his placeholder, strode right up to the head table and replaced Roger's with his own. "They ought to mingle at their own party," he said. "They're the hosts, after all."

As people began flooding in, most were already seated by the time Lynne and Roger arrived. When she saw Colin seated next to her, Lynne didn't make a fuss, but I could tell she was none too pleased. Whispers had made their way round the party, and by the end of it, everyone knew what Colin had done. Lynne's friends barely talked to me, which made me feel like a pariah. To make matters worse, Colin brought Cuddles – his dog, a Newfoundland – into the room at the end of the evening. A glance at Lynne told me she was no longer "none too pleased"; she was pissed. Cuddles wasn't a small dog, she was huge, and those who didn't like dogs fled the room.

"Colin, please put Cuddles away," I pulled him aside. "This is Lynne's night, not yours."

"How could anyone not like Cuddles?" he replied. "Look at her; she's making everyone smile."

"But not everyone likes dogs, Colin. Lynne is mad at you – and me, probably – for letting you bring a dog in. If you won't do it for her, do it for me, please." He simply ignored me, and it seemed no amount of pleading would change his mind.

So, instead, I went to apologise to Roger. He shrugged his shoulders in response, "It's not me you should be apologising to; it's Lynne. But you can't do that now, because she's left the room. Honestly, Rose, you need to convince Colin to act like a normal human being for a change. You're losing friends fast, and it's because of him."

Fat chance, I thought. *I'll never convince him to be normal.* In fact, it took another thirty minutes and most of the guests (including me) leaving the party room in support of Lynne, before Colin retreated to the campervan with Cuddles. To add insult to injury, the next morning, instead of apologising to Lynne and Roger, Colin let the dog run loose again in the breakfast room. By the time we left, Lynne and Roger were giving me the cold shoulder. But I didn't want to lose them.

As soon as we took a pit stop and I had a chance to get away from Colin, I called Lynne. "I just wanted to say, I'm so sorr—"

"Just a moment," Lynne cut me off. She handed the phone to someone, and Roger's voice filled the line.

"Lynne isn't prepared to talk to you, Rose. And I hate to tell you this, but we don't want anything further to do with you and Colin. It was Lynne's birthday for God's sake. His behaviour was completely out of line."

"I know it was," I agreed. "I'm so sorry. I apologise for the both of us."

"Colin is not apologising. And as long as you're with him, you're not welcome here. I hope this makes you come to your senses."

They were the last of my family who would socialise with us, and now Colin had effectively destroyed even their friendship. When I returned to the campervan, I was crying. I didn't care that Colin saw, and neither did he, as it turned out.

"What are you crying for?" he huffed.

"Your behaviour has cost us Lynne and Roger's friendship."

"Well, if it's lost on nothing..." he didn't care one iota, and even worse, he couldn't care less about how it might affect me to lose my brother. "Remember, Rose," he said, "I'm your family, not all those idiots. It's you, me, and Brendan. Everyone else is moot."

Cuddles –the name suited her when she was six weeks old!

22

THE LAST STRAW

Haslers was my saviour. I'd worked there in the early 80s, and when we'd returned from our trip, they called and asked me back. I was delighted to accept, not only to receive an income again, but also to get away from Colin. I parked the Kon-Tiki – my new home from Monday to Friday – at the Elms Caravan & Camping Park in the heart of Epping Forest. Being on my own made me happier than I'd been since the early days of Charlton House. I was even happier when I learnt Brendan had been accepted for Boot Camp as a band musician with the Coldstream Guards. But things started falling apart when I was away from Colin five days a week, and his controlling grip tightened round me.

"Where were you?" he'd holler into the phone if I'd arrived to the campervan a minute past 6.30 p.m. There was no right answer. If I told him I'd worked late or had been out visiting friends, he'd bellow like I'd run him over with my car. "We're going to look at houses near to Kneller Hall, where Brendan will be based," he told me on one of these blistering phone calls.

"I'm not agreeing to that," I replied, standing my ground. "You promised ages ago our next home would be near to where I work." A week later, lo and behold, he'd found a house near Brendan in Kew, one that was much too big for the two of us. I steadfastly refused to go ahead with it. "My journey would be at least an hour-and-a-half one-way and on two tube lines," I told him. "I don't see why I should have to be the one to suffer yet again."

He took no notice whatsoever, and before I knew it, we owned the Kew

How proud was my Mum and I seeing Brendan in his army uniform

house. I didn't remember signing the paperwork, and whilst I knew I could have done something about it, I already had one court case going, and neither was I ready to turn my whole life upside down and split from Colin and Brendan. Or so I thought.

***

On one of my weekday evenings, I went out to dinner with a friend. I knew Colin was out with Brendan so assumed he wouldn't call me until later, and although I had a missed call when I returned to the campervan, I decided to return it when I was ready for bed. Before I'd even undressed, he'd beaten me to the punch; he rang me again, and as soon as I heard his voice, I knew I was in trouble for something real or imagined.

"Where the hell have you been?" he screamed down the phone, loud enough for the whole campground to hear.

"Out with a friend. Why? What's happened?"

"Didn't you remember Brendan went for his first interview today?"

"Yes, but I knew you were taking him, so what's the problem?"

"You're the problem, you thoughtless bitch. You could have called to see how it went."

I ignored his verbal abuse, like always, and replied calmly, "I was just about to call you when you called me. How did it go?"

"As if you care. I can see your friends are more important to you. I bet it was Fiona, wasn't it? And don't lie to me, because I've got her number and will find out."

"No, it wasn't Fiona actually. I'm entitled to have a life of my own, you know. You try living away from home in a campervan alone in Epping Forest and see how you like it." *Where did that come from?* I thought fleetingly. *The worm is turning.*

"Don't speak to me like that. You're just lucky Brendan is home tonight, or I'd drive up there now, and believe me that would soon spoil your cosy little existence. Either way, you'll be sorry. Just you wait and see." And with that, he rang off.

I was trembling with anger and fear. Weeping, I didn't know what to do. I lay on my bed, unable to sleep. Reaching for my Dictaphone, I whispered into it and began addressing Colin's controlling behaviour. My little saying – "When he's good he is very good, but when he's bad he is horrid" – had taken on a whole new meaning, as I accepted that "the bad" was now intolerable. His outrageous scare tactics hit me like a physical pang in my stomach, and I wanted to scream. "He's abusive – verbally, emotionally, and physically," I whispered into my Dictaphone, "and I have to do something about it. I have to somehow break from this relationship."

***

PLUNK. I jolted awake early the next morning, when I heard a noise in the campervan – I'd knocked the Dictaphone off the bed.

At work, the first phone call I received was from Fiona. My heart sank when I heard her voice. "What's the matter? I can't make out what you're saying."

Fiona was emotional and talking rapid fire, "Colin called me last night and was just awful. He was like a madman, Rosy; he was ranting and raving and threatening all sorts of things. I didn't know if I should call the police. I've got Matthew to think of." Matthew was my godson and Fiona's only child; he was only six years old. "The stupid thing is I kept answering the phone, which is right by my bed, until I had the sense to unplug it. Then what did I do? The next time it rang, I went downstairs and answered it again."

"I'm so sorry," I apologised, I was so sick of apologising for this man. "He was angry with me, and now that he's shouted at you, he's probably gotten it out of his system. I'm so sorry you had to endure his wrath. I'm really at the end of my tether with him."

"You can't be safe with that man, Rosy. Promise me, you won't put yourself in danger."

"I promise I'll keep myself safe." I didn't know how, exactly, I'd keep that promise. All I knew is that history had shown Colin's rages were not often physical and were over and done with quickly. The abuse was then followed by a long period of calm. The calm before yet another storm.

***

"Have you ever noticed when Dad rants and raves, he invariably isn't even looking at us?" Brendan asked me one day, after we'd moved into the house in Kew.

The two of us had a loving and supportive relationship and had started discussing Colin. The two of us were the only ones who really knew what he was like.

"I know," I said, "that's why I'm so much calmer these days. I realise he is just in the mood for being angry, and it doesn't matter to him which of us he is shouting at, as long as he's making himself heard." Brendan nodded. "Let's just agree to smile, and know we are there for each other. It will make each incident less of a trial."

And so we were completely there for each other from then on, and we found there is power in numbers.

***

"I'm going to visit long-standing friends of mine in New York," Colin informed me one day while we were walking round an old-fashioned card shop in Richmond. "And you're coming with me."

I paused in step and, picking up a postcard, said, "You know I can't do that. It's a very busy time. I won't be able to get the days off work."

"Your work comes before me?" he grabbed my arm so tightly that his grip was sure to bruise. "I don't think so. You'll be coming with me and that's the end of it." I was so embarrassed, even though I didn't know anyone in the shop. *Why is it we worry about what other people are thinking in situations like this?* I thought. But I did worry. I worried enough to finally leave him.

By the time I arrived to the office on Monday morning, Colin had already been on the phone to Hasler's. He'd been put through to a partner and he told him that, in no uncertain terms, I needed a week off to go to New York. By that point, I was numb with it all. "I'm sorry that he called here," I was apologising for Colin again, this time to my boss. I sat across from him and explained some of our background. "I promise I'll be doing something about my relationship very soon."

"Go ahead and call Colin," my boss said after listening compassionately. "Tell him you've been given permission to take the days you need."

When I called him, he was over the moon. "We're going to have such a great time in the Big Apple!" he chattered excitedly. "I'll book our flights. I'm going to head there four days ahead of you." *Great,* I thought. *That'll give me three days to plan my escape.*

***

Once I knew I was going to leave him, it was amazing how quickly I went into overdrive, becoming altogether practical, efficient, and thorough. In thirty-six hours, I had driven down to Somerset, managed to temporarily rent a two-up, two-down house in Barkingside from a colleague, arranged moving vans to transfer the bare essentials to my new place, opened up a bank account and transferred half of the money from our joint account, written to our credit card companies to remove my name from those accounts, and had also spoken to our solicitor to inform him what was going on. Last but not least, I picked up Cindy and Goldie from the dog-sitter. My two best friends would no longer cower under Colin's feet. They would live with my mum in Durham while I sorted myself out.

I had one last important thing to do: explain everything to Brendan.

On the morning I was due to arrive in New York, I arrived in Kew, knowing Brendan would be home for the weekend. "What are you doing home?" he asked.

I was very tearful, and he looked concerned when I sat him down and said, "It's taken me a lot of courage to leave your dad, but I have to do it. I have to preserve my sanity."

He listened calmly to what I was saying, and when I'd finished, said, "Mum, I don't know how you've put up with it for so long. I know you stayed because of me, which I really appreciate; but you have your own life to lead, and you must do this."

Overwhelming relief flooded through me. I'd gone over so many scenarios in my mind as to how Brendan would react, and this surpassed the best of them. I took two Orange mobile phones from my bag and handed one to him. "Your dad is going to react one of two ways when I tell him what I've done. If he goes ballistic, the one thing he'll want to take from me is you, because he knows it would hurt me the most. He won't allow you to contact me, but I'm hoping you'll want to. We can keep in touch on these phones. But don't let him know you have the phone; leave it at work or hide it."

"Of course I'll keep in touch," Brendan said. By now we were both in floods of tears and, feeling emotionally drained, we sat and hugged, crying together.

"I've taken Cindy and Goldie somewhere safe. I was worried he might punish them." Brendan nodded; he knew the dogs had been my lifeline. "It's time I called your dad."

At the exact moment Colin would be expecting my call from the airport, I rang him. "Hello, you've landed. Great!" he sounded thrilled. "You're really going to love it here. How long do you think it will take you to get through customs?"

"Colin, I'm at home," I blurted out. "I'm not coming to New York; I've left you. I can't live like this anymore. I've explained everything to Brendan, and he'll be here when you come back. I haven't taken anything except a few pieces of furniture from our warehouse, my personal things, half of what was in our bank accounts, and Cindy and Goldie."

There was a long pause on the other end, and when he finally answered, Colin's voice was shaken and subdued, "Don't leave me. I can't live without you, and what about Brendan; he can't either."

No dice, this time. At that moment, I felt strong and in control for probably the first time in our relationship. "I've explained everything to Brendan, and he understands. Goodbye, Colin. I hope you can find some help to get you through this."

"Put Brendan on the phone," Colin said. He was crying.

I handed the phone to Brendan, who'd been listening, and I whispered, "He's upset."

Brendan did more listening than talking and, when he ended the call, he turned to me and said, without emotion, "Dad says he's going to get packed and take the next flight back."

"I am so sorry to put you through this Bren," I said, again, "but I just cannot live my life constantly being demeaned and controlled."

"Don't be sorry. Go, Mum, and don't worry about me. I'm not a little boy anymore. I'm much stronger than Dad now, and he is hurting, not angry. Just be safe and don't let him know where you are straight away. He'll be back tomorrow."

That jolted me back to reality – my feelings of strength, control, and euphoria gone, as fear crept in to replace them. But I remained outwardly calm, and I hugged Brendan, not knowing when I might see him again. Then I left the house for what I thought would be the last time.

***

On the way to Peter and Cheryl's, where I'd arranged to stay the night, I reiterated all possible scenarios that might unfold once Colin returned. If he wanted revenge, I'd already informed my office that Colin might turn up. I warned them that he was abusive. I told reception to put any calls through to me and not engage him in conversation. I had to face everything he did head-on and not run away from confrontation, with the proviso that someone was always nearby in case he got physical.

As it happened, all of that was unnecessary. By the time Colin contacted me again three days later, he sounded like the person I'd first met. He was calm, apologetic, and funny. "You've given me the wakeup call I so badly needed. I'd ignored it so many times before. But I won't now. I have to change completely for the better. I know it will take time to convince you I have, but I'm going to try." I listened and didn't respond. I was just so relieved I wasn't going to have to deal with a downward spiral of guilt and fear.

23

A CHANGED MAN

My life was very simple now. I got up, went to work, came home, cooked my dinner, walked the dogs, watched TV, and went to bed. For the first time in ages, I felt at peace. The only thing provoking disharmony in my mind was the knowledge that Colin would, at some point, turn up on my doorstep. I'd been taking his calls, and he claimed he'd found God and was going to church at least twice a week. He'd contacted all the people he'd fallen out with over the years and apologised to them. He was looking for a steady job. "I'm still holding out hope that you'll come back to me and Brendan," he said, almost pleadingly.

Late October 1997, six weeks after I'd made my escape, Colin asked me to go out to dinner with him. Brendan had confirmed with me over the phone that Colin's stories were true. "I haven't seen him lose his temper once, since you left our Kew house," he said. He didn't tell me his dad had asked him to call, but I'm sure he had, though Brendan had remained in touch with me of his own accord.

I rang Colin back. "I'll go out to dinner with you, but that's all. You mustn't read anything more into it than that."

Needless to say, at dinner he was charm personified, and the evening went by very pleasantly.

"I really do understand why you left me. I've been a total idiot and find it difficult to articulate what I was feeling during my rages." He paused, and with a sad look in his eyes, added, "I know it will take a while before you'll trust me again, but Brendan can confirm to you that I have changed. I've found comfort in the church and enjoy attending weekly services and being part of the community I grew up in. I didn't know I was missing God in my life." Then he turned the conversation around, "How are you coping on your own? You used to really dislike being alone."

I sat up and leaned forward, "I'm not alone though, am I? I have my two best friends with me."

"Of course," Colin smiled. "Cindy and Goldie must love having you to themselves. Cuddles misses them, you know."

By the end of the night, I was second-guessing my decision in agreeing to this dinner, and I was annoyed by my lack of willpower. I'd promised myself I would not let Colin back into my life. With each smile, it was apparent he thought he might win me back. But I had no intention of being won.

"Can I come in for a last coffee before I go home?" he asked when the meal was over. Without a word, I led the way. Cindy and Goldie darted away upon sight of him, but Colin won them over with a treat or two. I think he was shocked by how tiny my place was, but he didn't say anything apart from, "You've made it cosy."

Like me, I'm sure my dogs were happy when he left without incident, and it was just the three of us again. I resolved to make these visits few and far between. I sat before my cold coffee and thought to myself, *I mustn't let one nice meal change my mind about the monster Colin had become before I left him.*

***

We went out a few more times. During one of the evenings, I made the mistake of casually mentioning, "I'll need to move out of the house and find a new place. My colleague found a buyer for it."

Colin's eyes lit up. "Why don't you just move back in early December? Your mum can come and stay for the Christmas holiday. It will be great fun."

We'd already been talking about me spending Christmas at Kew with him and Brendan, and so when he suggested I move back, my willpower disintegrated and I agreed, "All right, I will. But only on my terms."

There's no point in me justifying my decision by claiming it was to protect Brendan. He was now almost six feet tall and more than capable of looking after himself. No, I did it because it was a quick fix to my problem of being homeless. I returned to the lion's den, convincing myself that the lion had been tamed. He certainly seemed it; he wasn't the monster I'd run away from and he was nicer than he'd ever been. *Perhaps the church has taught him humility and kindness*, I thought. Whatever he was, I'm sure if there'd been a vote that night in my little temporary home, I would have been outvoted two-to-one. But the dogs just wagged their tails and loved me anyway.

***

Colin made moving back easy for me, clearing the house in Barkingside and ensuring the Kew house was pristine and full of flowers when I returned. He was on his best behaviour every minute of every day. He didn't raise his voice, he didn't belittle my mum or me like he used to, he didn't even monopolise the TV or conversation. "When you left," he told me, "I had an epiphany of sorts; I realised how I'd been treating you. That's why I turned to the church. You wouldn't believe how the congregation welcomed me and encouraged me to talk about my mistakes. Clive has been a great support, as well. Since Karen left him he's been suffering too. But as you know, Clive calls a spade a spade. He told me what an idiot I'd been to let you go."

"And your list?" I asked. I was curious about the list of people Colin was reconnecting with – those he'd, at one point or another, treated poorly.

"I'm reaching out to everyone, trying to put things right. I know that's the only way I can move forward."

"Who have you managed to get in touch with?"

"Well, when I was divorced, I hired a young nanny to look after Brendan. I started a relationship with her, and she was under my spell. She assumed I'd marry her of course, but to me, she was just serving a purpose. I met someone else and unceremoniously dumped her. It broke her heart."

"So you found her?"

"Yes, I tracked her down and apologised to her. She was surprised and gracious. And I was pleased when she told me she was getting married."

Colin had used my friends as sounding boards in an attempt to unearth what it would take for me to come back. He mentioned Linda, and whilst I knew he'd been to see her, I didn't know what words of wisdom she'd given him, until she came to stay with us in Kew.

"When Colin asked if he could come to see me, I'll admit I was a bit wary, because of his history. But I invited him over, anyway."

"What did you talk about?" I asked, curiously.

"Well, he asked me for advice on how he could make you love him again. I was very careful in choosing my words. I told him that he had to just let it rest like a ploughed field and sow the seeds and hope that love grew again." She smiled as she said this. "All the time I was talking, I stirred a pan of soup like my life depended on it."

I laughed though I was somewhat annoyed Colin had put my friends in that position. Linda stopped talking about him, when Colin entered the room. "What are you girls chatting about? You haven't paused for breath."

"Nor have you and Clive," I retorted. "Are you putting the world to rights?"

He laughed and said, "Well, I shouldn't be asking you anyway. I'm sure you two have got a lot to catch up on." And he left us to it, something he wouldn't have dreamed of doing just a few months ago.

"I must tell you one more thing before we join the boys," Linda whispered urgently. "Something wasn't right with Colin that day, but I couldn't put my finger on it. Maybe it was my imagination, and I just couldn't believe he'd changed so much, but I still felt uneasy about him. As bad as it sounds, I had to tell you."

I absorbed this admission and then admitted, myself, "I'm treading on eggshells wondering when I might say or do something that will light his fuse. But he does seem to be a totally different person now. I want to believe he can change forever, and if he'd told me he'd been to a doctor for help, rather than the Church, I'd be more hopeful. As it is, I'm enjoying being spoilt, and unless he starts demanding sex, I'll support his efforts to change. Thanks for being such a good friend, Linda. I wish we lived nearer each other, but let's at least try and do this more often." As I spoke, Linda appeared as though she wanted to say something more, but she didn't. We'd been through a lot together and understood when the other needed to work things out in our own time.

She was right of course, but making love was the part of the relationship Colin wanted to resume immediately. I wasn't ready. Although we did sleep in the same bed and I knew it was difficult for him when I refused his advances, I couldn't bring myself to make love to him. Too many bad memories, too much history needed to wash from my system, yet. I'd cuddle and kiss him before turning over, but with my back to him, I'd pretend to sleep, although I was usually wide awake. I wouldn't let him try and break the rules. If I did, we'd be right back where we'd started.

***

Life was good again. Colin had managed to find a job as a computer programmer for an IT company. He claimed it was boring, but I knew that after ten years of unemployment, he was thrilled to be respected at work. Brendan was happy, Colin was happy, the dogs were happy, and I was happy.

It was after a particularly romantic meal with a glass or two of wine in me that I knew I was ready for Colin to make love to me again. So I seduced him.

"Are you ready for bed?" I asked.

When he turned to me, he found me already stripped down to my underwear. Tonight was the night. We held each other in the afterglow of lovemaking, and he said, "I've been waiting for that moment for three very long months." *Three months, is that all it was?* I thought. *Seems as though a year has passed.* Then he added, "I understand you need to take it slowly."

I was sure that he didn't understand, but I promised, "I'll do my best to satisfy your needs at least once a week." And that was what it had become for me: satisfying *his* needs. I was not being true to myself, and I was well aware of that. I didn't love him anymore, and thus I didn't enjoy what should have been the icing on the cake. I'd introduced a new problem now, one which would soon become a bone of contention between us; Colin wanted sex every night, and I did not.

***

My mum came for Christmas, and I had the best gift for her. I'd gone the extra mile this year and prepared stockings for Colin and Mum, while Brendan had his usual enormous one. My mum had once said that despite filling seven stockings each year, no one had ever done one for her, so I made hers extra special by replicating the contents of my own when I was a kid – nuts, an apple, Satsuma, sweets, chocolate coins, pencils, a rubber, a puzzle book, and a small toy. I remember the excitement of waking up to find it at the end of my bed, where I'd sift through the contents, waiting on pins-and-needles until I was allowed downstairs to open my main present, peeking from under the tree. I wanted Mum to experience the same. She was always doing puzzles, so I created her very own puzzle to solve. I provided seven clues that she must answer; the first letter of each answer, rearranged, would spell out her main present, hidden under the tree.

Come Christmas morning, I delivered her a cup of tea in bed, and there she was, pencil in hand, working out the clues. "You've spoilt me, Rosemary!" she said. "But I'm thrilled!" The smile on her face said it all. She'd had few surprises in her seventy-four years.

Time ticked by, and I called her down for a late breakfast where she ate hurriedly, in a rush to return to her puzzle. By two o'clock and after lots of cups of tea and nibbles, she said, "This must be something to do with a holiday, because I can spell 'case' but I can't make out a seven-letter word from these letters." She brandished the puzzle at me, with the correct letters guessed – r,s,e,a,c,u,i.

"You can't have the present if you don't work it out," I teased. "By the way, I didn't say it was only one word." While Colin cooked lunch, I enjoyed watching my mum puzzle it out, finally putting her out of her misery. "Whether or not you solve it, you can have your present after lunch," I allowed. "Besides, you'll have more work to do once you've opened it."

After we'd all eaten too much, as is tradition, we sat around the tree to unwrap presents. I didn't care about my own presents; all I wanted was to see Mum's face when she finally opened hers. Brendan handed her the thin package. "A magazine?" she guessed, with a quizzical expression, but as she opened it, her perplexity soon turned to sheer joy and a squeal of delight, "A cruise? Are you really going to take me on a cruise?" Mum had never been demonstrative, but she gifted me a big hug and a kiss. "Where are we going? And when?"

"Look inside," I told her. I'd written a formal invitation, inviting her to join me on a seven-day cruise of her choice in January to celebrate her seventy-fifth birthday. The rest of the day was spent flipping through the brochure from back to front and then back again. I'd never seen her so animated, and I can't remember another Christmas being so happy and different, without shouting, disagreement, tears (apart from joyful ones); with only laughter and smiling faces from the whole household – and, yes, even the dogs were grinning.

***

Christmas behind us, Colin said, "I want New Year's Eve to be extra special. Choose a local hotel where we can spend the night, just you and me."

After searching and finding the only available room last minute was a one-night stay at the Richmond Hill Hotel, I tried to persuade Colin against it. "The price is astronomical. We should just go out for a meal. Really, the rates are silly."

"No, no. Book it," he insisted.

To me, this was a complete waste of money. I had the cruise with Mum in January, and Colin had been invited to his friend's fortieth birthday in New Zealand, so we'd have to pay for the dogs to go on holiday as well. But I decided it wasn't worth arguing over. I wish I could have seen how easily I was slipping back into default: letting Colin get his way.

The four-star hotel was beautifully decorated and the staff, attentive. We ate and drank and danced the night away, waiting for the ball to drop. At 11:30 p.m., Colin unexpectedly whispered, "Let's go back to the room."

"Why?" I asked. I thought it strange. We were approaching midnight on New Year's Eve; surely, we should watch the ball drop and join in 'Auld Lang Syne'. But as always, I granted his wish. He seemed a bit nervous somehow, but I couldn't put my finger on why.

When we returned the room, he sat me down on the bed "The reason I wanted to be away on this particular night is that I've always had a burning desire to make love on the stroke of midnight on New Year's." My heart sank. *He's trying to control me, yet again,* I thought. *Why must he always get what he wants?* "You're the only person I'm ever going to get the chance to do this with. I'll never have another lover after you." He really knew what to say. And so I went along with his fantasy, allowing myself to be made love to, while he had no idea how I was truly feeling. I faked the orgasm at midnight, as any good wife would.

***

We were out with friends one night early in the New Year and chose to go to our favourite Italian restaurant in Kew, which was walking distance from the house. Martin was Colin's friend from his days in the Scouts, and he'd married Marianne just two weeks before our wedding

To my horror, he decided to share intimate details of our relationship with these two. "Rose is reluctant to perform in the bedroom," he put in, completely off-topic. He turned to his friend, "Would you put up with Marianne not agreeing to oral sex?"

Martin laughed, "I'm going to plead the fifth. Look at Marianne's face; she'll kill me if I say one word on the subject."

I went bright red but didn't say anything. Inside, I was furious and fuming; I couldn't believe what he'd just told the entire table, but I knew why he'd said it: oral sex was the one thing I absolutely could not bring myself to do, and it was the one thing he said would prove I loved him. But I didn't, and despite the wonderful times we'd been having, at some point I knew the relationship would self-destruct.

The nagging doubts I had about Colin kept coming to the fore, whenever I noticed the slightest chink in his armour. When his rages had started to manifest back in 1991, I'd considered whether medical help was necessary but knew if I'd voiced my opinion, I would've been roasted alive. Perhaps I'd been wrong, and he could change. But I found it hard to believe, having lived with him for twelve years, that he could have changed so completely. And I berated myself for not believing in him and for not being happy. Apart from the disagreements in the bedroom, a cross word was rarely spoken between us. However, these disagreements in the bedroom were becoming more frequent. *Is it too good to last?* I asked myself. Of course it was.

***

Colin left for New Zealand a few days before Mum and I would head out for our cruise. Under normal circumstances, apart from business trips, Colin would never have sanctioned me going anywhere abroad without either him or Brendan accompanying me, but now he was trying so hard to please me that he didn't make a fuss. And yet, the cracks in his façade were broadening, and the old Colin kept shining through now and again. I could sense he was becoming quietly bitter, so I was glad for the time apart.

Mum and I had a lovely time on the cruise and returned in late January. She busied herself by putting all our holiday snaps into an album so she could show them off to her friends. She really had just been on the best holiday ever she told me with delight.

Colin was due back five days later. It was straight back to work for me, and the time flew by so that I was soon picking Colin up from the airport. He wasn't as chatty as normal, but I just put his silence down to jetlag. Then out of nowhere, he said, "I thought a lot about my life while I was away. I still have things I need to do, before I can feel I've righted most of my wrongs."

"What kind of things?" I asked with concern; his demeanour was unusually subdued.

Colin on his visit to New Zealand

My Mum and I with the Captain

"I want to be reconciled with my father." Colin never could accept Val as his step-mother (she was only three months older than him), and he bore a grudge relating to his inheritance. Because of this, he hadn't treated Val well, and he and Ben had fallen out over it. "I've now realised how cruel I've been to the two of them, and I need to talk to him about it before the anniversary of my mum's death."

"I can arrange to meet Ben and try to persuade him to heal the rift," I replied. Colin's mum's death day was soon, on the 6th of February. I knew it would definitely take some persuading, because up until this point, Ben had steadfastly refused to meet him.

"I'll wait in the wings, in case you can change his mind."

***

I was fairly confident Ben would agree to have coffee with me, as we'd always got along. Sure enough, he was waiting for me in the café, where I'd set our date. After some small talk about my recent cruise and Val's latest health issues, Ben asked, "How's Brendan? And how are you feeling, living back in Kew?"

"Well, to be honest, I think Colin's a changed man," I lied a little, because somehow I knew he wasn't changed where it mattered – inside. Anyway, I wanted the two to forgive and forget, so I touched upon faith, because I knew Val was religious. "Colin's found God, Ben. He's been contacting people he's upset in the past. He really has demonstrated that he wants to change." I held my breath before going all in. "Please will you talk to him, if only for five minutes?"

Ben hesitated, "He's here, isn't he?" I nodded. He looked cross at me, shaking his head. "I know why you've done it, but you should have told me." I bit back tears, but then he mumbled his assent, "Okay, I'll talk to him, but not for long. Go and get him."

Colin was waiting by the menswear department, as pre-arranged. He walked towards me when he saw me approach and asked eagerly, "What did he say?"

"You have five minutes to talk to Ben. Don't try and be over-affectionate," I advised, "and, more importantly, don't mention Val, other than to ask how she is. You don't want to ruin your chance at reconciliation." Colin hugged me, and we returned to the café, where I took their drinks order and left them to it. What was supposed to be five minutes became over twenty before Colin came to find me. "It went well." Relief flooded his face. "You can go say goodbye."

I returned to Ben's side, and he smiled at me. "Colin doesn't deserve you," he said. "Thank you for being the intermediary. I've agreed to meet him at the crematorium on the 6th, but we have a lot more making up to do before our relationship will be as solid as it should."

When we left, Colin reiterated this to me. "Everything must happen one step at a time," he said. "I'll be forever in your debt for getting me and my dad on speaking terms again. I'm glad to have a happy ending."

***

The first week in February was cold and dreary. Colin made it more so.

"I'll be driving up north on Friday after work to go to the fiftieth birthday party I told you about. I'll take Mum home at the same time."

"I told you before, you're not going without me!" he bellowed. He knew he wasn't invited and wouldn't be allowed anywhere near the party because of his past behaviour.

"I told you I was going, and I am," I said, furiously. Colin grabbed my arm and went to hit me but realised in time what he was doing and let go. Instead, he did something else he knew would upset me: he targeted my mum.

He stormed into the bathroom, where he knew she was in the bath, and screamed, "Do you know what that daughter of yours has done? Some mother you must be to have brought up a daughter who won't respect her husband's wishes. Get out of the bath and talk some sense into her."

"How dare you talk to her like that?" I shouted, mortified. "She's seventy-five years old for goodness sake."

He stormed out of the bathroom and hammered downstairs. Mum was crying, and the dogs were cowering on the landing. I stood seething with anger. This was too much. After helping Mum out of the bath, I dressed her in her nightie and suggested, "Why don't you stay in your room, while I sort things downstairs?"

She was more than happy to agree. "Be careful," she cautioned, "I saw something sinister in that man's eyes." I knew what she meant, but I had to face him, otherwise I'd be letting Colin think he'd got away with treating me like garbage yet again. I'd buried my head in the sand one too many times. But no longer.

For once, I felt strong and determined. He was in the lounge, and when I walked in, he turned to me and sobbed, "I can't believe that just happened. I'm so sorry. You have to believe me; I won't do it again. Say you'll forgive me."

"Colin, you know as well as I do that you can't control your temper. I'm not prepared to stay here with you and live in fear."

"Please, just give me another chance. I promise I won't stop you from seeing friends on your own. And I won't keep making unreasonable demands in the bedroom."

I breathed in deeply. "I'm emotionally drained, Colin. I can't deal with this. I'm going to bed. If you have any sense, you'll seek professional help, instead of thinking you can cure yourself just by going to church."

I went upstairs, checked Mum was okay, and laid in bed, feeling surprisingly free and at peace.

***

"How about you take us all out for dinner tonight at our favourite local Italian restaurant?" I heard Colin talking to Brendan in the kitchen when I plodded down for my morning coffee.

"Yeah, that sounds good, Dad," Brendan agreed.

As I walked into the conversation, Colin turned to me, "You'll be there, Rose?"

"Yes, sure," I decided to go along, as if last night had never happened. "I'll look forward to it."

It turned out to be a strange evening. Colin was buzzing and over exuberant. "This is the first meal my son's bought us, so it's a momentous occasion," he explained to the maître d.

Brendan and I just looked each other and grinned. Colin was night and day, and in this moment, he was day – at one with the world and glowing with positive energy. Mum had kept out of Colin's way and was in bed by the time we arrived home from the restaurant. But Colin didn't want the day to end.

"Brendan, why don't you dress up in your guards uniform, so we can take some family photos?" Brendan reluctantly went upstairs and got changed to please his dad. We'd all consumed a glass or two of wine, and Colin was clearly keen to ensure all of us were looking happy, posing for the not-so-special occasion. The dogs joined in the frivolity as well; they'd had no wine, but they were drunk on life, it seemed.

The next morning, Colin woke early. When Brendan and I came down for breakfast, we were surprised he'd laid the table out as if we were eating in the dining room at Charlton House. He'd used all of the formal crockery and cutlery and had cooked us a full English breakfast.

"I hope you're not going to tell us you're thinking of turning the house into a B&B," Brendan joked.

"I just want to make you happy, is all."

I then remembered it was the anniversary of his mum dying, and he would meet up with his dad at the crematorium in Surrey later that day. I assumed he saw this extravagant breakfast as a good reflection on his mum's remembrance; everyone being happy together. I was too busy thinking about work to pay any attention when he seemed to take longer than usual to say goodbye to us both as we set off.

I was sorting through the incoming mail at Haslers, when I received a call from Colin. "I'm just phoning to tell you I won't be there when you come home tonight," he said strangely.

A proud Dad with Brendan

A proud Mum with Brendan

"Where are you?" I asked.

"Outside," he said. I assumed he meant outside in the open air; he'd have met Ben at the crematorium, and they were likely to have spent time on the grounds. "Even though I won't be there, I want you to know I love you."

"Okay, well, drive safely and call me later," I rang off. On reflection, it was a strange conversation, but everything about Colin had been strange in the last thirty-six hours, and so I thought nothing of it and carried on going through my paperwork. I was surprised when, twenty minutes later, someone said, "Rosemary, they want you in reception. There's someone here who needs to talk to you."

I had no idea who it could be, and to my astonishment, I found it was a policeman. "Excuse me, are you Rosemary Bensley?" I nodded. "I need to talk to you about a personal matter. Would you please step outside with me for a moment?"

Flustered and confused, as soon as I was met with the fresh morning air, saw blue flashing lights and Colin's Range Rover on the green, a sense of foreboding dealt me a swift blow. "Colin Bensley is your husband, correct?" the policeman asked. I nodded. "I'm sorry to tell you he's shot himself with a double-barrel shotgun. But he's still alive, and an air ambulance is on its way."

"Wh-what?"

"Your husband has shot himself in the stomach. Had he shot himself in the head, he would have died instantly, but there's hope. With immediate medical help, he may live. But I must tell you the wound is life-threatening; he has a slim chance of survival."

In complete shock, questions, one after another, surged through me. *How had he managed to drive here from Surrey so quickly? How long has he been planning this? Why here? Why put Brendan and me through this?*

"Who else is Colin close to?" the policeman asked. "And where would they be? We need to make sure he hasn't harmed anyone else."

"Brendan is his son; he's in the Coldstream Guards and will be at Kneller Hall. And Ben – his father." *And maybe the last person to see him alive,* I thought. "Also, my mum was at home when Colin left the house this morning." He scribbled the telephone numbers.

I was scared now, and when I told him about the conversation I'd had with Colin earlier, he replied, "It's just as well you didn't come out. He had two bullets in the gun. It's not unusual in these cases that the person wants to take someone else with him."

By now I was a complete wreck, shivering and crying and numb. He steered me towards a police van that had pulled up on the green and sat me down. "You can't see Colin now, but you'll have an opportunity to see him at the hospital. As soon as the air ambulance takes off, we'll get someone to drive you there."

I was so surprised when Haslers head of financial planning, joined me in the police van. He'd come to calm me down, and I was grateful. He'd just lost his wife and daughter in a car crash and knew exactly what to say to me. "Stay strong for Brendan," he held my hand. "I'll be here for you if you ever need to talk."

After what seemed like hours but was really no time at all, I was brought to London Hospital in a police car. A nurse ushered me into a private room where I was to wait for news of Colin. The police had already told me everyone was safe, and Brendan and Ben were on their way to join me. Colin's brother was the first to arrive and because I hardly knew him, I found making small talk irritating. I'd probably only met him three times in thirteen years – he and Colin weren't close – but I appreciated he wanted to be there for Ben. *Ben must be feeling absolutely dreadful, having just seen Colin earlier,* I thought. I felt awash with warm relief for having reconciled the two of them, otherwise he'd probably have been even more overwhelmed and conflicted.

Brendan showed up next, and after embracing, he said, "Sorry it took me forever. The sergeant major allowed me to come to the hospital, and arranged for a driver to take me to the hospital, unfortunately it was not known territory and we did get lost."

When Ben arrived, he walked straight into the room and came over to me, without a glance at Brendan or his son. He cupped my face in his hands, looked me straight in the eyes, and said, "Don't you dare blame yourself. You are the best thing that happened to Colin since Brendan was born. He is wicked for putting you through this." I can't pretend I hadn't been thinking the same.

Time passed, and the four of us were running out of things to say. I excused myself to call my friend. She was expecting me at the house tomorrow in Yorkshire for her birthday. She answered the phone, and when I greeted her, she was very animated. "Hi, Rosy, are you on your way already?"

I took a deep breath and said, "I'm sorry, I can't come after all."

She must have sensed my distress, as she immediately asked, "What's that bastard done now?"

"He's shot himself."

24

THE SCARS REMAIN

We were receiving little feedback from the hospital staff, and it was almost 10:30 p.m.; eleven-and-a-half hours since the attempted suicide. Eventually, we were taken upstairs to the intensive care unit, where we were once again sat waiting in a small room. None of us could believe what had happened. We were even more surprised anyone could have survived a double-barrel gunshot wound at such close range.

Finally, the consultant entered. "We're prepping Colin so that you can see him, but you must prepare for the worst. He's on two life-support machines. He's not conscious but could come round; we just don't know at this stage. If he does come round, I'm sorry to tell you he'll be an invalid for the rest of his life."

After everyone left the room, Brendan immediately turned to me. "Mum, we should let him die; he wouldn't want to live like this." As soon as he said those words, alarms went off in the ward, and I knew Colin was giving up the ghost.

Sure enough, the consultant returned just after midnight and informed us that Colin had passed. "You may still see his body if you wish, but we don't recommend it." We all agreed we'd rather not.

A sombre atmosphere enveloped the four of us when we were alone again, until Brendan said, "Mum, I'm starving. Can we get a pizza or something?" This lightened the mood, and we did find a late-night pizza place close to the hospital. We kept the conversation going, as you do, while making little reference to the terrible event that had occurred.

It was 3 a.m. when we eventually arrived home, and Mum was dozing in the chair, a puzzle book in her lap. "I've been worried sick about you," she woke with a start.

"He's passed, Mum." I could tell she was relieved. "It was a blessing, really, as he would have suffered for the rest his life."

"Yes," she agreed, "considering the circumstances, it's the best outcome for everyone. He left envelopes for you on the table, and there's a message on the stereo."

I dragged my feet to the stereo and lifted the note, which read, "Rose, please play track three and think of me." It was Nilsson's 'Without You', and although I started to play the track, I could barely listen to the words, I was so overwhelmed with the day's events. I switched it off, deciding I'd leave everything else until the morning. I was exhausted.

The aftermath of Colin's death began the next day and included calling all of the people in his address book. I thought it would get easier with each call, but it didn't. Everyone was shocked, although not always surprised. Clive made calls for me to shared friends and acquaintances of theirs. I appreciated it, as I appreciated everything he did for me in those awful days leading up to the funeral, including encouraging me to walk the dogs every day in Richmond Park. He was incredibly supportive, and I recognised his being involved probably allowed him to grieve without looking like he was. They'd been friends for over thirty-five years, and it must have been hard for him to lose a best friend just after the break up of his marriage.

I didn't stop finding notes from Colin until about a week later. I found them under the pillow, in the pockets of my clothes, in the bedroom drawers, in the kitchen – everywhere, it seemed. The letters he'd left in the lounge included written instructions regarding his funeral requests and a list of the people he wanted there. He also left two suicide notes: one for me and one for Brendan. They were each four pages, typed on A4 paper, long letters full of pain and regret.

"Dearest Rosemary, I love you so very much. I do love you from the bottom of my breaking heart. I am so lonely when we are apart. I am so truly sorry for the totally unacceptable way I have treated you especially during last autumn. I had absolutely no excuse, save that of boredom and probably a little envy over your career. You are such a wonderful person in every respect. I sincerely wish I could have shown you the life you deserved all of the time. I had no right whatsoever to expect you to give me yet another

Happy memories – Colin with Clive 1990

chance. I do thank you for continuing to try to be my loving friend, but I need more. I would like you to have tried to be my loving wife."

He went on to talk about our many fond memories together and then wrote about our finances and how I was to deal with them. He also wrote a lot about his feelings for me, and how I'd enhanced his life. He wanted me to know I wasn't to blame for what he'd done; he'd hoped to free me from his controlling nature, saying, "*Rose, I have definitely not performed this dreadful act out of spite, but far rather to give you an absolute, complete break from my continual domination of your life.*"

In Brendan's letter, he emphasised this point, saying, "*I ask you to treat this as a life lesson to yourself to help you learn to treat all females with love and respect. Being really kind, fair, just, faithful and, above all, loving. Love is your greatest asset, please believe me, and you will be happy.*"

What a terrible state he must have been in, I read the notes through my tears. He'd been planning his suicide since we started living apart in October 1997. I recalled him mentioning he'd written a suicide note back then, but at the time, I thought his intention was to pressure me into forgiving him. He'd chosen to die on the anniversary of his mum's death so that they could both be on the same crematorium page in the Book of Remembrance. He only just achieved this by ten minutes; he died just before midnight on the 6th February 1998.

It was many years later that I found out that Linda wasn't the only one of my friends Colin had turned to; he'd also asked Cheryl for advice and two days prior to his suicide, he'd arranged to take her out for dinner locally in Kew. I recalled the bizarre event, "Can you please wait round the corner until Cheryl and I have left the house?" he asked me. "I don't want her to see you here, because then she'll expect you to eat with us. I don't think she'll be as open and honest about my behaviour if you're there. "

I agreed I wouldn't come home until they'd left. In fact, I sat in my car nearby, waiting for them to go out together, which was strange, really. I knew Cheryl had my best interests at heart, and she wouldn't be shy about being honest with Colin. She knew I had misgivings, and I'd told her I wouldn't stand for any more of his nonsense.

They weren't out too long, and Cheryl popped in before heading back to Maidenhead. "Colin is so happy now that you're home. He spoke all night about how he knew he must keep his temper in check and spoil you if he wants the reunion to last." Cheryl admitted that she thought that Colin's behaviour was not normal but did not expect him to take his own life.

***

Before the funeral, Brendan and I went to see Colin at the funeral parlour for the last time. He'd been dressed in his wedding suit and looked serene and at peace. Neither of us cried, which is a sad indictment of how Colin had hurt us, and I, for one, felt relieved I was at last free of his control.

On the journey home, I said, "Bren, we must talk about the bad times as well as the good. I don't like when death means we don't remember a person as they were, but as we wanted them to be. What was the worst thing your dad ever did to you?"

"He used his belt on me once when I reversed the mini-tractor into the garage door. I lied about it and I still have the scar to show for it. You never told me about how he hurt you either," he said. "I was as scared of him as you were and knew we'd both be in trouble if I said anything."

Of course, Brendan was right. To keep the peace, we danced to Colin's tune, 'Without You', and I wondered when I'd feel normal again.

***

One of Colin's final requests was for Brendan to wear his Coldstream Guards uniform to the funeral, and he'd been given permission. He looked so grown up, but he was much too young to have lost his father. Then again, no one is ever really ready for loss.

The church was packed. Colin had been a regular churchgoer for five months, so many of the congregants attended, along with several of Brendan's friends and their parents, and many of my own. Clive read from the bible, and Martin did a tribute, focusing on Colin's good deeds with the scouts, of which there had been many. After the Reverend Arthur arose to read the blessing, an ear-splitting *bang* broke out to the right of the church, startling everyone. Inexplicably, a chair had fallen over, though no one stood near it. *Colin is making his presence known,* I thought, *even while he's gone from this earth.*

On the same day as the funeral, the *Somerset Western Daily Press* headline read, 'Torment of West Tycoon'. A photo of Colin splashed across the front page, and on page three, they'd printed a family portrait of us with the article, along with one of Brendan in his army uniform. The Charlton House photographer must have provided the photos. I was quoted in the article, though I don't remember talking to a reporter. "He did not know what to do with himself anymore," I supposedly said. "By thirty-seven he had achieved more than most people do in a lifetime."

The national papers picked up on the story the next day. *The Mail, Telegraph* and *Express* all delivered dramatic headlines to exploit our tragedy, despite never having spoken to anyone: '*Death by boredom*', '*Suicide of high flyer who opted out of the rat race*', '*Millionaire killed by his own success*'. I was so incensed by their callousness and the fact that they got their stories wrong that I couldn't read newspapers for months.

The days were a blur, and I was on autopilot. My emotions were conflicting; I felt compelled to be sad, but I wasn't. I was relieved. No more temper tantrums, no more dread in walking into my own home for fear of what mood Colin might be in. I recalled how different I'd felt when Brian had died. I wouldn't be running away this time, that's for sure. I would stay put and rebuild my life again.

25

A NEW LIFE

Colin's death breathed new life into me. As devastating as suicide is, the man I'd spent thirteen years of my life with was not happy or psychologically well and, at last, he was free. I was free too: free from his psychological and physical abuse. I felt guilty that I wasn't mourning in the traditional way. Although I wasn't mourning how everyone wanted me to, I hadn't been acting normally, racing around doing a million things at once. My friends knew what I'd been through during those years but others didn't. I certainly was not acting like a grieving widow, and my colleagues at work tried to encourage me to grieve.

"You don't have to put on a brave face all the time, you know," Janet consoled me. She'd lost her brother not long before, and he'd been around Colin's age.

"I know, Jan, but I feel like a hypocrite when I cry. Who am I crying for? Colin or myself?" I became subdued. "Perhaps I should be more emotional, but I'm too busy rebuilding my life. There's so much to sort out. I'm also really angry at Colin. He killed himself. He hurt everyone who loved him. His dad is now a shadow of his former self. Suicide is a sin, as far as he's concerned, and he can't mention that word to anyone." I was working myself into a state, just thinking of Ben, and with Pandora's box opened, I burst into tears and sobbed, "I hate Colin for what he's done to all of us!" Jan didn't say a word; she just wrapped her arms around me.

I wanted and needed a fresh start, so I sold the house in Kew and the surplus of vehicles we'd accumulated – the Range Rover, Honda motorbike, Ford pickup, and Kon-Tiki campervan. It was like shedding skin. I adorned

243

myself in new, lighter skin, finding a home nearer to work. Within a few weeks, I'd decided on a house in Mayfair Gardens, Woodford Green, which is where I'd lived with Bob after Brian had died. Strange, I was drawn back to that place following yet another death.

After the funeral, Clive had remained in my life, as both a friend and an advisor. Before I signed the papers, he walked through the new property in order to offer me his expert opinion. "It's a great location, Rose. The work needing done can be done quite quickly." I was glad to have his advice, because though I'm good with numbers, what I find difficult is thinking long-term and looking beyond the quick fix outside my scope. Instead, whether intentional or involuntary, on self-reflection, I realised I often followed three tried-and-tested steps when handling nearly any life issue thrown my way: 1) Identify the problem; 2) Find a solution; then 3) Don't hesitate, just do it. Whether this is the most effective approach or not, at least it's efficient. And at that point in particular, efficiency was pertinent; I was in a rush to feel settled again. So after being given the green light by Clive and other trusted advisors, I didn't hesitate. I just did it.

The freedom I felt lifted me through. I had the rest of my life ahead of me and no limits abounded. I could do whatever I wanted, whenever I wanted. And yet, Colin continued to try and control me from the grave. The list of requests he'd left me, regarding what to do following his death, not only established his funeral arrangements, but detailed financial instructions as well. Despite the fact that I was entitled to the proceeds from the house and our possessions, Colin instructed me to split the assets we'd accumulated during our thirteen years together with Brendan. For once, I agreed with Colin. Although friends advised me that the legality of his request was null and void, I was happy to do it. I didn't want Brendan to resent me then or ever, and I wanted to honour Colin's wishes. The issue between Colin and his father over his own inheritance remained unresolved upon his death. I knew Brendan was not like his father, but I didn't want any seed of contention between us; I wanted to be happy, free, and all the rest.

***

"What do you think about going abroad for Easter?" I asked Brendan early in the New Year. With everything that had happened, I thought we'd both benefit from getting away. "I was thinking the south of France; Nice, maybe. We could come back with a nice Mediterranean tan."

"Do you think my friend, Simon, can come along?"

I didn't mind, so I arranged for both Simon and my friend, Josée, to join us. Not only was Josée a good travel companion, but she spoke French, so her company would be particularly advantageous on this trip. In April, we set off for our ten-day holiday, in which we'd be staying at a four-star hotel on the Promenade des Anglais. I was very much looking forward to some rest and relaxation in the sun.

However, the sun must have been on holiday elsewhere, because it decided not to show. Every single day of our stay was rainy and cold… and the people colder. Perhaps a stereotypical observation, but the French were not the friendliest; they were generally rude, unhelpful and seemed to look down their noses at us Brits. Even worse, Brendan got food poisoning from some seafood and was out for the count on day three. But food poisoning wasn't the only thing that would take him out on this trip.

Josée and I were in our room mid-holiday, when we heard a strange retching noise coming from the boy's room next door. After about ten minutes, we thought we'd better investigate. I knocked four times before Simon answered the door, and when he did, it was no wonder they'd been so reluctant: the sight and stench that greeted us was unbelievable. The room looked as though they'd been hosting a rave; empty bottles of vodka and other spirits spread haphazardly across the bedside cabinet, clothes strewn across the floor, and a rancid smell of vomit throughout.

"What on earth is going on in here?" I shouted at Simon. "Where did you get the liquour from? And where's Brendan?" Simon pointed to the bathroom door, which was shut. The sound behind it frightened me. If one poisoning wasn't enough on this trip, I thought he might now have alcohol poisoning. This wasn't the time for shouting and laying down the law; the post mortem could come later.

"Would you please take Simon out for a walk in the cold air to try and sober him up while I sort Brendan out?" I asked Josée. With them gone, I knocked lightly on the bathroom door. "Brendan, open up. I'm not mad," I lied. "I just want to help."

When Brendan finally managed to cease retching enough to crawl to the door, he looked absolutely dreadful. His face was pallid and clammy, wet with tears and sweat, and his eyes were bloodshot. "I want to die. I want to

Brendan and I loved having Josée join us on the holiday

die," he croaked over and over again. "Dad would've killed me, if he saw me like this."

I put him under a cold shower, wrapped him up in a towel, and sat him down near an open window so the fresh air might whip him back into shape. Then I held him. He was shaking and crying so much, all I could do was hold him, until he got everything out of his system. Sitting there, cradling seventeen-year-old Brendan, I realised neither of us had processed Colin's death quite as readily as I'd thought; we'd been masking our feelings until they ate away at us. Brendan had discovered a way to unmask these feelings and let out some of the anger and hurt… but his method wasn't particularly constructive, and I worried for him. I busied myself in order to give him time to calm down, cleaning up the messy room and ordering fresh towels from housekeeping, and when he was in good enough shape to get dressed and go out for a walk, we went together. Nothing more was said about the incident, and I'm sure we were all glad when it was time to go home.

***

The previous year Clive had separated from his wife, Karen, and was not coping well emotionally. They'd been married for over twenty years, and they had two children together; they were a family. So when their relationship fell apart, Clive was devastated. In fact, I may have been somewhat culpable in its demise. I'd encouraged Karen to return to work after being a stay-at-home mum, coaching her in bookkeeping and helping her out wherever I could, so I felt a tad responsible.

Despite having major problems of our own, Colin and I had tried to support Clive through the separation. It was therefore natural for him to now try and support me. We'd been friends for around twelve years by that point, and with neither of our spouses in the picture, the friendship developed. We got into the habit of meeting up for a meal once a week and going to the cinema or theatre together. He'd also been busy renovating his house in Teddington, which was only a fifteen-minute drive away, and I felt he needed the company as much as I did.

One evening, when he came round for a drink, he brought a newspaper with him and pointed out a coupon. "Have you seen the '2 for 1' flight offers for Ryanair? What a deal!"

"Yes, I have. I saw flights to Zurich. I was thinking of taking advantage, as an old friend of mine has moved there. I thought it would be a good idea for me and Brendan to visit some weekend."

"If I start collecting the tokens, would you like to join me on a trip somewhere?"

"That's a great idea," I agreed. "If we both collect, it won't take long before we have enough to book the first trip. A short break will give me something to look forward to."

Clive browsed through the destinations and seemed to settle on one. "What do you think of Rome? I have a travel consultant friend who can organise the whole thing – hotels and all that."

Having known Clive for so long, I had no doubts that we'd get along fine for a three-day trip. Neither did I assume there would be romance, even in such a hopelessly romantic city as Rome. Neither of us had ever shown any interest in the other, apart from friendship, so I suggested we save on costs by booking a room with twin beds.

When I told the girls at work about our plans, they insisted on teasing me about Clive's intentions, "Come on, Rosemary. He's a man; they always have an ulterior motive."

"Don't be so cynical. Clive has known me for so long, he probably thinks of me as a sister."

"Until he sees you with your see-through nightie on!"

"I don't wear anything in bed, actually," I joked.

"What will you do if he makes a move?"

"He won't. Anyway, I'm big enough and ugly enough to deal with that if it happens."

Even though I was being honest with the girls about our platonic relationship, I found myself thinking, *But what if he does make a move?* We'd become close friends, but I'd convinced myself that if Clive really wanted more, he would have swept me off my feet by now. It wasn't as though he had no opportunity to do so. We went out together at least once a week, and he'd done nothing more than kiss me on the cheek. I shook my head, feeling stupid that the girls had gotten into my head. *We're travelling as friends*, I thought, *nothing more, nothing less.*

***

I relaxed into our trip and was looking forward to exploring the historic city of Rome, as I hadn't ever been there, and neither had Clive. The family-run hotel Clive's friend had booked for us was within close proximity to the main sights, and our room was on the top floor. As I strode in, the alarm in my head went berserk: a double bed, rather than twins.

"I am so sorry," Clive walked in behind me and discovered the error. "I specified that we needed twin beds. I'll go down and see if they have another room."

"I saw a 'No Vacancies' sign outside." He looked mortified, and I didn't want him to feel bad. "Never mind, I always sleep on the edge of a bed anyway. If you're okay with this arrangement, I am."

"Are you sure?"

"Don't worry. I won't leap on you in the night, if that's what you're afraid of," I replied with a wicked grin on my face. He breathed a sigh of relief.

I knew Clive was probably concerned I might think he'd done this on purpose, but he was such a gentleman, the thought never entered my mind. As we unpacked, we discussed our plans for the rest of the day.

"I read some tour guides," I put in, "and they said to accept – straight off – that you won't see everything. They suggested making a shortlist of sites you definitely want to visit and to leave plenty of time for simply wandering around."

"Have you made a shortlist?"

"No, you?"

Clive laughed. "What do you think of this: for the rest of the day, we visit some of the sights nearest to the hotel and finish up by having a meal somewhere along the way?"

We did this. We walked what seemed like miles, *oohing* and *aahing* at the Trevi Fountain, climbing up and down the Spanish Steps, and visiting various churches before enjoying a pizza. We covered a lot of ground and chatted easily together. *I like Rome,* I decided. *It's lively and fun, and it's nice to see Clive relax for once.* He truly was a lovely man, even if he was backward in coming forward. If Clive did have ulterior motives, he was certainly keeping them to himself. We were two weary travellers arriving back at the hotel that night, and neither of us took any rocking to get to sleep.

I slept on the very edge of my side of the bed, and Clive on his. Apparently, I'd drank too much wine, because I found myself needing to go the bathroom around five o'clock, so I slid out of bed as quietly as I could, hoping I wouldn't disturb Clive. I climbed back in and perched on the edge with my back towards my bedmate. Just when I was drifting off to sleep, his arm laid across my body. I froze, unsure if this was an accident or premeditated and whether or not I should respond. With all the teasing from my workmates, I'd wondered what I'd do if Clive made a pass at me. But now I knew what I'd do. I reached for his hand, and suffice it to say, Clive was not asleep.

Turns out we didn't need to make a shortlist for sightseeing; we ended up spending a lot more time in bed during our mini-break than was planned.

***

We'd continued to collect travel vouchers, and without pre-planning it, we found ourselves in Norway in June when the sun didn't set, a strange but incredible experience. We didn't go to bed to sleep these days anyway, so all-day sunlight mattered not.

On our first evening in Norway, we talked over dinner about how I was feeling now that four months had passed since Colin's death. "I feel so much happier with him gone," I talked openly. "He made me feel small and insignificant, undermining everything I did. I never felt good enough for him."

"I often berated him for being such a bastard," he told me. "I could never understand why he was the way he was. He always had a tendency to go through rough patches, where he seemed adamant about upsetting people. In fact, one occasion, Colin and his first wife joined Karen and me on a couples' holiday in Spain. As normally is the case, we couldn't agree on what to do, and it got to the point that we ended up falling out. Not unusual, but the timing was unfortunate; Colin was supposed to be my best man, and he ended up not even attending the wedding." He shook his head, thinking about it. "I have to ask – why did you stay with him? You're strong, you have a successful career, and you're optimistic and happy. How could you have put up with Colin for so long?"

I'd thought long and hard about this myself and had only ever arrived at one conclusion. "The simple answer is that my love and concern for Brendan was always my priority; I couldn't leave him while Colin was still able to control him. And Colin wouldn't let me go. He still won't." I held up my left hand, "I can't get my wedding ring off." As I said it, I reached for the ring, turned it, and it slid from my hand. I gasped. I'd been fighting with it for months, and the ring hadn't budged. As I placed it on the table, I felt light as a feather.

***

A month later, we planned a last-minute birthday party for Clive. Clive never did anything by halves and had organised a DJ and erected a small marquee in case the weather was bad. I hadn't met many of his friends and was looking forward to it; the only problem I foresaw was we hadn't told Susan, Katie or Brendan that we were more than just friends these days. Turns out, it wasn't a problem, because Clive ignored me all night, and I ended up playing hostess and babysitter rather than enjoying the party. If any of the kids suspected we were romantically involved, they would have to have been incredibly intuitive.

At one point, I was called upstairs, because one of the girls was being sick in the bathroom. I managed to coax her out and clean her and the bathroom, before rushing downstairs to join in the dancing. 'My Heart will Go On', the theme from *Titanic*, a big hit at the time, had started to play. I wanted to dance with Clive, but I was too late; he was already dancing with another Rosemary he'd once dated, and as she pulled him close, it was clear *this* Rosemary was intent in keeping Clive for herself tonight.

I sulked. I was upset and hurt more than I should have been. Clive hadn't come looking for me once, and on top of all that, he had the gall to approach me at the end of the evening. "I'm going to walk Rosemary home, but I won't be too long." When he returned to a cold shoulder, he couldn't understand what all the fuss was about and came back at me with the cliché, "But I came home to you, didn't I?"

I guess the honeymoon is over, I thought. Our relationship meant more to me than friendship, but I was confused as to what it was. I tried to put it into perspective. *We're two good friends who enjoy good sex together. That must be all this is. It's certainly all it is to Clive. What I mustn't do is think he is going to fall madly in love with me, and we'll live happily ever after.* By that point, I had come to accept that happily ever afters didn't exist... not for me, anyway.

***

Throughout his tenure at the Coldstream Guards, my relationship with Brendan was solid. I knew how upset and incredulous he'd been when Colin took his own life without having seen him play publicly, especially since Colin had been the one to encourage him to join the band in the first place. I always made sure to stay involved in his life; I attended his first public concert, and I asked Clive to accompany me. When I saw Brendan playing on that stage, I'd never been more proud. I wanted to do something special for him.

Before Brendan's eighteenth birthday, I contacted his bandmaster, "Brendan's had a rough year, and I'm wondering if it would be possible for me to surprise him and the band for his birthday when you play in the Edinburgh Military Tattoo. I'll supply enough champagne and cake for the whole party."

"Sure," the bandmaster agreed, "this can be arranged, and you may join in as well. I'll ensure that the champagne is on site."

I was thrilled and asked Clive, again, to accompany me for two nights in Edinburgh, while I arranged to meet Brendan for a birthday lunch. At the lunch, Brendan – oblivious to the surprise that night – apologised to me, "Sorry, Mum, I won't be able to see you between performances tonight; we're having a meeting, and we're not permitted to leave campus."

"Well, that's unfortunate," I pretended to be upset. "And after we came all this way..."

That night, when the "meeting" was underway and I was hidden out of sight, I watched Brendan from my hiding place. He seemed disinterested and bored, until, that is, the bandmaster made a brief speech and mentioned it being a special occasion. Brendan's ears perked up, and once he saw the champagne flowing and the glow of the candles on the cake, realisation dawned. His face was a picture. He caught me out of the corner of his eye and made a beeline for me, acknowledging the thumps of congrats from officers and friends along the way. Wrapping his arms around me, he gave me the biggest hug ever. Whilst I managed to keep my emotions in check, I could have cried when I thought, *Look at what Colin is missing.*

26

FENG SHUI OF THE MIND

Clive always liked to be out and about doing something new. Money was no object, and if there was something he heard about, he'd try it. One thing he'd heard about was The White Elephant on the River, a restaurant with dancing, situated on the north embankment of the Thames. The White Elephant was the haunt of London celebrities and socialites and was also frequented by quite a few of London's more notorious criminals. The restaurant was upstairs with a balcony overlooking a stage where the band played, with a small circular dance floor in front of it. Neither of us were dancers, but after being wined and dined, I wasn't going to let Clive get away with not whirling me around.

Even though we were having a lot of fun, I realised I wanted more, but I felt trapped in the "friend zone". Clive was never a demonstrative person, and despite the fact that we enjoyed a healthy sex life, he was not keen to acknowledge to anyone that we were anything but friends.

One Sunday after lunch, I asked, "Do you want me to stay for the evening?"

He was silent for a moment then answered, "Well, as we don't have any plans, you may as well go home early and see Cindy and Goldie, you know they miss you. I have plenty to do here to keep myself busy." I put up no argument, but as I was driving home, I felt a sense of loss. We'd come together at a time when we were both grieving, but I was now recognising it had been a relationship of convenience, not one that would last. And yet, I didn't want it to end.

I never discussed this with Clive, and we carried on with our routine of talking on the phone every night, seeing each other at least four times a week.

The passion that had ignited between us was still there, but unfortunately, it was no longer making me happy.

***

"You're doing what?" Clive laughed when I told him my remodelling plans. The current rage for homes was to hire a *Feng Shui* expert to go through each room of your home and give advice on good karma. "What mumbo jumbo. It's just a way for consultants to make a living off of women who have nothing better to do with their money."

I knew he would react to this news cynically. He was a man's man, and maybe he was right; but I was ready to consider anything that would help lift my feeling of gloom and disaster. Even if he didn't see it in me, I recognised I wasn't coping. And so, *Feng Shui* it was.

When I received the report, I had mixed feelings. I embraced the points about placing money trees in the right places and that mirrors should never face the bed, but one thing I couldn't bring myself to do was paint my lounge bright red; and I mean postbox red. When Clive saw the results, we had a good laugh about it. "You know, it's *you* who has to change your own life," he said, "not some stranger who's learnt his trade from briefly studying the finer points of the latest craze." I had to agree, and in November 1998, I eventually took a work colleague's advice to go to the doctor.

I had tried so hard to fight the overwhelming feelings of helplessness, and when I broke down in therapy, she asked me how I was feeling. "My husband killed himself," I answered. "He was psychologically abusive, so I'd expected everything in my life to be wonderful now he's gone. But I'm not happy. And I don't know why."

"You're suffering from depression," she immediately responded. "I can prescribe you Prozac."

I picked up the prescription at the local pharmacy, but something was telling me not to take the tablets. I didn't tell Clive about it. He should have been the one to confide in, but he wouldn't have been sympathetic; not because he was unkind, but rather because he wouldn't understand why I was feeling down. He believed pulling yourself together and getting on with life could overcome any mental illness. If it hadn't been for my experiences with Mark and now Colin, I would probably have agreed with him.

You can fight this without becoming a zombie, I convinced myself.

You have an important job to do, your dogs to look after, and friends and family who need you. That was all well and good in theory, but when sleep deprivation set in, it became increasingly difficult to cope. I'd go to bed by ten o'clock but be awake after a fitful few hours of sleep. I'd look at the ceiling and reiterate what I needed to do the next day; from the time I'd awaken to the time I'd lay in bed for my next restless night's sleep. *The first thing I have to do is choose my clothes for work,* I'd think to myself, and without fail, each morning I'd look for the particular clothes I'd chosen in my mind, but they were never there... or at least, I couldn't see them.

I became obsessive about things being in order. One Sunday morning, Brendan and my brother, Paul, came downstairs to find me still in my nightclothes, surrounded by my extensive video collection, muttering to myself about putting them back in strict alphabetical order.

"Rose, does this need to be done right this second?" Paul asked, exchanging a worried look with Brendan.

"Mum, why don't we go out for a walk?" Brendan pitched in. "You don't need to do this right now."

"No, no," I said, reluctant to be persuaded. "I've no time for a walk. This has to be done."

The boys humoured me, and we completed the tedious project together. Neither of them openly acknowledged that I was ill and getting worse, but no doubt they noticed. Paul had been working with me and had seen first-hand that I'd not been firing on all cylinders lately. He was aware I'd started visiting my friends less, and I wasn't sleeping. In response, he'd taken over the morning dog walking and had assumed greater responsibilities at work to help cover for me. But this latest episode particularly concerned him.

At the office not long after this incident, I was sorting the opened post – on average, over 100 letters – separating them by department manager and placing urgent documents in a pile for the partners, when suddenly, I started to panic. All of the pages were completely blank. I blinked. There was not one single word written, pages and pages of blank letters. I raced upstairs to my boss's office, sat down, and as I started to explain my problem, the tears flowed and wouldn't stop. "There's nothing on these letters," I said, nearly hysterical. "They're blank. Aren't they blank?"

My boss looked worried and attempted to calm me. "Rosemary, I think I know what's happening – you're having a delayed reaction to Colin dying," he said. "My wife died of cancer last year, and I took it hard. I felt totally bereft and alone. To restore myself, I went away to a spa hotel for two weeks. You need to do the same. Complete rest and relaxation will restore you."

As it happened, I was going to Ragdale Hall in Leicestershire to meet up with my two nieces, Julie and Angie, and their step-mum for a two-night spa break that weekend. I decided to book myself into Ragdale ahead of the others. I had the court case on Monday, which had been going on for two years and where I hoped to get resolution to the injustice done to me in 1996. I knew I'd need a holiday after dealing with it.

I'm sure all would have gone according to plan had it not been for the phone call I received from my lawyers, informing me that the court case had been postponed. This was the last straw, it broke my back, and as irrational as this may sound, my feelings of complete helplessness were compounded by that call. *I'm being punished,* I decided for reasons I couldn't work out. I tried to pull myself together; I didn't want to be a mess when the girls arrived. I didn't want to ruin their fun.

My idea was fine in theory, but not in practice. Whether I chose to be alone or with the others, I felt hollow and sad. I wanted desperately to be upbeat, but they saw right through me. It was obvious to them that I was ill. We talked nonstop, and they tried their hardest to cheer me up, but nothing worked; the underlying despair just wouldn't leave me.

On the journey home, I stopped for a coffee and called my friends, Peter and Cheryl. I'd planned to stay with them on Monday, as they lived near the courthouse. "I won't be needing to stay, Cheryl. The court case has been deferred."

"No matter, forget about the court case, but come still," Cheryl said. "I insist."

And so I went to visit Cheryl, who had known all I'd been through with Colin. When Cheryl opened the door I handed her my case and my handbag. "Can you take care of these I just can't cope with my life anymore."

The next morning she said to me, "Do you have private medical insurance?"

"Y-yes," I answered, caught off guard.

"Do you have your membership card with you?"

"Yes, right here I keep it in my purse." I gave it to her without even wondering why she wanted to see it.

"I'll be right back, Rose." She went away for a short while, and when she returned, she said, "Have I ever told you about the close friends of mine who benefitted from counselling at a local clinic in Windsor. They needed support at a time when they were going through emotional turmoil, and their stay there helped them put things into perspective." I still honestly had no clue what Cheryl was getting at until she said, "I just called the counsellor at Windsor and booked you an appointment for this evening."

She'd called my general practitioner, explained to them what was happening to me, and gave them my insurance details, so they could call and authorise my stay in the Cardinal Clinic. I don't know about you, but I don't think many people would do that for a friend, and I'll be eternally grateful to Cheryl for taking my life in her hands.

*＊＊

The psychiatrist looked at me over his glasses and scribbled something on a pad before saying, "Please take five minutes and tell me about the main events in your life so far."

"My dad died when I was fourteen. My first husband was schizophrenic. My sister and boyfriend died in a car crash several years ago. And, most recently, my husband, Colin, committed suicide." When I said it like that, I wondered how it was possible I hadn't landed myself in a clinic long ago.

The psychiatrist listened intently, and after a pause, said, "So you are coming to stay with us then?"

"Oh no, I just came in for a chat."

At this, he sat back in his chair, picked up his notes, and repeated them to me. "If someone else told you all of these events had happened to them, would you believe them?" I shook my head. "I didn't think so. Now perhaps you can understand why you are feeling so low. Anyone who had gone through just one of these events would be feeling down, let alone one after the other. You couldn't make it up. You don't need a chat; you need to come and stay here, so we can try and get you back to your normal self again."

So there it was. I'd officially been deemed psychologically unwell; I'd become an inmate of a mental institution. *What has my life come to?* I thought. *Have I gone mad?*

The Cardinal Clinic was a safe haven

***

As part of the therapy, I had to write down how I was feeling. I was not a good writer and just felt more pressure was being put on me. *How in the world will this help me?* I asked myself. But I was a complacent patient, and I surprised myself by being able to articulate exactly what I was feeling with little effort.

During some of the black moods I've experienced recently, I've found it very hard to remember what my life used to be like when I was happy. Deep down, I know that the majority of the time, there was a lot of enjoyment despite all of the hard work that was necessary to maintaining a comfortable standard of living. I'm finding it difficult to comprehend why I feel so unable to cope but hope by being honest with myself and by accepting that the events in my life are extraordinary, slowly things will get better. At the moment, I feel useless, but I know this, too, will pass, and I will be able to achieve fulfilment. What does fulfilment mean to me? Nothing very exciting! To be in a position where I'm happy with my environment, can perform well at work and have time to spend with friends and family. First of all though, I need to bury the ghosts that are haunting me –those preventing me from going forward.

By the end of the first week, I was already feeling much better. I was a model patient, did as I was told, and followed the programme to the letter each day. Apart from an occasional visit from the psychiatrist, we had meditation, group therapy sessions, art classes, videos, flower arrangements, exercise routines, and socialising with other inmates to entertain ourselves and fill the time. Others gravitated towards me, if they wanted to discuss their problems with someone other than the staff. I was a good listener as well as a good talker, and I even considered training to become a counsellor.

One of the patients was Peter. He was there, because he'd attempted suicide after his wife had asked him to leave her and his four children. "There's no way I can carry on if I'm separated from them," he told me.

"Whatever happens, nothing and no one is worth taking your life over, especially when you have children," I replied, speaking from personal experience.

He adored his children, which was clear when his family came to visit. And over time, he seemed to accept that his wife's affair was to blame for the breakdown of his marriage. Whilst he maybe could have handled it better, he was the wronged party. I tried to make him see he wasn't at fault, because he seemed intent on blaming himself.

Clive came to the clinic to visit and took me out for the day shopping. He had no idea how I was feeling and still insisted I should 'pull myself together' and get on with life. I knew there wasn't much point in discussing it with him, but I was pleased he came.

"I'm planning something special for your birthday," he said. My birthday was the following month. "I'm banking on you being back to normal by then." *Normal?* I thought. *Who defines that, I wonder.*

***

My brother, John, had a horse running at Lingfield and called me up to ask if I'd be allowed out for the day. I received permission, and when I was telling some of the other residents about it, I felt a bit guilty and so asked if anyone else would like to join us. "I'd like to come if the invitation is still open," Pete approached me timidly after dinner that night. And so, we were off to the races!

"I bought you a little gift," John handed me a gift bag upon his arrival the next day. I opened it to find the video, *One Flew over the Cuckoo's Nest*, and as I started laughing, I thought, *How typical of him to make fun of the situation, but it's just what I needed.* I was well on my way to returning to normality, so when I laughed now, it was genuine and not something forced.

Pete was surprisingly knowledgeable about horse racing and was relaxed, for the first time, in my company. At the clinic, he always kept himself to himself and didn't tend to join in anything unless he had to.

"So, Rosey, what complicated system do you have for choosing the winners?" Pete asked. He smiled, and it made me feel good to see him in a positive mood.

"Well, I'm certainly not going to give my secrets away to a relative stranger, now am I?" Pete laughed a laugh that was infectious, one that started John and me off.

"I hope you're both going to put your money on Sihafi," John interceded. "Rosey won £400 last time she went to the races with me, all because Sihafi won a five furlong race easily. I can't promise he'll do that today though, so don't bet your shirt." John had made a small fortune on Sihafi, and the event he was referring to happened at Windsor Races, not long after Colin died. Clive had accompanied me that time, and thinking about it made me wonder why I hadn't invited him along today. No conscious reason, apart maybe from the fact that he didn't like seeing me in the loony bin, as he referred to it.

Regardless, the three of us had a great day at the races, and I was glad Pete had ventured out and was able to enjoy himself.

***

I felt stronger and stronger with each passing day and welcomed any and all visitors to break up the clinic's routine. Visits reminded me that I could be myself again. Cheryl came a few times to check up on me. I'd progressed so much that she was pleased she'd decided to get me help, and as far as I was concerned, she was a friend in a million. My American girlfriend, Jo, also took time out of her busy life to come. I realised (not for the first time) what great friends I had. They boosted my self-esteem and advised me to proceed with caution. "You need to take things slowly," Cheryl encouraged me. "Don't just assume you're better, because you're smiling again." I heeded their advice, but I also knew I wouldn't be able to stay at the clinic once my brain kicked into gear.

Sure enough, I soon grew concerned about all the things I needed to do at work, home, and with the family. By the end of week three, I was more than ready to face the big bad world again. My stay had convinced me to take better care of myself and not ignore my mental health. In fact, I'd learned two very valuable lessons: to look after myself, because no one else would, and to learn to say 'no'. I was always agreeing to things I didn't necessarily want to do, so this second lesson was imperative when it came to putting myself and my health first, at least until I was better.

I was provided medication and assigned a psychologist to visit weekly. All that was left was to say goodbye to everyone I'd grown close to, all the tormented souls. As my birthday and Christmas were around the corner, eight of us agreed to meet up for dinner in Windsor.

After leaving the clinic, I'd intended to take an extra week before returning to work but decided there was no need. So my professional life back on track, I instantly got back into the swing of things in my personal life, which included seeing Clive. In the clinic, I'd managed to put things in perspective where he was concerned, and I now felt differently about him. Part of this was because I'd enjoyed chatting to other men in the clinic. Whilst Clive and I had been good together, there were 'plenty of fish in the sea', not that I was looking to dip my feet in just yet. I'd only determined not to assume he was ever going to want more than we already had.

On my evening out in Windsor with my ex-inmates, I spent most of the night chatting with Pete, who had positioned himself by my side.

Pete and I waiting for food at the Christmas Dinner

"Do you know when you'll be escaping the Cardinal?" I joked.

"They let me out for Christmas, so not long now," he sighed. "I'm not sure what I'm going home to though. That's the problem."

"I know you're anxious about it, but you need to enjoy the time with your children. They love you to bits; I could see that."

"That makes it worse, somehow. I hate to see them upset, and the situation upsets them. Anyway, let's not talk about that now; we're here to party. What are you drinking?"

He was a different person to the one who'd cried on my shoulder, and we spent the evening laughing together and agreeing to stay friends. I drove him and two others back to the Cardinal, and when I got out of the car to say goodbye, Pete decided to stay behind and chat some more over hot chocolates.

"So how are you feeling since you left the clinic?" he asked. "Are you feeling anxious at all? I confess, I'm not looking forward to it."

"My circumstances are a lot different to yours. I only have myself to worry about. I'm lucky, because no one – other than my dogs – relies on me."

"You are so positive about everything, and yet, from what I've heard, your life has not been without drama. What's your secret to surviving trauma?" Pete seemed genuinely interested.

My favourite photo of my faithful friends

"Ever since the love of my life, Brian, died in a car accident when I was twenty-seven, I decided to make the most of my life. The problem is, I seem to have made a number of wrong decisions since then, one being my late husband. Colin was controlling and abusive. I wasn't happy with him. When he committed suicide, I thought I'd be instantly happy again, but life isn't like that, is it?"

Pete nodded. "Well, I was happily married for twenty years, but now my wife is cheating on me, and I know I won't win her back. Not long ago, life didn't seem worth living, but now look at me, chatting away so easily to a very lovely young lady." He smiled so broadly, I could have hugged him; compliments of any kind were few and far between these days.

I glanced at the time. "Oh dear, I didn't realise how late it was. I'm sorry, I have to run. I have work tomorrow." As I moved to get out of the car to say goodbye, he pulled me towards him and kissed me passionately. I was shocked. I honestly hadn't been expecting it and was beyond taken aback. Although all the passion was his, the kiss certainly wasn't unpleasant for me either.

"I'll be leaving the clinic in two days," he said. "Promise you'll call me. We can meet up again before Christmas."

27

JUGGLING

I wasn't sure how to handle this – two men interested in me at the same time? I'd never been in this situation before, but I decided I didn't want to waste too many of my newfound brain cells thinking about it, so I'd just let matters unfold. *I'm not doing anything wrong*, I thought. *Not yet, anyway.*

At my first outpatient visit with my psychologist, Jane, we talked mainly about Colin and my feelings regarding what happened. "I'm coping," I said, "but there are so many bad memories, it's difficult not to keep re-evaluating them. At one point in our relationship, I recorded a tape. I'd made the decision to leave him and wanted to remind myself why."

"Yes, I've heard the tape. It's part of your file." She dug the tape out of a drawer and handed it to me. "When you feel ready, you should destroy this tape, and while you're destroying it, speak aloud about how Colin cannot influence your life any longer, and how you're now your own person and have a new life to lead."

"I already feel this is absolutely the right thing to do."

"I must caution you about continuing your relationship with Clive," Jane added. "He was so much a part of your life with Colin, he serves as a constant reminder of him, which is unadvisable. I also recommend that you leave your job. No matter how much you consciously think it's okay, walking back and forth past the spot where your husband shot himself every day will affect you subconsciously."

I nodded. "I haven't told you yet about Pete," I decided to be 100% honest with Jane. "He kissed me."

She raised a brow. "He did? And how do you feel about this?"

"Honestly, I think it's doing my ego good having two men interested in me."

She was quiet for a moment and then, to my surprise, said, "In the long run, a relationship with Pete would be unadvisable. I hope your interest in him and from him is fleeting."

***

Clive took me to the Oatlands Park Hotel in Weybridge for my birthday. Normally, he knew how to treat a lady and his chivalry never ceased to amaze me. However, his chivalry must have been hibernating on this occasion.

"*What* are you wearing?" he asked as soon as I showed up. "Why are you dressed like *that*?" I wore the track suit I'd normally wear to walk the dogs, but I'd had to drive from Essex to get there and, anyway, he wasn't supposed to arrive before me. Clive was a master of sarcasm, so I shouldn't have taken any notice, but I did. "I'm glad I scored a good deal on the hotel, otherwise we'd probably be in the local B&B."

I was disappointed he'd set the tone for the night. Moreover, I have to admit the affection from Pete made me question why I was here with Clive in the first place. I felt rather guilty, not only for seeing both men, but because Jane had recommended I see neither.

My prearranged lunch meeting with Pete on Christmas Eve ended up being a disappointment as well. We met at The Poachers at Sindlesham Mill, and as Pete lived in Wokingham, only fifteen minutes away, I'd agreed to call him when I was approaching. Thank goodness we'd made this arrangement; the traffic from Teddington was diabolical, and a journey that should only have taken me forty-five minutes took 2.5 hours. By the time we met, Pete and I were both stressed out, as we had commitments to other people – me to Clive and him to his family. All we had time for was a sandwich and a drink before parting. We discussed getting together for New Year's Eve, but I didn't want to make that decision. Clive was expecting me to spend it with him, and I was seriously considering taking a break from both of them and flying solo.

In the end, I flew solo. I accepted an invitation from my friends, Jim and Jayne, who were having a fancy-dress dinner party. I'd never been any good at this sort of thing, and I had only a few days to sort out a costume. But as luck would have it, for some stupid reason, I found a bright orange tracksuit in my wardrobe… it seemed my taste in dress hadn't improved much past my schoolgirl days of bright lime coats.

I approached one of the girls from my office who was an amazing seamstress, "Janet, can you help me transform this fashion faux pas into an outfit that at least looks like I've made an effort?"

"I think I can design something," she eyed the orange jumpsuit, "and we'll call it 'I've been tangoed'." The outfit was head-to-toe orange, and I wore it to the party with something like pride.

I'd been questioning my decision to avoid Clive and Pete, but the minute I was immersed in all the fun and frolicking, I knew I'd made the right choice. Jim and Jayne were aware of what I'd been through, and they were determined that I was going to have a hell of a good New Year's Eve… which I did for the most part. But even they couldn't take my mind off the fact that I'd upset both Clive and Pete by turning down their invites. *This is the new me,* I insisted. *I have to stop putting everyone else before myself. Let them be left to their own devices once in a while. They're grown men, after all.* Still, their own devices seemed to infringe on mine, as they both called me regularly throughout the evening.

To put it mildly, I was confused, and to compound my confusion, that spell in the funny farm made me feel like I could very well be a bit crazy. *You're being stupid,* I thought, *putting undue pressure on yourself.* I became so anxious about my relationships that I thought it best to discuss these issues with my psychologist on my next weekly visit. *She might have some pearls of wisdom to offer me.*

"I'm getting close to Pete," I told her, being open and honest, though I knew Jane disapproved of our relationship. "I'm looking forward to spending a night at the Savoy Hotel with him."

Jane's lips pressed together; she was not pleased. "Rosemary, you should think very carefully before embarking on any type of relationship with someone who already has personal relationship issues to deal with. Once again, you're choosing a man who needs you. You have consistently shown that you like to be with someone who needs you. You, in turn, need to be needed, so it's easy and even satisfying for you to fall in line with what they want; but doing so is usually to your detriment."

"I don't know that I agree," I replied, not wanting to see what she saw.

"Mark was schizophrenic and needed you to care for him. Brian was divorced with two young children and ambitious; he needed someone who had a career and was financially stable. Colin was a single parent, and you've already told me he wanted to find someone financially stable who fitted into his life. He was also mentally unwell and no doubt saw in you someone that was strong. Listen to me, you need to break this chain, and I'm here to help you do that. I hope you take my advice and do not pursue this relationship with Peter. Remain friends, but nothing more."

I nodded along, but I didn't agree with her when it came to Pete. He was only unhappy because of his relationship deteriorating, just as I had been in the past when things fell apart. *What's wrong with him looking for happiness with someone else?* I thought. *We're both mature adults, and I'm sure I can cope with whatever else life has to throw at me. And so can he.*

***

I went ahead with our date at the Savoy and phoned the receptionist before Pete's arrival. "My boyfriend will be arriving before me," I told her, "but the night away is a surprise for him. I'll take care of the bill, so please don't ask him for a credit card or let him know what everything is costing." I didn't know Pete's financial situation, but I surmised that with a soon-to-be ex-wife and four children to support, he was unlikely to have money to burn for a night away. The call paid off; we'd been upgraded to a suite big enough to live in, with its own lounge, mega bathroom, and separate bedroom, laden with all the luxury one could desire – dressing gowns, slippers, and complimentary fruit, chocolates, and flowers.

"I've booked a table overlooking the Thames for six o'clock," I told Pete, "and we have tickets for the evening performance of *Boogie Nights* at the Savoy Theatre."

"Beautiful," Pete answered. He took it all in his stride, and if he felt awkward about me funding the evening, he didn't show it. On reflection he was a bit quiet, but I put that down to his anxiety over what the New Year was going to bring. Life was anything but easy for him right now, and all I wanted to do was lighten his load.

By the end of the evening, we were both exhausted, but we gave it a shot. I'd forgotten we were both only just out of the clinic and were on medication, so it shouldn't have come as a shock to me that our first night in bed together was unremarkable. On top of the exhaustion and pills, Pete was nervous. Needless to say, the earth certainly didn't move for me.

***

I finally talked to Clive about Pete.

"I know already. That's the guy from the clinic, right?" I nodded. "Are you sure you know what you're doing?"

His face fell when I nodded. I'd decided to be honest with him, and he wasn't taking it as well as I thought he would. I'd thought he would be somewhat indifferent, but he seemed more down about it than I'd expected.

"I should have shown you more affection, Rose, but my family has never been demonstrative. It's just the way we're built. I wish I'd tried harder. Your friendship is important to me. Will we still keep in touch with each other and go out occasionally?"

I agreed. And he kept his word. He called me the week after my date with Pete and asked if he could take me to The White Elephant on the river. I accepted his invitation. The truth was I missed him.

And so Clive took me out, and during dinner, he excused himself from the table. He returned with a twinkle in his eye, reached for my hand, and led me down to the dance floor. I smiled at Clive, for once, he was truly being romantic, and as we smooched to the music, I thought maybe I hadn't given him a chance.

When we returned to his house, I expected him to whisk me upstairs to bed so that we could resume where we'd left off only two weeks previous. But he did no such thing. "You can sleep in the spare room," he said and that's where he left me, giving me a gentle kiss goodnight. My head and heart were in turmoil. I had no idea who I wanted to be with. I lay awake for ages, hoping Clive would return to my room, take me in his arms, and ravish me. But he steered clear of me. And lying there awake, waiting for him, I convinced myself that Clive didn't want me in his life.

***

A week after our date at the nightclub Clive had driven Brendan and me home after a night at the theatre. I was surprised to find Pete waiting for me. "My wife packed all my belongings and told me to leave the house," he mumbled, his eyes red. I glanced over his shoulder toward his car; inside were seven black bin liners filled with clothes and other personal items. I looked at him. He was completely shattered. There was no way I could send him away.

I was embarrassed that Clive had to see this, and so was he, he took off in a hurry.

"Come in," I said to Pete, unconvinced that I was making the right choice for either of us. As I reached over to him for a kiss goodnight, I wondered what Jane would say. I'd see her in two days' time, so I didn't have long to find out.

***

"Pete's moved in," I told her at our next appointment.

Her response was immediate, "You have to stop this now for the reasons I've already explained to you. I am trying to help you, but you don't seem to be taking any of my advice."

"He needs me."

"And you need to be needed. Pete needs to work through this problem on his own. You have to be cruel to be kind, Rosemary. Send Pete back to his family."

"But his wife doesn't want him there, and his children are suffering over their fighting. I *am* listening to what you're saying, but I can't ask Pete to leave. We've become good friends, and he's happy when he's with me." As I said this, I fleetingly wondered if it was true or if I only wanted it to be.

"Good friends or lovers, you cannot open your home to Pete. He will begin to rely on you, and you'll only become his crutch. What will happen when you leave him?"

"Why would I leave him?"

Jane breathed a sigh. "If you won't cease the relationship, then don't bother coming back to see me. I cannot help you, if you won't heed my advice, and I'm sorry to say that I see this relationship ending in disaster."

I left her office, full of anger at her parting words. I thought counsellors were meant to stick by their patients, not cast them aside at the first sign of trouble. I never returned for more counselling, and I stopped taking my medication.

A week after Pete had moved in, Clive called me on the phone. "Can I take you to lunch?" I agreed to meet him. This was the first time he'd ever done this; the journey from Teddington to Woodford Green took forty-five minutes, so he'd be away from his business for three hours. *He must have something important to tell me,* I thought.

He seemed a bit on edge and not his usual jokey self when I arrived, and while we were waiting for our meal to be served, he spoke in a low and serious voice, "Rose, I miss you. I can't tell you how much I miss you. I can't believe I've been so stupid."

"Stupid? How so?"

"I know this is going to sound mad, but my friends told me I shouldn't settle down with the first woman I fall for, and I was stupid enough to listen. They said I was a good catch, since I own my own house and business, and I should enjoy being single for a while. They kept saying I could go out with a Claudia Schiffer lookalike if I wanted to."

"Well, no wonder you didn't settle for me then," I laughed. "I bet Claudia wouldn't put up with your snoring though."

He reached across the table and took my hand and, to my utter amazement, asked, "Will you stay with me?"

Oh, boy.

"I can't," I answered after a moment of shock. "Pete has moved in with me. I love you in my own way, and I promise to stay friends forever, but you know I can't."

Clive looked broken. "All right," he said, defeated. "Let's do stay friends and visit at least once a month to keep our friendship going."

On my drive home, I couldn't believe what had just happened. *Had he asked me to stay with him the night we'd gone dancing at The White Elephant, I may well have said 'yes',* I thought. *I seem to have a habit of finding men who only appreciate me after I leave them.* I hoped Pete would be the one to appreciate me while I was around.

***

Our whirlwind romance progressed quickly, but I found that Pete and I were at different stages in our rehabilitation. My time at the clinic had sped my recovery, and whilst I was back to being my old self again – and even an improved 2.0 version of myself – Pete was struggling with everything he had on his plate. And his plate was piled high: four children to visit and support, an ex-wife who was horrible to him, and now a long commute on the M25 in rush hour to Mars in Slough, where he worked. I tried my best to make things easier for Pete. I didn't pressure him as far as our relationship was concerned, and I even went so far as to organise some treats to cheer him up, including a trip to Disneyland Paris with his children and, even better, a couple of birthday surprises. But nothing I could do would lessen his load.

Work was so consuming that I just let my relationship with Pete jog along, ignoring the times when he was distant and putting his lack of interest in the intimate side of our relationship down to his troubles. Before long, I'd disregarded nearly everything Jane had advised and reverted back to my standard in a relationship: compromising to please my partner.

But I didn't disregard all of Jane's advice. One night when Pete and I were at home enjoying a quiet evening on our own, I dug out the tape I'd dictated about Colin. "Jane said I should destroy this when I'm ready to let go," I told Pete. I pulled the thin, shiny brown tape out of the reel, pulled and pulled until it was just a crumbled heap on the floor. "Colin can't control my life anymore. I'm my own person and have a new life to lead." Pulling that tape, saying those words, was cathartic and freeing. I was proud I'd put myself back together, and I could talk about my three weeks in the clinic as the best days of my life.

I took another piece of Jane's advice and spoke to my boss about needing to find a new job. Not only did he understand, he found me a consultancy job with one of Haslers' clients. I put the house on the market and found a buyer in an instant, recovering my costs and feeling no pressure in finding somewhere else to live. On the downside, I had to say goodbye to two of my best friends in the world – my dogs, Cindy and Goldie. Being twelve-year-old Golden Retrievers, they were old in doggie years and slowing down. There was no way I could leave them alone all day while I went to work. I called my mum and told her what was happening. She had recently suffered the loss of Toby, her own dog, and so she was only too happy to take in Cindy and Goldie until I got myself sorted.

Pete's commute to work would now be much shorter, as we'd found a house in Maidenhead, close to Slough. My intention was to continue in my consultancy job, until I'd settled into my new home, and then look for a local job. I still had doubts and anxieties about my relationship with Pete, and now his four children would live close enough to come and stay on a regular basis. I wasn't sure whether I could play 'happy family' that easily. But of course I ignored my gut instinct, something I've learned you should never do. I did approach my concerns in a new way, however; I discussed them with my partner.

"If we move in together, I expect to sign a pre-nuptial agreement to protect your money," Pete responded to some of my concerns. "As long as we're both going into this with our eyes open and are prepared to work through our anxieties as they manifest themselves then, as two intelligent adults, we should be able to make it work."

And so, we moved into Redcliffe, a modern five-bedroom house on Lower Cookham Road, situated across from the Thames. My longstanding lawyer, Richard, filed all the legal work for me, including a cohabitation agreement. Pete wasn't yet divorced, and a pre-nup isn't valid unless you get married, an arrangement we had yet to touch on.

***

Pete's fiftieth birthday was approaching, and I wanted to surprise him with not one, but two birthday meals – the first on his actual birthday with friends, and the second with family. I invited Peter and Cheryl, Pete's best friend, Gerry, and his wife, Sue, my American friends, Jo and Wally, and four more of Pete's friends.

"I can't believe how lucky I am to have met Rosey!" he exclaimed, in excellent form and delighted with all the trouble I'd gone to. "I'm so excited we're now living together. I've just… I've never been happier!"

These words were repeated the following weekend, when he got over the shock of arriving at the pub in Oakley Green, which we favoured in our clinic days, where he was cheered by all of his immediate family.

When he walked into the surprise, he started to cry. "I'm sorry," he said. "I'm just overwhelmed. I can't believe you're all here."

As for me, I was as pleased as punch that I'd managed to pull off two surprises without Pete finding out. On top of these parties, I'd also arranged for the two of us to go to Sorrento for a week's holiday, where we had a romantic time visiting Capri and Pompeii, and driving down the Amalfi coast, enjoying the scenery and the sunshine. *I wonder if I'll ever be able to top this,* I thought to myself, smiling. Then another voice answered, *Who are you kidding, Rosey? You most certainly will.*

Pete & I ready for a night out

28

THE RELATIONSHIP FALLS APART

Pete's children became regular visitors. Not long after we'd moved in together, the youngest boy asked his dad if he could come and live with us. "You're one of the reasons he wants to come and stay," Pete told me, delighted. I didn't quite believe that, but I could see how having his dad all to himself, together with his choice of bedroom in a new house, would appeal to him.

He settled in very quickly and was no trouble; he was bright, loved school, and did his homework without being told. I was no longer used to a teenage boy being around all the time, but soon I fell into the routine. Pete took charge during the weekends when the others visited, so I wouldn't have to deal with the hectic organising of four children, and I even enjoyed getting to know the girls better. Not many weekends went by without us visiting the garden centre, and everyone chose koi carp for the fishpond and plants for the garden. The youngest, in particular, liked going to the gift shop; Beanie Babies were in vogue, and more often than not, she was able to persuade one or the other of us to buy her one. Apart from the times of sibling rivalry when both the girls were vying for Pete's attention, life chugged on harmoniously.

But I was surprised at how often we had the children. I'd been warned that when couples split up, visiting rights are invariably a point of discord, but not with these two. Pete's ex even approved of us having them for the October half term, and so the six of us went on holiday to Majorca. Pete had told me he loved going abroad, and from what I could gather, family holidays were one of the reasons they'd both accumulated heaps of credit card debt. This debt became a point of discord in our own relationship.

"I'm against debt of any kind, other than having a mortgage or interest-free credit," I told Pete when I found out he owed £3,000 on his cards. "I've drawn up an interest-free loan document between the two of us so that you can clear the debt."

"I'm not comfortable with this," Pete replied, looking over the agreement. "How will I ever pay you back? And how can I survive without using the cards? I have to pay maintenance for the children, and at the end of the month, I don't have much money left. I won't be able to pay you."

"But it will be a great help not having to pay the exorbitant interest. You can still use the cards, but as part of the agreement, they must be paid off in full each month going forward."

Eventually, he agreed, and he always had the cards paid off, while also ensuring he paid for half the household bills and the mortgage. Though his finances were regularly stretched thin, we never had a single disagreement over money.

In fact, I took great pleasure in buying Pete extravagant presents. One of his dreams was to own a sports car, and whenever we were out driving, he would point out different cars he liked – BMW Z3, Jaguar XKR, and his favourite, the Mercedes SLK with a hardtop sliding roof. I was so intent on trying to make Pete happy, I'd made up my mind that whatever he wanted, he should have. As most generosities do, the gift would serve me as well; I was excited about the prospect of seeing the look on his face when he received the present he'd never in his life expected. And so, I did what I do – I went all-in.

The problem was I knew diddlysquat about buying cars, especially expensive ones. I considered asking Clive, but eventually called my brother, John, who was a mechanic by trade and who now owned Autovision, his own car and caravan warranty business. One of his agents found the right car for me. "It's the model you want with only 25,000 miles on the clock," he said. "But I don't know about the colour. It's an unusual shade of green and apparently some people just don't like green cars."

When I looked at the colour, 'Calypso Green', in the Mercedes brochure, it was certainly eye-catching, but would Pete like it? As luck would have it, when Pete and I were out shopping later that day, I spotted a car; the same model and colour. "Look at that," Pete pointed it out to me. "What a beauty!" In my mind, this was a sign that it was meant to be.

I called John, got all of the details, arranged the finance, negotiated a good deal on the insurance, and registered the car in Pete's name. The following weekend, Pete and I set out to visit my mum and brother, Peter; we were then to travel on to John's house in Bardon Mill. "I've always wanted to visit Hadrian's Wall," Pete said, looking forward to our trip with no real idea as to what was in store.

As we drove up the long winding drive leading to John's house, we were chatting about the trip we had to Lingfield the previous year and about the success Sihafi was having in the current racing season. I was too excited to focus and kept the conversation going only in order to keep Pete's eyes from wandering to the cars parked at the side of the house.

John and Joyce were there to greet us, and we were soon presented with a cup of tea, followed by lunch. I don't know how I kept everything in. I was fit to burst by the time John said, "Rosey, why don't you show Pete around the house and garden, while we clear up?"

At last. I'd barely eaten a thing, I was so excited. We toured the house, and as I led him out of the conservatory into the garden, Pete's eyes found the car.

"Wow, look at that," Pete whistled. "It's the exact car I'd choose if I ever win the lottery. Is it John's?"

"No, I don't think so. He drives a Jaguar."

John had followed us out and joined in the conversation, "One of my sales agents brought it here yesterday and said it would be collected today. It's quite something, isn't it?" Pete peered inside at the cream leather interior. "You wanna take it out for a spin?" John asked.

Pete looked completely taken aback, "I'd love to, but knowing my luck, I'd put a dent in it and then we'd all be in trouble!"

"Oh, go on," I encouraged him to take the keys from John, which didn't take much doing. Completely star struck, he opened the door and sat behind the wheel. He was in love. "You can take it out," I allowed, "but no longer than ten minutes."

It was a glorious November day, and the first thing Pete did after starting the car up was put the electric roof down. He drove away, beaming, with the breeze blowing through his thick black hair. I couldn't wait for him to return, so I could see his face when I told him it was his. After taking it for a spin around the countryside, he pulled back into the drive and stepped out from behind the driver's seat. "Wow," he breathed. "It drives beautifully."

"Do you like it?" I asked.

"Do you have to ask?"

"Well, Pete, it's your lucky day, because she's all yours."

Pete looked at me with the face I'd been picturing for weeks, a face that was so much better in reality than I could ever have imagined. "Don't wind me up," he said. I only smiled, but my expression was enough to convince him that this was for real. "You've got to be kidding! I can't accept this." But he did accept it. He picked me up, spun me round, kissed and hugged me, and then turned to John. "How could you let her do this for me?" he admonished him for being a party to the surprise, though he was smiling through it all. Why wouldn't he be? He now owned a Mercedes SLK. And as for me, I secretly hoped he'd be able to show me a bit more affection than he had been recently.

***

In November 1999, I'd managed to talk myself into a permanent position working for a German Water Treatment company, Hydrotec (UK) Limited. The company was based close to home in Marlow. I was surprised to be hired, actually. The interview with the MD, Mike Darvill, started off with him saying, "I must warn you, I've more or less made up my mind to hire one of the candidates I've already seen. Unfortunately, you've come into the interview process at the last minute, and I'm basically sold on one of the previous qualified candidates."

Hearing this only made me more determined to win him over. If I was going to impress Mike, I'd need to demonstrate my grit. "Does this small company have plans to grow? I want to determine how I can make a difference here."

"Yes, our products are innovative, and the company has promising growth potential." He spoke more about the products and the company's future and sold me on Hydrotec, so that I was even more eager to win him over.

"I've demonstrated my negotiation skills through my experiences with Hogan Systems, as well as during my current dealings with Haslers and their clients. I even negotiated a finder's fee for Haslers when I joined Hogan, so they weren't so disappointed about me giving my notice in. As you can see on my CV, I firmly believe that developing people to their best potential produces results. I have experience in introducing policies and procedures, which is essential for a growing company, and my financial skills and ability to think outside the box has been demonstrated in my progression to Deputy Managing Director when I was only thirty-four and then MD when I was in my early forties, despite having no formal qualifications."

"So you'll have your eye on my job then?" Mike smiled.

"No, one thing I've learned is I prefer to be the best number two I can possibly be, not the chief. You wouldn't regret hiring me, I can promise you that."

When I walked out of that interview, I felt like I'd blown it out of the water. I was quietly confident I'd be called in for a second interview – which I was – and that I'd talk my way into a job –which I did. The owner of the company was a hard nut to crack, according to Mike; but crack him, I did, and I even negotiated my salary to my liking and was pleased I now had a local job with potential for growth at last. A year on from my spell at the clinic, life was looking good. Too good to last?

***

If I'm guilty of one thing, it's my willingness to spend money on others. As far as I can see, there's no point in having money if you can't enjoy it. I love to plan trips and presents for both my enjoyment and others'. And the year 2000 was no exception. Pete and I had so many plans – a trip to the US with two of the boys and my nephew Matthew, ten days in the Caribbean planned for April, and a two-week trip to Crete. All of these travel plans were well and good, but I'd soon find that if a relationship is starting to show cracks, you're bound to fall through them.

In Barbados, we fell through. Pete's brother and his wife joined us on our idyllic getaway. They were complete together; they'd been married for twenty-five years and were as loving a couple as it was possibly to be. Pete and I were the opposite. We'd been together a year, and we may as well have slept in separate rooms for all the affection he showed me. The intimate side of our relationship had never been good, and I should have realised Pete would never get over his wife. But I loved him in my own way. It would be difficult not to; he was a lovely person, kind, considerate, and a good conversationalist. "I love you," he repeatedly told me, "but my medication affects my libido." Although I accepted this and contented myself with the infrequent occasions we did make love, I needed intimacy in my life.

Understanding how things were between us, I don't know why I expected our Crete holiday to be any different. To me, our dynamic was a complete disaster, and it affected my sleeping pattern to the extent that I'd wake up crying, get out of my single bed, and lie in the empty bath, trying to work out what I should do. Pete was completely oblivious; he slept through the night like a baby. Neither of us acknowledged that anything was wrong. I'd never been good at talking through my feelings with my partners. I could never understand why they weren't picking up on them themselves; they must have shown on my face and in my behaviour. *Surely Pete must realise I'm unhappy and need more from him?* I thought, lying in the cold, hard tub. *If he sees, why isn't he responding?*

As soon as we returned from Crete, Pete's favourite brother and sister-in-law asked us over for lunch. They'd confided in me previously about how worried they'd been when Pete was going through his issues. They told me they were grateful to me for making him happy again. Normally, I'd be looking forward to seeing them, but returning from that trip, I couldn't escape the despair I felt. On the way to their house, I broke down in tears. "Stop the car," I said, choking as I cried.

"What's the matter?" Pete was completely taken aback. "Why are you upset?"

"Do you honestly have no idea?" Pete shook his head. "So you hadn't noticed I was upset most of our holiday then?"

He appeared as though he was thinking back and reliving our entire trip, "Well, I suppose you did become withdrawn and quiet, now you mention it."

"And why do you think that was?"

He shook his head again, and then slowly he realised, "Was I distant?"

"Distant? You may just as well have been in a different country. I may just as well be your sister. Turn the car around. I don't want to visit anyone. I'm too upset."

He was visibly shocked. "I had no idea. Honestly. What can I do to make things right? I'll try a lot harder to show my love. I promise. I'll take care to consider your feelings rather than falling into my own world all the time."

"Who's in that world of yours? Your wife?"

Pete took a breath. "I'm over my wife. Her feelings for me died long ago. Listen, as far as I'm concerned, we have a great life together. There's nothing I wouldn't do to make you feel wanted and needed."

I calmed myself, but deep down I knew I couldn't accept this. Although all that he said sounded great in theory, the physical side of our relationship would never be put right. Whether the drugs or something else was inhibiting his performance in bed, I wasn't convinced our sexual relationship would change and I knew, from experience past, I needed this deeper, more intimate connection to feel whole in a relationship.

***

While learning about the water treatment business and strategizing further profitability, my life was as busy as always. Pete and I continued to muddle along, but I didn't like the way Pete was acting; he was withdrawing further from not only me, but his children too. It wasn't long after he told me he'd try harder that Pete had a mini-breakdown.

"I don't understand why I still feel so low, when I have everything I've ever wanted – a loving partner, a beautiful house, my children, my job. Money isn't even an issue anymore. Why can't I be happy?"

Though I was frustrated with our relationship, my compassion for Pete was strong. I tried to console him, "Only eighteen months ago, you felt far worse than you do now. Whether you realise it or not, you've made progress, Pete. Keep with it."

"But you're not happy."

I felt awful that he felt awful. "Our relationship started off with good intentions on both sides, but I think we can agree we were both guilty of rushing into it without due consideration." I knew he'd just read the book by Helge Pedersen, *10 Years on 2 Wheels: 77 Countries, 250,000 Miles*. He'd marvelled about how fascinating it would be to see the world. "Why don't you take some time off work and travel solo, like the Pedersen guy?" I suggested. "You've just earned yourself a six month sabbatical. *Use* it. I'll fund your travel, and I know it will be money well spent if you come back having cleared your mind of all of the baggage you're currently carrying."

He looked at me like I was crazy. Although he did understand I was deadly serious, he didn't even consider the proposal. I was beginning to accept that I could not help him.

***

The following week, Clive asked me to attend a Mason's function with him, as his current love interest had cancelled on him. I jumped at the chance to see him. I asked Pete if he minded; I'd be staying overnight at the venue with

Clive, and I didn't want him to be uncomfortable. But he wasn't. He knew Clive had always been a good friend, and I don't suppose he ever saw him as a threat to our relationship. "It will do you good to have a chance to catch up with him," he agreed.

When I arrived at Lensbury and checked into my room, I smiled when I saw Clive, ever the gentleman, had arranged for flowers and champagne. For all his faults where I was concerned, he certainly knew how to treat a lady. I wanted him to meet someone who would make him happy.

For one evening, I was able to put my personal concerns out of mind. At the end of the night, Clive walked me to my room, and I invited him in to finish off the champagne. We were both somewhat inebriated but in control, because although the chemistry between us was alive as ever, we kissed a friendly good night, and he went to his room. We both knew we could have got together and blamed it on the drink, but neither of us was like that. Or so I thought.

Clive called me later that week. "We have some unfinished business to discuss," he said. "Want to get together next weekend?"

I knew exactly what he meant and agreed to meet up with him anyway. I had a business meeting in London the day after his birthday, so I booked a hotel room for the night and arranged to meet up to give him his present, a painting to complement his newly decorated front room. Again, I didn't keep it secret from Pete that I'd be visiting Clive.

"I've bought this painting for him," I showed it to Pete. "What do you think?" Again, Pete agreed it was a good idea; but I did keep secret what I knew was going to happen when Clive and I met up.

I felt guilty for deceiving Pete but justified it in my mind by telling myself I had needs he couldn't fulfil. *He'd probably agree to the liaison if I told him anyway,* I convinced myself. He made it easy for me, really. His parting words were, "Don't rush back; it will be nice for me to have a night on my own for a change." *More like he won't need to conjure up an excuse for going straight to sleep tonight,* I thought.

Clive joined me at the hotel and I gave him the painting, which he loved.

"I'm going to take a bath before we go for dinner," I said. "All I seem to have done today is rush around, as usual."

"Do you want your back washed?" Clive asked, with a wink. "I seem to remember you liked that."

As he held me close, I was left in no doubt that tonight would be a good night.

29

MEETING A LEGEND

"The Mind Sports Olympiad is being held at Alexandra Palace in August," I told Pete one day in April 2000, "and there's a backgammon tournament taking place."

I'd started playing tournament backgammon again after nineteen years. A weekend tournament was held once a month in Coventry, and I'd often go with my brother, Paul. Pete and I had just returned from our holiday in Florida, so he jumped at the chance to concentrate on the children without me being there.

"Sure, you can go. You'll have a lovely time. And don't worry about me; I'm looking forward to having the girls here."

I called Clive. "I'm going to be at Ally Pally, and I'll be visiting Peter and Cheryl in Suffolk on Sunday."

"Well, how about I join you for the weekend? You can leave the arrangements to me." He surprised me by taking the initiative, and when I agreed to it, we both knew what it meant. I realised I was about to embark on yet another act of infidelity, and if it was half as exciting as the last one, I was in for a good time. Of course the excitement I felt was tinged with guilt, but I kept telling myself, *It's not as if I'm with someone new. Pete has likely guessed Clive and I are more than friends, anyhow.* Pete hadn't attempted to make love to me for over a month, and I'd lost the need for intimacy between us. We got along great as friends, and so my guilt dissipated, and excitement for backgammon and sex took over.

I arrived at the tournament, and who should I run into but Bob, who I'd lived with in Mayfair Gardens for two years. I'd taught him how to play backgammon on our first holiday together in Malta, and he'd broken my heart briefly by marrying his love interest from work.

"I started running a small backgammon club in Kent," he told me over a cup of coffee, as we caught up with each other's lives. "You know, I've always kept track with what you were up to over the years. I hear you were living with a guy called Pete."

He'd been surprised when I introduced him to Clive earlier, and he didn't hide it. "Clive's a good friend," I said, not willing to admit that I was going to be spending the night with him. *Why should I? Bob is nothing to do with me anymore,* I thought. *But, then again, let's be honest; the truth is I don't want him to know.*

***

Dice rattled throughout the hall, row upon row of players, deep in thought, contemplating their next roll. The backgammon scene at this time was rife with colourful characters, none more so than John Clark (JC) and John Slattery (Slatts). The first time I'd ever seen the two backgammon legends was at the Hilton Coventry. Two guys carrying backgammon boards, wearing black leather trousers and waistcoats, strode into the Hilton as if they owned the place. JC was over six feet tall, good-looking, and single, while Slatts was average height, not particularly good looking, a chain smoker with terrible teeth, and married. But they had one thing in common: they were at the top of their game and commanded respect from most of the backgammon community.

JC had earned the title 'Backgammon Grandmaster' which was no mean feat. Peter Bennet (who it turns out was also christened John) and Slatts both also went on to receive that accolade. I played Peter in the first round at Ally Pally and lost; but it was a surprisingly close match. He went on to win the tournament that day.

Slatts agreed to engage in a £100 side bet with a player, in which they'd guess how many players would enter the tournament. Harmless fun, you would think, and the money was peanuts to them. It was not unusual for the wealthier players to gamble amongst themselves.

"eighty-five players have entered," Michael Crane, the tournament director, announced to the gathered crowd. Cheers and groans abounded, as Slatts immediately handed over one of his coveted Scottish £100 notes to the other player, who'd guessed within two of the total.

Not long after the money-changed hands, Michael revealed that the winner had asked him how many entrants he expected just before the deadline for registering. As word spread like wildfire through the backgammon hall that the bet was won by cheating, Slatts just shrugged his shoulders and carried on with his game.

The £100 note was not returned, and whilst the two of them continued to play backgammon together, a backgammon friendship that had once been strong evaporated in an instant.

Regardless of evaporating friendships, I was having a blast. For the first time in ages, I felt truly happy and carefree. I was even feeling frisky, and at one point, ran my finger down Slatts's back when he was in the queue in front of me. Heaven knows what possessed me to do it, as I'd barely said two words to the icon before. He just laughed it off, thank goodness.

After watching the professionals battle it out for a place in the final, Clive said, "Let's head off for dinner." I think we both knew it wasn't dinner that was uppermost in our minds. I was looking forward to some love and attention, and Clive was more than happy to provide it. I knew I was acting totally out of character, but the clinic's motto, 'Look after yourself, because no one else will', came to mind. Life was too short to be living unfulfilled.

**

In September, Pete and I had a trip planned to Reims, the champagne region in Northern France. Josée was visiting from Canada, and we were looking forward to seeing each other again. Pete had read *Birdsong* while we were in Crete and was interested in visiting the WWI battlefields of the Western Front. He was the happiest I'd seen him in a long time, probably because I'd withdrawn from him in the bedroom, so he didn't have to pretend anymore. The truth was if Josée hadn't been visiting, I wouldn't have agreed to the trip. I was now the one feeling low, or more specifically, I was feeling guilty. I knew the writing was on the wall, but I couldn't get my head round what to do. I had no one to talk to about our relationship and my infidelity; the only person who had any inkling at all was Gerry, Pete's best friend, and he was going through his own issues, primarily the dissolution of his marriage. So with no one to confide in, I continued on with my secret love affair, feeling at once guilty and fulfilled.

At the monthly BIBA backgammon tournament in September, I played one of the quieter players, Jules Minwalla, who was intelligent and had a style of play that was aggressive without being reckless. I lost the match but found a good friend. He informed me about a weekly tournament at The Bell, Hampton, a local backgammon club run by John Clark. I decided to be brave and go along the following Tuesday, and this became a weekly routine. Several regulars, including Slatts, played there. I arrived quite early one evening and found Slatts sat at a table with his head in his hands, looking like he had the weight of the world on his shoulders.

"Hey," I greeted him, "you look down in the dumps. Can I buy you a coffee?"

He lifted his head and, in his broad Scottish brogue, said, "Aye, that would be grand."

After a brief back-and-forth, he dropped a bombshell, "Sorry if I look miserable, but I'm just trying to get my head round the fact that my wife has just run off with all my money."

I'd seen his wife, for the first and only time the week before. She'd lived up to my expectations, as people had described her as 'mutton dressed as lamb and loud with it'. She'd totally ignored me, not that I was particularly bothered, but as so few women played, I thought she might have wanted to chat. She was one of those proud women who gave the impression that the rest of her gender was not worth passing the time of day with.

I didn't know what to say to Slatts, so I asked, "Are you planning to attend the BIBA tournament in October?"

"I will if I can find someone else to travel with."

Without a second thought, I offered, "Well, I'll be going if you get stuck for a lift."

"That would be great. When do you need to know by?"

"As long as you let me know the Thursday before the tournament, I'll come and collect you around three o'clock on Friday."

We left it at that, and I couldn't believe my boldness. But I felt sad for Slatts. No one deserved to be treated so badly. I was keen to get to know him better and be part of the elite inner circle as I saw it.

Clive arrived to have dinner with me before the game started. He didn't play backgammon but had taken an interest in these weekly meetings since our recent illicit liaisons. We hadn't slept together since the Ally Pally, but I'd told him I was booked to go to the Irish Open the last weekend of October, and we discussed the possibility of him coming along. Clive had begun to have stronger feelings for me, so now not only did I feel guilty about Pete, but I felt guilty about him. We had fun together and satisfied something in each other, but I knew he wouldn't want to take it any further. I didn't want him to accompany me on the trip to Dublin.

***

I saw Slatts again at the next weekly meeting. "Rosey, I'd like to take you up on that ride to Coventry, if the offer's still on the table."

"Oh, good," I replied, "but I must warn you that mine is a non-smoking car."

"Don't worry, I'll manage. But if you notice me start to twitch then you should stop at the next services; you don't want to see me when I'm in need of nicotine."

In reality, when we were about an hour down the road, having endured it without nicotine, he saw a sign for 'services' and said, "Let's call in. I'll buy you a coffee and a cake." Slatt's company on the journey was without any embarrassing silences; he was a good storyteller, and having led a colourful life, he had many to tell.

"I'll let you do the talking, since I've heard many a tale from the backgammon players about how you came to be as good as you are."

"Well, I was a successful blackjack player, earning myself a lot of £100 notes a week, before I'd even heard of backgammon." Slatts's voice was loud and deep, and his Scottish accent charming. "A friend gave me a set for Christmas a few years ago, and it intrigued me. I love a challenge, and backgammon became something I wanted to master. I'm happy when I succeed, and this was to be no exception."

"How long did it take you to get to your present level? I mean, you're well-respected by nearly everyone."

"Thanks for that, you sweet talker," he grinned. "Not that long, really, as I paid good money to fly the best players to compete with me at my home in the wilds of Scotland. We'd play for high stakes and would barely pause for food or drink for days on end. I lost over £100,000, and now it's payback time, I'm pleased to say."

I'm sure I only heard a fraction of his stories, and of course I was intrigued to hear more and patted myself on the back at having the nerve to offer him a lift. Before we reached the Hilton, I ventured out of my comfort zone again and asked, "Would you like to play Doubles with me on Saturday night?"

"I don't usually play the doubles," he muttered, "because I'll be playing a professional game." I knew this meant he'd be playing someone in a match for anything between £50 and £1,000, depending on the number of points played. I couldn't fault him for saying no; this was something far beyond my abilities, and I accepted he was a professional backgammon player and earned a living this way. *Earning is probably uppermost in his mind now that his wife has done the dirty on him*, I thought. I also wondered what it was about me always attracting men whose wives had left them – Brian, Colin, Clive, Pete, and now Slatts? *I'm sure Jane, my psychologist, would have something to say about it*, I considered. And so I set about the tournament, separating from Slatts, but with our conversation rattling in my brain.

On Saturday, I was grabbing a drink in the bar before dinner, when out of the corner of my eye, I spotted Slatts approaching… not surprising, since his voice was like a megaphone as he played to some of his followers. If he was one thing, he was a showman, and loved the limelight. "If we're going to be playing doubles together, lassie," he said as he approached, "we'll have to register a name." I don't know what made Slatts change his mind, but I didn't question it. I was thrilled.

My excitement was short-lived, because we were out in the first round. Obviously, neither of us was a lucky charm for the other. But it wasn't a complete loss. "Do you think you could give me a few backgammon lessons on seven-point matches?" I asked him. "I'm still in the consolation tournament."

"In lieu of a taxi fare," he joked. "Do you mind playing in my room? I'm rather partial to wacky baccy."

"As long as you don't expect me to join in," I agreed. I hadn't got to the ripe old age of forty-seven to be led into temptation now, after all.

Slatts lit up in his room, and we sat down to two matches. He turned out to be a good teacher, and after we'd finished, I stayed in his room to have a coffee and talk about life. Out of the blue, he asked, "Why isn't your boyfriend here?"

"He isn't interested in backgammon and is at home looking after his children who are visiting him this weekend."

"Doesn't he mind you attending an event that is 95% male dominated?"

"If I'm honest, he's never been that interested in backgammon and so probably isn't even aware that's the case."

"More fool him. You are a very well liked and respected player. He'd better watch out."

The longer we talked, the more I divulged, and soon I found myself telling him far more about my life than I should have done, including the fact that two partners had died. He looked aghast. "And my relationship with Pete isn't any better. In fact, I think it's drawing to a close."

"So why are you wasting time on someone you think you'd be better off without? Life's too short, as it is. What's on your 'bucket list'?" *Bucket list?* I'd never heard the expression and it showed on my face. "The film with Jack Nicholson and Morgan Freeman," Slatts explained. "A 'bucket list' is a list of the things you want to do before you die. So tell me three things you'd like on your list."

I gave it a moment's thought and then said, "I want to swim with dolphins, cruise through the Panama Canal, and win a backgammon trophy."

"Well, the first two are easy enough to achieve; you have money to do them, so do them soon. Don't waste your life regretting that you didn't. As for the backgammon, that might take you a bit longer, but you'll get there eventually."

We talked a while longer, and at the end of the night when I got up to leave, he rose too and stood in front of the door. "Sleep well," he said, before kissing me gently on the mouth. "Can I be cheeky and ask you to call me in the morning if you don't see me downstairs by 9:30?" He shut the door behind me and to say I was in shock would be an understatement. *Where did that come from?* I wondered. *Was I giving him signals to precipitate that? I don't feel like I was.* Maybe he'd interpreted my ramblings about Pete as 'The Confessions of a Sex-starved Backgammon Player'.

I found myself unable to fall asleep and kept thinking about the evening, my mind working overtime. *That was* not *the impression I'd intended to leave him with at all.* By the time I drifted off, I had visions of Slatts walking into the sunset hand in hand with me.

***

Slatts had to eat his words on Sunday, because I won my first backgammon trophy! It wasn't the runner-up trophy either; I actually won the consolation tournament, beating Dod Davies, a top-ranked player in the quarter final, Slatts in the semi-final (and believe me there is no way he let me win, the league points were far too important to him), and David Nathan in the final. I was elated, and the fact that everyone was so happy for me was an added bonus.

Once I received my trophy, I went to leave. Slatts was travelling up to Blackpool with Jerry Limb, so I didn't have carpooling to worry about. But before I had a chance to slip out, Slatts steered me towards the disabled bathroom and kissed me again. "I couldn't let you go without congratulating you properly," he said. "You did amazingly well, and I'm very proud of you. I think you and I will be spending a lot more time together in the future, and I shall look forward to it." Again, he left me standing there in shock. The image of the two of us walking off into the sunset suddenly seemed to brighten. I almost laughed at the absurdity of it.

I returned to the lounge, hoping I wasn't looking too flushed while I said my goodbyes. Jerry winked at me. Jerry was a thalidomide baby and had no arms, but he didn't let that hold him back; he was married to a beautiful blonde, had two children, was a mouth-and-foot artist, and played backgammon with his feet. He was also the comic of the group. I pulled him to one side, "Did you put Slatts up to that?"

He laughed and said, "You've got to be kidding. Slatts doesn't need me to recognise a winner when he sees one."

I drove home smiling.

30

SOMETHING TERRIBLE HAS HAPPENED

"Are you ready to consider getting to know me better?" Slatts called me three days later. I knew it was wrong, but I needed some excitement in my life, and Slatts was exactly that. He was unlike anyone I'd ever been with before. He didn't need me, that's for sure, and at this point, I didn't need to be needed.

"I will certainly consider it, but I'm not sure you're my type."

"I understand it is a bit quick, but didn't I hear you say life is too short? Don't think about it long; you don't know what you'll be missing out on." He paused, "By the way, there's something you need to know about me: I have an insatiable appetite for sex." He laughed, which made me laugh.

"Well, I'll have to ponder your offer even more then. I don't want to be a disappointment in that department."

"There's a fortieth birthday party coming up in Richmond next week. I'll book us a room."

As far as sex was concerned, I went from accepting nothing to being rapacious. We met up a few times and Brendan, of all people, was a willing accomplice to this affair. He let me and Slatts use his spare room when we were in the area. Of course I knew it was wrong. I knew I had to bring things with Pete to a head. But I also knew I had to do it when I was ready.

***

The Irish Open tournament was coming up, and when Clive asked me if he could come with me, I made an excuse as to why he shouldn't. I hadn't had the heart to tell him about this latest episode in my life. *What am I playing at?* I thought. *This isn't me at all.* But, then again, maybe it was, because I was doing it.

I spent most of my time in Dublin watching Slatts play backgammon. I played in the tournament myself but didn't win anything and was happiest whiling away the tournament as a spectator, as Slatts played into the final. My flight home was before the final, and I wouldn't be able to catch it if I stayed to watch, so I rescheduled for the morning.

Slatts with his bling ready for a game of backgammon

"One of my friends has made it to the final," I explained to Pete over the phone. "A few of us are staying to root him on. I hope you don't mind. I'll see you Monday." Of course he was fine with it.

Our support didn't push Slatts to number one; he came second to Sean Casey, the Irish champ. The ranking was still excellent of course, but not what Slatts had striven for. As for me, I was well and truly hooked on the buzz of it all. Even the windstorm that battered the UK and caused a delay at the airport didn't alter my mood. But on the flight home, I thought about this double life I'd been leading. Slatts had told me he wanted to see me on a regular basis, and I was totally enamoured with him and bewitched by the lifestyle I'd just been a party to. *I can't carry on with this any longer. I have to bite the bullet; I have to talk to Pete this week about ending the relationship. I'm not being fair to him, and I hate lying.*

When and how I was going to tell Pete was decided for me. He confronted me late Monday night after my phone rang, and I took the call upstairs. He'd guessed that something wasn't right, and Sue, Gerry's ex-wife, who was downstairs with him later told me Pete had tried to listen to the conversation. It was obvious to Sue that something was wrong. "Do you know what's going on?" he'd asked her. But of course she knew nothing, nor did anyone else. After she'd left, Pete asked me outright, "Are you seeing someone else?"

Taken aback, before I could lie, I told the truth. "I've just started having feelings for someone," I admitted, apologetically. "We need to accept that our relationship is over. It's not working. I love you in my own way, but it's simply not working. You know that."

He was visibly upset but said, "I accept that I'm to blame for it. You need more from a relationship than I can give."

"You and the boys can stay in the house for as long as you want," I offered, "but you'll have to move to another bedroom." Pete nodded in agreement and, wiping away our tears, we held each other and cried together.

I was relieved Pete had accepted my decision, but I was also concerned about his state of mind. On Tuesday, I called Gerry first thing to tell him what had happened.

"Pete has already called me," he said to my surprise and relief. "We're meeting up after work tonight, and I'll meet you for lunch as usual on Thursday. Until then, don't beat yourself up too much."

Easier said than done, I thought, but I consoled myself with knowing I'd put my all into trying to make the relationship work and couldn't have done anymore. I'd wanted to make Pete happy; I'd invited his children into my life as if they were my own. No expense had been spared to make them feel loved and welcome in our home.

I also turned to Slatts for reassurance. "You've done the right thing," he said. "I'll arrange to take the train to Reading on Friday." We were going out to dinner with Clive's ex, Karen, and her new partner, another Scotsman called John, and would stay the night at their house. I knew he was biased, but I felt better after speaking with Slatts. I still had the rest of the week to get through.

When Pete arrived home from seeing Gerry, he came to my room, "I'm sorry for being so stupid. I realise that everything is my fault, but I can change. I'm committed to you. Will you marry me?"

A familiar question entered my mind: *Why does it take me breaking off a relationship for my partner to realise they should have treated me differently?* I'd been through this too many times before; I had to be honest. "It's too late, Pete. It will never work. I'm sorry, but I've moved on."

***

Thursday evening, I managed to put Pete out of my mind at the Reading backgammon club. In fact, my mind was so focused on the game that I did my best playing and won the tournament. When I returned home, Pete was still up. "Gerry has invited me to live with him for a while. I'll probably move some of my things out at the weekend."

"I think that's best, but there's really no hurry as far as I'm concerned."

We slept in separate rooms. At 5 a.m. the next morning, Pete entered my bedroom. "Can I get in beside you to talk?" he asked. "You've no idea how sorry I am to have let you down and put you through the trauma of another failed relationship, when you're the last person on earth that deserves it." He held me, and we reminisced about the good times we had together. "My boys have really enjoyed having you as a sort of step-mum," he said. Unlike Colin, I knew Pete wasn't using his children to pull my heartstrings and make me stay. He was genuine and sincere, and I appreciated him for it. "I recognise that backgammon has become a driving force in your life. The fact that you've started winning tournaments shows me you're as clever as I always thought you were."

Later, when he popped his head round the door to tell me he was leaving for work, I said, "I won't be around at the weekend, as I'm going to stay with friends."

"Thank you for letting me know," he smiled sadly. And off he went.

As I drove to work, something didn't quite feel right. I thought back on our conversation, reiterating in my mind his words, the expression on his face. I decided to call him at work around noon. "Pete's gone home," the receptionist told me. My mouth went dry. He hadn't said anything about having a half-day, not that he needed to tell me, but his leaving work made me feel uneasy.

I called Gerry, "Would you please call round to the house and check Pete is okay? Give me a call back and let me know." I also left a message to the same effect on Pete's brother's phone.

My phone rang at almost two o'clock, sharp. I was sitting with my beautician, having my weekly manicure. "I've just left Pete sitting in front of his computer with Molly, the cat, on his lap," Gerry informed me, to my great relief. "He's fine and told me I shouldn't be wasting my time worrying about him."

I returned to work, breathing easier, and at 3:35, received a call from Pete, himself. "Hey, Rosey," he slurred into the phone.

I'd only ever seen him drink once, so I knew instinctively that something was seriously wrong. "Pete, what's the matter? Why are you drinking in the afternoon? I hope you're not thinking of doing anything silly."

"I can do what I like," he muttered. "I'm the only one at home."

"One of the boys will be home soon."

"They wont; they're going to their mum's."

"Not anymore, I said I was worried about you being on your own, they will come and spend the evening with you."

"You had no right to do that!" Pete roared into the phone. I'd never heard him so furious. "You had no right to do that! I'm nothing to do with you anymore!" The receiver slammed. Nothing left but a dial tone.

I was shaking and tearful when my boss, Mike, entered my office. After explaining what was going on, I asked, "Why is it I always feel like I'm being blackmailed somehow? I know Pete expects me to come home to him now, and why should I?"

"Go home to him, Rosey," Mike replied. "You'll regret it if you don't."

He was right. I got in my car and was immediately on the phone to Gerry. "Pete is not okay. Can you meet me at the house as soon as possible?

I have a bad feeling and suspect he's overdosed on alcohol." I also called the Cardinal Clinic, explained the situation, and asked if I could bring Pete round, as he needed help.

"You can't," I was told. "You must take him to his GP."

When I arrived at the house, I sat in the car for a moment. I had a sense of foreboding; it built and built until I turned the key in the front door. As I walked into the hall, I dropped my shopping and screamed. Pete was hanging from the loft space. I raced up the stairs. I tried to lift him up but knew I was too late. I'd spoken to him only thirty minutes ago. How quickly death takes us.

Shaking with sobs, I called the police. I was so shocked; I couldn't really get my head around Pete doing this terrible thing in the house he loved. I went outside looking for Gerry. I needed him to tell me it was not my fault, just as Ben had when Colin took his life. Tears wouldn't stop, and I felt cold and clammy, while the same questions ran over and over again through my mind: *Why me? For goodness sake, why does this keep happening to me?*

The police arrived and Gerry followed five minutes after. He took one look at my distraught face and the shopping strewn on the hall floor and immediately understood this was more than just a cry for help from Pete. "Where is he?" he asked, and as I glanced up the stairs, he saw his friend's legs dangling, just as I had. The difference was he knew there was no point in trying to get him down. He pulled me to him and tried to console me, when all he really wanted to do was scream like I had. Pete had been his friend for over thirty years; they'd worked together, lived together, got drunk together, been out on the pull together, and helped each other through hard times.

"How could he do this to me, Gerry?" I sobbed into his shoulder. "He knew how much I went through after Colin's suicide."

"I don't know, Rosey. I was just selfishly thinking the same thing about myself. I only saw him two hours ago, and he was so calm and in control. How could I have been so unaware of how he was really feeling? I have to assume he was researching how to do this on the Internet."

The police took over and arranged for the body to be taken away, and after asking me about Pete's state of mind that morning and whether I had any idea why he would want to take his own life, they turned to Gerry. "You were the last person to see him alive. Is there anything you can add to Mrs Bensley's statement?"

Gerry just reiterated what he'd told me earlier. "Pete was on the computer with the cat on his lap. There was no suggestion at all of what he'd planned to do."

Gerry called everyone to inform them of Pete's death. I was so grateful he was there. I called Brendan and left a voice message for him and also rang Karen to let her know what had happened. Brendan must have picked up his message straight away, as I received a text immediately: "Mum, where are you? I need to be with you." Karen offered to bring Brendan along when she drove down with John.

I was in such a state when they all arrived, life spun around me – people coming and going, asking me if I was okay or passing me by – while I just waited, not knowing how to move or what to do. It wasn't until my mobile rang for what was at least the third time that it suddenly dawned on me: *I'm supposed to be at Reading station to meet Slatts.* I moved out of the chair I'd been sitting in for what seemed hours and went to take the call.

It was Slatts. "I'm really sorry. Something terrible's happened, and I can't meet you tonight."

"What's happened? Can I help you? You sound dreadful."

I remembered how he'd reacted when I'd told him about Brian and Colin dying and knew this would probably be the end of our early relationship.

"Pete has committed suicide," I blurted out and, hearing the sharp intake of breath on the other end of the phone, I sobbed, "Just take the next train back to Bristol."

"Put Brendan on the phone," he said. When he wouldn't take no for an answer, I handed the phone to Brendan. Between them, they decided the best thing for me would be to have close friends and family around me. In the end, Karen took charge.

"Get a train to Maidenhead and call me when you get there," she told Slatts. "We'll come to pick you up."

The last thing I wanted was to be on my own, so I went along with the plan. Karen organised an overnight bag for me, and as soon as Slatts rang, she bundled me in the car. We drove far away from the scene, while Pete's lifeless body and his pointless death remained tattooed in my mind.

Pete died on the 3rd of November 2000. Gerry took me to the inquest; it was no comfort to me that it was Pete's marriage breakdown that was blamed for his early death.

EPILOGUE

My journey writing my life story has been cathartic and is something I would recommend anyone to do. I have been reunited with friends after thirty-five years and whilst I didn't initially intend to publish my book I am hoping that it will enable others that have had to endure tragedies to see that life can go on if you feel positive.

Here is an update on my various relationships and I am so pleased that I tracked down so many friends from the past.

My mother died on 1st May 2015 after choosing to stop eating. My brother Peter and sister Joan were visiting her in the Care Home the day before she died and despite not having spoken since a stroke four years earlier, when Joan asked her if she was ready to go she said 'soon' and pointed to my dad's photo. It made it easier for us six siblings to accept her passing and helped build a stronger bond between us.

Royal Wanstead School, closed down in 1971 due to lack of funds. Sawbridgeworth became luxury apartments and the Boys school became Snaresbrook Crown Court. I am currently the treasurer of the Friends of Royal Wanstead School and am part of the team that organises reunions for past pupils. I also support the charity RNCF Royal National Children's Foundation and have had the honour of attending dinners with Princess Anne at Buckingham Palace and St James's Palace.

After thirty-five years I met up with my first husband, Mark. Not long after we had separated he was involved in a near fatal car crash. This changed his life and his schizophrenia abated but he has been left with damaged limbs, which cause him constant pain. He went on to marry and have three children. Whilst that didn't last he enjoys being part of his children's lives. He is still playing musical instruments and is part of a band enjoying what he has always done. We will now stay in touch with each other.

I am still in touch with Brian's oldest son Darren and his brother Michael. Both his parent's and youngest son have passed away but Jim made his 100th birthday; he really was an amazing man.

Bob now runs his own backgammon club in Kent. I see him at backgammon tournaments and we always reminisce about the people we met and the places we visited.

Brendan is now living in the Philippines with his wife Gurlee and three children. He has built a wonderful house and I am pleased to say it has a Mum Rosey's room there for me. I visit as often as I can and keep in touch on Skype. Colin's father died on his ninetieth birthday and his wife Val died nine months later.

I introduced Clive to my friend Rita in 2004 and they are two of my closest friends. I am lucky enough to be able to stay with them when I am in the South of England and we have had a lot of adventures together.

The time spent in the clinic had put my life in perspective, and I still refer to the lessons I learnt there in times of indecision. I admit to still making terrible decisions where men are concerned, but my positivity through the darkest of times sees me through. I was grateful to Pete's employer for supporting me through the aftermath of his death. Gerry and I remained good friends until he died from cancer in December 2013. I was by his side two days before he passed. He whispered to me that he was scared of dying, and I'd like to think my reassurance that death would find him reunited with his parents and Pete comforted him.

I now spend a lot of my time in Thailand where Slatts runs his condominium business. I get lots of backgammon practice while I am there.

I realised that money can't buy happiness, but it did allow me to achieve my goal of playing backgammon around the world. This became the focus of my life for seven years… But that's another story.

ACKNOWLEDGEMENTS

I want to thank The Book Guild for making this book happen as well as all my friends and relatives that have contributed to my life story and put up with me during this long process – I wish I could mention you all.

Jessica Holom who was my initial editor and who spent far more time than she should have to turn my ramblings into something readable.

Brendan for spending many hours reading my manuscript and contributing some extra wording he felt should be included about his dad.

Cheryl & Peter who allowed me to use them as sounding boards and Cheryl in particular, who has been my rock ever since I met her in 1985.

Clive and Rita for putting up with me dropping in with minimum notice and I am really grateful for their friendship and am looking forward to more holidays with them.

Julie, Michael and Angie for joining me in Prague and giving me that lovely framed photo of us all in Lanzarote in 1981.

Mark, who spent time going through his chapter adding things I had forgotten and who, despite the drama in his chapter, still let me publish it.

Jim Loch, who I met on an Arvon course, for giving me the encouragement to write the book after I had misgivings when I realised how big a challenge it was.

Doris for reading some of my chapters and readily asking for the next one.

Anne Atkins, who I met at a charity cricket match and she indulged me by listening to my life summary and went on to encourage me to write the book.

Jonathan Lamb and his wife, who read some of my early ramblings and who always came back to ask for more.

Gemma, who was very forthright when she heard that I wanted to call the book *Something Terrible's Happened* – she thought it was too harsh and wanted 'Rosey' to be in the title.

I have Tim Parfitt to thank for being the inspiration behind the title, even though I initially thought he was criticising me when he wrote on Facebook "*Life isn't all Rosey*".

All of my Facebook friends who gave me encouragement and my backgammon friends who always looked like they were interested when I gave them updates on the book's progress.

My final thank you though has to go to my sister Joan, who allowed me to take over the lounge floor on many an occasion while I was sorting our photographs and for putting up with me full stop.

A lot has happened since the year 2000, so maybe in a few years time I may write Rosey's book two.

THE AUTHOR

ROSEMARY BENSLEY